Brand YOU

MARKETING
REAL PEOPLE, REAL CHOICES 7e

Michael R. Solomon

SAINT JOSEPH'S UNIVERSITY

Greg W. Marshall

ROLLINS COLLEGE

Elnora W. Stuart

THE UNIVERSITY OF SOUTH CAROLINA UPSTATE

Boston   Columbus   Indianapolis   New York   San Francisco   Upper Saddle River
Amsterdam   Cape Town   Dubai   London   Madrid   Milan   Munich   Paris   Montreal   Toronto
Delhi   Mexico City   São Paulo   Sydney   Hong Kong   Seoul   Singapore   Taipei   Tokyo

Dedication

To Phil, the greatest brand I know.
Thank you for your inspiration.

Editorial Director: Sally Yagan
Editor in Chief: Eric Svendsen
Acquisitions Editor: Melissa Sabella
Editorial Project Manager: Kierra Bloom
Editorial Assistant: Elisabeth Scarpa
Director of Marketing: Patrice Lumumba Jones
Senior Marketing Manager: Anne Fahlgren
Marketing Assistant: Melinda Jensen
Senior Managing Editor: Judy Leale
Project Manager: Becca Richter Groves
Senior Operations Supervisor: Arnold Vila

Creative Director: John Christiana
Senior Art Director: Blair Brown
Media Project Manager, Production: Lisa Rinaldi
Media Project Manager, Editorial: Denise Vaughn
Full-Service Project Management: S4Carlisle
   Publishing Services
Composition: S4Carlisle Publishing Services
Printer/Binder: Courier/Kendallville
Cover Printer: Lehigh-Phoenix Color/Hagerstown
Typeface: 11.5/16 Palatino

Library of Congress Cataloging-in-Publication Data
Solomon, Michael R.
   Brand you : marketing real people,real choices / Michael R.Solomon, Greg W.Marshall,
Elnora W.Stuart.—4th ed.
      p. cm.
   ISBN-13: 978-0-13-038853-7
   ISBN-10: 0-13-038853-X
   1. Career development.   2. Marketing—Vocational guidance.   I. Marshall, Greg W.   II. Stuart, Elnora W.
III. Title.
   HF5381.S64618 2011
   650.1—dc22   2010050469

10 9 8 7 6 5 4 3 2 1

Prentice Hall
is an imprint of

ISBN-10:   0-13-038853-X
ISBN-13: 978-0-13-038853-7

www.pearsonhighered.com

▶Contents

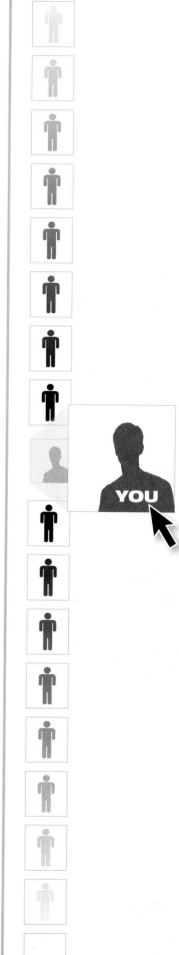

▶ Introduction

You are about to take on the mission of marketing the most important brand in the world—YOU.

Great careers don't just happen. They are carefully researched and planned, just like great brands. Even though it seems as though some brands just "happen" overnight, there was a lot of research, planning, and modification that took place before brands like Facebook, iPad, and Droid became household words and brands of choice. Using these same marketing principles for your personal brand, *Brand You* will guide you through the process of how to become the brand of choice for your target employers.

You are in control of your brand and your career *right now*. Whether you are a freshman just beginning to think about your future, a sophomore beginning to explore different career considerations, a junior looking for an internship, a senior looking for the right first job, or an experienced executive looking to make a change, *Brand You* can help you determine the direction you want to take and how to get the job you want.

Planning your career and finding the right internship or full-time job is a process. Just like a great marketing campaign, you need a plan. You need to determine what direction you want to take, how you will position your brand, how you will advertise your brand, and how you will "close the sale" by securing the job offer you want. *Brand You*, a supplement to *Marketing: Real People, Real Choices*, by Solomon/Marshall/Stuart, follows the same marketing process that unfolds in your text. You'll apply each step of the process to create and market your own unique brand.

If you want the right internship or full-time job, take charge and start building your personal brand NOW!

How to Use This Book

Planning your career and conducting a work search are part of a process. *Brand You* is designed to be an interactive workbook as well as a reference book that you can use throughout both your academic and professional careers. It employs a proven process that works for real people that you will meet throughout the book. And the process works as well for people looking for an internship as well as for those looking for a full-time job or a career change.

Meet Real People

Brand You is your path to the real world. In fact, the book follows a real student, Amanda Burd, through the Brand You process. Amanda asks questions and shares her experiences during her career search. Since Amanda is a real student, chances are that her questions are the same questions you may have. And in each chapter, a professional shares his or her insights in response to Amanda's comments. You'll meet professionals with different experience, from different disciplines, in different roles, with different educational backgrounds, and are different ages. Some knew exactly what they wanted to do when they graduated from college. Others found their path after trying different jobs and even different career paths. As diverse as they are, they all have one thing in common—they have harnessed the power of building and maintaining a strong personal brand to be successful in their careers. They all willingly share their insights to help you as you craft your own personal brand. You'll meet all of them in Chapter 1 and you'll read their personal profiles and see their video profiles in chapters throughout the book.

Watch Videos and Complete Activities on www.mypearsonmarketinglab.com

The video interviews with Amanda Burd and the professionals can be viewed at **www.mypearsonmarketinglab .com**. The videos are short clips designed to give you real-world insight on key issues that will help you develop your personal brand. It's the best way to learn how real people use personal branding practices that work and share their advice for success.

In addition, all activities that are included in *Brand You* are live at **www.mypearsonmarketinglab.com** so each one can easily be completed online.

Follow the Five Steps to Real Success

To maximize your benefits from *Brand You*, read each chapter at least once. Then complete the activities in that chapter before moving on to the next chapter. To help you follow the process, the book is divided into **The 5 Steps to Real Success**.

- Step 1—Choosing Your Path (Chapters 1–3)
- Step 2—Researching the Market (Chapters 4–7)
- Step 3—Creating Your Value Proposition (Chapters 8–11)
- Step 4—Communicating Your Value Proposition (Chapters 12–14)
- Step 5—Delivering Your Value Proposition (Chapters 15–16)

The 5 Steps to Real Success is a step-by-step process that may take place over the course of months or years. And chances are you will go through the process more than once . . . even before you graduate. For example, you may choose a career direction, send out résumés and interview for an internship, then repeat the process again when you are looking for a full-time job.

Brand You Toolkit

As a companion to **The 5 Steps to Real Success**, *Brand You* also includes a comprehensive Toolkit at the back of the book. The ***Brand You* Toolkit** includes valuable activities and practical examples that will provide an excellent reference for you throughout your career search. The *Brand You* Toolkit includes the following:

- Getting Started—Creating Your Action Plan and Timeline
- Recommended Web Sites
- Your Digital Brand: Dos and Don'ts of Online Job Searching and Social Networking
- Networking Made Easy—10 Tips You Should Know
- Internships 101
- Sample Résumés and Cover Letters
- Portfolios and Professional Web Sites
- Interview Checklist
- How and When to Provide References
- Sample Thank-You Notes
- FAQs

The *Brand You* Toolkit should be used frequently as it is one of the most important parts of the book.

A Book That Works

What makes *Brand You* different is that it is more than a textbook. Building your personal brand is a process that never ends. So use *Brand You* now, throughout your academic career, and after you graduate. You will want to revisit many of the activities at various times during your work search. You should reread many of the chapters such as those on interviewing and evaluating a job offer as you are experiencing those steps. And the information and activities in the ***Brand You* Toolkit** will be helpful to use again and again. Just as you use GPS when you travel, use *Brand You* to help guide your career choices.

Brand You is much more than a book; it's the GPS for your career.

Welcome to *Brand You*!

▶ About the Author

Kimberly Richmond is a senior marketing executive with over 25 years of marketing and branding experience. She was Executive Vice President, Marketing at FAO Schwarz and has held senior marketing positions at other major corporations including Kraft Foods, Zany Brainy, The Right Start, Charming Shoppes, and Sears.

Ms. Richmond is currently a principal at Richmond Marketing + Communications, the marketing consultancy firm that she founded. Her practice focuses on the integration of traditional marketing and branding with online and social media.

She is also an adjunct professor at the Haub School of Business at Saint Joseph's University in Philadelphia, PA, and a member of the Advisory Board and the Thought Leaders Panel for the Center for Consumer Research. She serves on the Board of Governors of the Philly Ad Club. Ms. Richmond speaks frequently at industry and academic events.

Ms. Richmond's experience in branding, leadership, and mentorship in several industries provides real insights into how companies make hiring decisions. And her involvement in the academic arena provides valuable perspective from the student and faculty point of view.

▶ Acknowledgments

Great brands inspire people. There have been many great brands that have been the inspiration for this book.

Many thanks to the professionals that have been so generous with their time and spirit. Their personal stories and advice are invaluable to students and young professionals who are starting their career. Each of them added something special to the book. I truly appreciate them sharing their personal brand insights.

Marc Brownstein, President and CEO, Brownstein Group

Janée Burkhalter, Ph.D., Associate Professor, Saint Joseph's University

Karen Carroll, Executive Recruiter, Blue Plate Minds

Stephen Facenda, President, ViaMark Advertising

Vince Giannini, General Manager, WPHL 17

Kristin Kane, Director of Social Media and Recruiting, Kane Partners Staffing Solutions

Monica McIntyre, Musician and Entrepreneur

Ike Richman, Vice President of Public Relations, Comcast-Spectacor

Carla Showell-Lee, Television Personality and Host of "Attire for Hire" Workshops

Brian Wiggins, Director of Circulation, *Philadelphia Business Journal*

Jennifer Wolf, Event Planning Manager, *Philadelphia Business Journal*

Creating your own personal brand is a journey. Many thanks to Amanda Burd, student at Saint Joseph's University, for sharing her personal experiences throughout her brand-building process. Amanda's openness and willingness to share is a special dimension of her personal brand that will serve her well throughout her career and life.

My students have been a huge source of inspiration for me. It's a thrill to watch great brands come alive. I want to especially thank those students who participated in the student video.

Daniel Altieri
Megan Ceselsky
William Camacho
Juliana Dos Santos
Erika Piraino
Anne Schreuders
Courtney Scardellette
Caitlin Walsh

Being a great brand means providing great leadership. Melissa Sabella has done that consistently throughout the process from inception to publication and beyond. *Brand You* is more than a book, it's an experience that helps students think and feel differently about themselves and their futures. This is possible only because of Melissa's vision and support.

Brand You is an extension of one of the great brands in the industry—*Marketing: Real People, Real Choices*. Special thanks to Mike Solomon for conceiving and creating the perfect platform for the book and for taking it to new levels in each edition.

Thanks to the professors who adopt *Brand You* to help give students insight about themselves and the working world. All students have the ability to succeed; it's those who gain the confidence to tell their brand story that flourish.

And to all of the students who read *Brand You*, I hope you will use the concept of personal branding now and throughout your career. The world is waiting to hear your brand story.

Choosing Your Path

Step 1

(Chapters 1-3)

This is the beginning of the development of the most important brand that you will ever market—**You.** Successful brands don't just happen. They are developed as a result of research, fact-finding, insight, and thoughtful consideration. Then, the brand positioning is determined and the brand message is crafted and communicated. **The 5 Steps to Real Success** outlined in *Brand You* will help you follow the same process to develop your personal brand.

Do you cringe whenever someone asks you, "What do you want to do when you graduate?"

Do you give a half-hearted answer and hope you can find a job?

Do you have several areas that you want to pursue, but you don't know how to explore each one?

Do you have an idea of what you want to do, but you are not exactly sure how to get a job in that field?

If you answer yes to any of these questions, *Brand You* is the perfect place to begin to answer these questions. Finding the right internship or full-time job is a process. It doesn't just happen. Getting started is the first step. And it's never too early to start.

Step 1—Choosing Your Path includes Chapters 1–3. These chapters are filled with information, activities, and resources to help you get started planning your future. Your career will most likely span decades. It's worth taking the time now to learn about what's available in the real world and which path will be best for you.

Real success starts here! ➤

1

Welcome to Brand You:
A Framework for Your Career Search

Brand

A name, a term, or a symbol that identifies one firm's products and sets them apart from the competition.

Are You a Great Brand?

Nike, Nintendo, Starbucks. Each of these companies has a strong brand name. Even if you haven't worn the shoes, used the gaming console, or tried the coffee, you probably have a clear image of each of these companies and their products and services. That's the power of branding.

Great brands are all around you. Your personal brand can be as powerful as these brands. Developing a powerful brand is a process that considers the needs of the target audience, establishing the value of a product, and creating a message that is compelling to customers. This book uses the same marketing process to create **Brand You**—your own personal brand. Your brand will help you to present yourself to employers as you seek internships and jobs during college, and later to differentiate yourself from all the other new college grads seeking work.

Great brands offer something that is different and unique. But to establish how their brand is different, marketers first get to know their products and their customers inside and out. *Brand You* **walks you through the steps of discovering what makes you unique.** You'll discover not only your talents, but also the benefit of those talents and the ways you can add value for your customer—your employer. When you create your own personal brand, you'll see the workplace from a different perspective, one that allows you to see more clearly the importance of how you perform and present yourself.

Many people create brands for themselves. Entertainers and athletes, for example, create personal brands. We like stars we think we know, so their branding increases the popularity (and sales) of their team or musical group. If you think about political candidates, you'll realize they brand themselves, too. When candidates develop their brand, they create slogans and issue messages so that we'll know something about their political views. Then they develop marketing strategies targeted toward their constituents so people will take action and vote for them. Businesspeople create personal brands too. When you hear the names Steve Jobs (Apple's founder and chief executive officer), Bill Gates (Microsoft's founder and philanthropist), and Oprah Winfrey (entertainment mogul who can make or break a product), you have immediate images of their personal brands as well as that of the companies for which they work. These unique personal brands attract employees and investors, and even help win high-level negotiations.

You may not aspire to be famous, yet the same strategies can help you build your career. Creating your brand now will clarify what you can do as a student to prepare for the world of work.

Meet Amanda Burd, a Real Student

Building a personal brand may sound a little overwhelming. You might wonder if other students face the same challenges you face in this area. To help you see why and how to develop your personal brand, this book follows a real student through the process of developing her personal brand. Amanda Burd, a senior at Saint Joseph's University in Philadelphia, shares her insights and perceptions about the personal branding process. Each chapter includes some thoughts and questions from Amanda as she goes through the process of developing her personal brand.

Amanda
Burd's Brand

See Amanda's video profile at www.mypearsonmarketinglab.com.

▼ **Q & A** with Amanda Burd, student at Saint Joseph's University

Amanda's Profile

College: Saint Joseph's University

Year of study: Senior

Major: Marketing

Hometown: Pittsburgh, PA

Why I chose Saint Joseph's University: It has a good business school with a relatively small student body and a collegial environment.

How I chose my major: My dad was an entrepreneur so I got a good exposure to business at an early age.

What I like about marketing: The combination of creative thinking and quantitative analysis.

Career goal: Brand management.

Brand key word: Focused.

Brand image: I'm competitive, but collaborative; I won't run over someone just to get what I want.

What I want to learn about personal branding: I never thought of myself as a brand before; I think it's a good idea and I'm looking forward to the process.

Real People, Real Brands

To help you get additional insights about the process of creating your personal brand, each chapter also includes insights and advice from real people who are in the workforce. They each have different backgrounds, different types of jobs, and are different ages. Some are currently in jobs that are related to their majors in college, while others are engaged in completely different careers. Some are new to the workplace, others have many years of experience, while others have made profound career changes. Although all of them are diverse, they all have one thing in common—they all believe in the power of personal branding. These professionals will share their background along with their thoughts and recommendations for best practices in personal branding. A profile of a different professional appears in each chapter. Short video clips are available on www.mypearsonmarketinglab.com and are indicated in each chapter.

The professionals you will meet throughout *Brand You* include:

 **Marc Brownstein**, President and CEO, Brownstein Group

 **Vince Giannini**, Vice President and General Manager, WPHL 17

 **Carla Showell-Lee**, Televison Personality and Host of "Attire for Hire" Workshops

 **Janée Burkhalter**, Ph.D., Associate Professor, Saint Joseph's University

 **Kristin Kane**, Director of Social Media and Recruiting, Kane Partners Staffing Solutions

 **Brian Wiggins**, Director of Circulation, *Philadelphia Business Journal*

 **Karen Carroll**, Executive Recruiter, Blue Plate Minds

 **Monica McIntyre**, Musician and Entrepreneur

 **Jennifer Wolf**, Event Manager, *Philadelphia Business Journal*

 **Stephen Facenda**, President, ViaMark Advertising

 **Ike Richman**, Vice President of Public Relations, Comcast-Spectacor

Starting the Brand You Process

This is it . . . the beginning of your personal branding process. Because this is a new process for you, it will be helpful to follow someone through the process. Hear how Amanda Burd, student at Saint Joseph's University, began the process of creating her personal brand.

The journey of developing your personal brand will help you answer many key questions, such as: Do you know what kind of job you want? Have you thought about the kind of company for which you want to work? Do you know what steps to take to prepare for your field? Have you even thought about your future in terms of a career as opposed to what job you want when you graduate? Reading and working through the activities in *Brand You* can help you find courses that teach needed skills, as well as other steps to your value to employers—such as landing an internship or finding a mentor. And, of course, marketing strategies will help you succeed whenever you search for work—you'll be able to communicate your value with a clear, dynamic message.

brand **YOU**

A unique identity and coherent message that sets you apart from the other job candidates.

"I've never really sat down and thought of myself in terms of a brand."

—*Amanda Burd, student at Saint Joseph's University*

"A personal brand is really important because when you are graduating from college, you really need to set yourself apart from everyone else because everyone else is knocking on that same door that you are. You need to differentiate yourself and prove to someone why they should select you as a candidate as opposed to the next person that's knocking on their door.... It's really important to start building your credentials the day you start college."

—*Jennifer Wolf, Event Manager, Philadelphia Business Journal*

Watch a short video including insights from several professionals about why a personal brand is important at www.mypearsonmarketinglab.com.

Real Questions, *Real Answers*

Q. I'm not a marketing major. Why do I need a personal brand?

A. No matter what type of career you want to pursue, creating your personal brand is critical. Whether you are planning on working for a company in any position or going out on your own, a personal brand is a must because it helps you determine who you are and what you want to do. In addition, it provides a framework for you to quickly communicate to a prospective employer or client what makes you unique and why he or she should choose you for the job. Although branding is a marketing concept, it is not limited to marketing majors. Consider Venus Williams, the professional tennis player, Eva Longoria, the actress, or Ludacris, the rapper. None was a marketing major, but all have very powerful personal brands. Without a personal brand, each of these people is just one in a million. But with a personal brand, each is distinctive and stands out for a special reason; that's why each is a household name.

For you, a personal brand can help distinguish you from the many students or recent graduates applying for an internship or full-time job. A personal brand sets you apart and gives you focus and helps you quickly tell your personal brand story, whether you are applying for a job in accounting, operations, human resources, sales, teaching, nursing, or any other area.

The importance of branding doesn't stop with your first professional job. By maintaining and refining your brand over your lifetime, you will thrive no matter what the future holds. As the CEO of your own personal brand, you'll be in charge of your career, always looking for special projects and experiences that will increase your value in the marketplace.

The Real World

Creating your own personal brand is more than an idea in a book. It's a necessity in today's workplace. Welcome to today's real world—a constantly shifting arena where there's no guarantee of employment, where jobs change faster than the click of a mouse. It's a world where new markets, new technology, and new business models will frequently alter the way you work. To adapt to new challenges, you'll need to master new subjects, quickly establish effective working relationships with a changing cast of players, and communicate with team members from different functions, often without the benefit of face-to-face interaction. This work environment requires flexibility, continuous learning, and self-management to ensure your employability. In the workplace, you can expect:

- Increased pressure for innovative products and services
- A global economy and worldwide opportunities
- A networked world where work flows from one member of a virtual team to the next, sometimes spanning the globe every 24 hours
- More work options. At times, you may have a so-called full-time job, but just as likely, there will be times when you'll be an entrepreneur, indie (independent contractor or freelancer), free agent, or job sharer
- A social networking environment that allows you to solve problems using the wisdom of people all over the world (think: YouTube, Facebook, Flickr, Digg, Twitter, Foursquare)
- To retire later than age 65, or not at all. As we live longer, healthier lives, people will be willing to work longer, provided they can have alternative work options
- More alternative working arrangements like working from home or in alternative locations

Whether you are looking for an internship or a full-time job, you'll need a twenty-first-century mindset, one that's in tune with the current environment. You're at risk if you're expecting a permanent job that will last a lifetime. Instead, set realistic goals—strive for continuous employability. In today's workplace, you'll have to constantly re-earn your right to employment. You will need to prove and reprove continually that you have the right skills and know-how to be the "best person" for the job. Sounds like the same challenges marketers face to keep their products moving, doesn't it? The contemporary work world will require continuous marketing of your brand. You'll always be on the lookout for the next assignment and finding ways to prepare for it.

The good news is that this is an exciting landscape where new job titles are created every day. Just as jobs such as interactive marketing manager, chief learning officer, video game designer, social networking specialist were unheard of just a few years ago, you can't even imagine the new jobs that will appear in the next decade. Although you can't make any assumptions about job retention, you will still have security—the security that comes from being a career activist, security you create by constantly scanning the horizon for new opportunities to add value.

Whether you are self-employed or working for a firm, you are in charge of your career. The days of corporate career paths are over. It's just as well, for you can adapt to changes in the workplace much faster than a corporation can. People who count on a company to tell them what skills they need usually discover they've become obsolete when the ever-changing economy takes a new turn. That way, you are in charge of your destiny and your happiness.

Here's a comparison of the old career mindset and the mindset you'll need as you enter the workplace. Be ahead of your competition and get your head in the game.

Former Mindset	Brand You Mindset
Loyalty to a company	Loyalty to your network and profession
Job security	Lifetime employability
Career ladders	Successive projects based on skills
Learning happens at school	Learning happens everywhere, all the time
Years of experience determine your pay	Your contributions determine your pay
Boss controls your career options	You control your career options
Base work options on past experience	Base work options on emerging opportunities
Master a body of knowledge	Learn how to learn and adapt to new tasks
Stability	Mobility

How Does Branding Increase Your Success?

Fundamentally, a brand is an identity that sets the product apart from the competition. We usually associate a brand with its logo (like Target's red bull's-eye) or with a tagline (like Nike's "Just do it"). In fact, some brands are so powerful that advertisers need few words to describe their products—all we see is the brand name and pictures that evoke an ideal lifestyle. Your brand can be as powerful as these. But figuring out the identity you want to communicate to your customers (potential employers) makes a lot of sense. You are a complex human being with many talents, interests, and viewpoints. Discovering which ones you want to bring to the world of work and which ones are important to employers are concrete benefits you'll achieve when you develop your own personal brand.

To develop a brand, marketers study the product to find out what the product can do. They ask, "Why would I want it?" They find the answers in the product's features. What you can do depends on your skills and knowledge. These are your "features." In building your brand, you'll want to answer the following questions: **Why would an employer want your skills? What problems can you solve?**

Next, marketers explore the benefits of the product. They ask, "What will this product do for me?" and "What can I get from this product that's better than the other products on the market?" To develop your own personal brand, think about questions like these: **What value can you add to an organization? What results will your skills achieve? What is the benefit of your solution to problems?**

When your brand is clear to you, just like a marketing expert, you'll know what to communicate to your customer. Because you will have discovered your customer's needs, you'll have confidence that your messages, whether delivered in a cover letter, a résumé, or an interview, will hit the mark. You'll have an effective, coherent message that will entice hiring managers to take action and hire you.

Benefits of Your Own Personal Brand

- A strong identity that you communicate to advance your career
- A focus on your customers' (that is, potential employers') needs
- An understanding of the benefits of your skills, knowledge, and experience
- The development of effective strategies to reach targeted employers
- A new attitude that puts you in charge of your career, able to adapt to change and maintain lifetime employability

Build Your Brand Online

The Internet provides many opportunities to build your brand. Check out the Do's and Don'ts of Online Job Searching in the *Brand You* Toolkit.

Applying Marketing Concepts to Brand You

Of course, developing a brand identity is only the first step. Once a brand has been created, it needs to be marketed. Here are three ways marketing concepts apply to your own personal brand:

Marketing is about meeting needs.   Jobs exist because employers need people who accomplish tasks and solve problems. Your first step in creating your own personal brand is to discover what kind of employer you want to work for and what kinds of skills and knowledge are needed to accomplish the goals of the position.

Marketing is about creating utility.   Utility creates value. The goal of your own personal brand is communicating that your skills and knowledge will be useful to employers (that is, will meet their needs). A person is hired when the value of his or her skills is perceived to be greater than the cost of his or her salary. When it comes to looking for work, you have a decision to make: Do you want to be a sales machine that blankets the whole market with generic résumés, or a market-driven person who finds out who is most likely to "buy" your skills and knowledge? If you decide on the second course, your challenge is to find a target market, uncover the benefits that those employers look for in job candidates, and then develop the skills that will deliver those benefits. That's why it is important to create your own personal brand now. The more you know now about the needs of employers in your target market, the more useful you'll be when you graduate. To communicate utility, marketers develop a *value proposition*—a statement that sums up the value the customer will realize if he or she buys the product. *Brand You* will guide you in developing your own personal value proposition tailored to the wants and needs of the employers you're targeting.

Marketing is about exchange relationships. Work is the ultimate exchange relationship—you exchange your skills for learning opportunities and compatible work arrangements as well as financial rewards. In an exchange relationship, it's important for both the buyer (your employer) and the seller (you) to be satisfied. Job seekers sometimes make the mistake of taking the first job offered to them. But remember, you won't do your best if you don't like the work, the environment, or your boss. You'll spend at least 2,000 hours per year exchanging your skills for pay—that's a very long time if it doesn't fit your needs!

Achieving Return on Your Investment (ROI)

How will you measure your success as a brand? Many students' ROI (return on investment) scorecard focuses on two outcomes: their new job title and the salary they attain after graduation. (Certainly, that's not the only way to evaluate ROI—what about learning for its own sake, increased self-esteem, or the discovery of new ideas?) Like a marketing manager, you can achieve a valuable return on your investment, however you measure it, through planning. A good marketing plan is the foundation for success; it points the way to profits and return on investment. Good career planning can do the same for you. You'll avoid occupational mismatches (jobs you hate) that can lead to stress, discontent, and even depression. People who take the time to make informed career decisions are engaged in their work, committed to results, and passionate about their mission.

Stepping through the Personal Branding Process

Creating and marketing your own personal brand is a decision process, just like any other type of marketing venture. With *Brand You*, you'll work through the steps of the process and make your own decisions about the kind of work you want—whether it's an internship or a full-time job—and the best ways to get it. Real people, people just like you, have found that this decision process actually works. Figure 1.1 shows a thumbnail sketch of the process.

STEP 1 Choosing Your Path

Every great brand starts with a plan. When company executives develop strategic plans, they look at both the external environment and their internal strengths to evaluate their market position and product plans. For the career planner, the building blocks of your plan are recognizing your strengths and deciding which skills you want to use. In this step, you'll get to know your product—you—and how you can apply your skills, interests, and knowledge in the workplace. You'll determine your mission, evaluate your skills, create career objectives, and identify the environment in which you work best.

Figure 1.1 The Brand You Process

Step 1—Choosing Your Path
(Chapters 1–3)

Values
Mission statement
Skills assessment
SWOT analysis
Career objectives
Company culture

Step 2—Researching the Market
(Chapters 4–7)

Industry research
Research resources
Informational interviews
25 target companies
How the hiring process works

Step 3—Creating Your Value Proposition
(Chapters 8–11)

Unique selling proposition
Elevator pitch
NAB (Need, Action, Benefit)
Entrepreneurial opportunities
Compensation

Step 4—Communicating Your Value Proposition
(Chapters 12–14)

Résumé
Cover letter
Getting the word out
Networking
Professional social networking

Step 5—Delivering Your Value Proposition
(Chapters 15–16)

Interviewing
Negotiating and accepting the right offer

STEP 2 Researching the Market

In this step, the focus is on your customer, the person who has the power to hire you. You'll discover the general characteristics employers seek in new hires. In addition, you'll examine job descriptions to uncover the specific benefits your customers are looking for. You'll look at 10 key industries and identify specific resources where you can find out more about the industry, how it functions, what kinds of jobs are available, and where you can learn more.

STEP 3 Creating Your Value Proposition

In this critical step, you'll develop a statement that summarizes the value you add to an organization. You'll learn techniques for using your value proposition during your search for work and to promote the development of your career.

STEP 4 Communicating Your Value Proposition

Your value proposition becomes the basis for writing dynamic résumés and cover letters. There are samples and guidelines included to help make this easier. You'll develop an integrated marketing communication plan to get your résumé to all the right people at the right time.

STEP 5 Delivering Your Value Proposition

Here's where you will learn how to prepare for and make every interview successful. And, when you get job offers, you'll have tools with which to evaluate them to make the right decision. Also, you'll understand the process of how to negotiate and accept the offer that's right for you.

Getting to Know Your Product—You

What makes you unique? This question may seem surprising, but each of you is unique. Your individuality is based on your particular constellation of characteristics—that is, your skills, interests, and personality. In the next few chapters, you'll have an opportunity to discover what makes you unique. Armed with this information, you'll be able to present yourself to employers in a compelling way. After cataloging your talents, you'll be able to describe the types of problems you can solve and the value you bring to an organization. This is an important step in creating your own personal brand.

There's another important reason to discover your talents. You may know precisely what you want to do upon graduation, but many college students have only a vague idea of their career goal, such as, "I want to go into business." But what exactly do you want to do in the business world? Do you want to manage a brand, acquire venture capital, or supervise a production team? Employers expect you to know what work you want to do, and they're likely to ask you why this career field interests you. So whether your career goal is quite definite or you're not sure at all, completing the activities in *Brand You* will increase your confidence in your goal or help you discover a goal to pursue.

Defining Your Personal Values

Employment is an **exchange** relationship between you and an employer. People find satisfaction in their work when they know what they want from the exchange. Many people want more than "just a job." They want work that feels important, that makes a difference, and even work that is meaningful or provides a sense of calling. Your work will matter to you if it is aligned with your personal values. **Values describe the beliefs that define you.** For example, you might feel strongly about the environment, or perhaps you are passionate about animal rights, or teamwork and collaboration might be important to you. These are examples of values. It's important to identify your personal values so that you can understand what motivates you. And, when you are aware of your personal values, you can be sure that you work for a company whose values reflect your values. In other words, if a healthy lifestyle is an important personal value, you might choose to work for a company that provides health-conscious products and services and offers benefits such as an on-premise fitness center and nutritious dining options.

Real People, Real Advice ... About Values

"I got my values from faith, family, friends . . . just where I came from. . . . They are the foundation of my interests, my personality, my work ethic, and things of that nature."

—*Amanda Burd, student, Saint Joseph's University*

"For me, most important was honesty and integrity. . . . There are companies that push the envelope farther on (let's call it) regulatory issues than others. That's not an environment I'd want to be in and I'm not comfortable with that."

—*Vince Giannini, Vice President and General Manager, WPHL 17*

Watch Amanda Burd and Vince Giannini discuss values in short video clips at www.mypearsonmarketinglab.com.

Tricks of the Trade
Personal Values

Values are critical to help you choose your career path. Consider Maria and Richard, two people who have different values. Their personal values are reflected in their work environments.

Maria is part of an organization that is structured around teams rather than a typical organizational hierarchy. Work is distributed to more than 100 project teams. Team members are located around the globe and meet on social networking sites to work creatively and solve problems. Team roles are defined by each person's expertise. The team operates with very few rules. The ability to get resources and results depends on Maria's ability to persuade others to support her. Maria enjoys the variety of projects, her role as team leader, and developing leading-edge skills.

Richard's work centers on the belief that the world and its inhabitants deserve respect and care. He's constantly on the move, working in different places around the globe. His knowledge and education assist people with improving their environments and communities. His organization promotes economic development and sustainability. Richard's work is filled with unexpected events requiring mental flexibility. He is free from routine activities and predictable work schedules. Richard is passionate about being an active player in the movement to create a green, sustainable world. For Richard, success means following the direction of his heart.

The activity which follows on the next page gives you an opportunity to identify those values that are important to you.

Speaking of Values . . .

Instructions: Read the values and descriptions listed below. Circle the 10 that are most important to you.

Value	Description	Value	Description
Achievement	To accomplish important things	**Helpful**	To be of service to others; to contribute to the well-being of others
Advancement	To reach the top in an organization or profession	**High income**	To be financially successful
Adventure	To take risks; to discover new things	**Influence**	To have influence over decisions; to influence people through my work
Autonomy	To set my own schedule and priorities	**Integrity**	To stand up for my beliefs; to be honest
Balance	To be able to balance my work life with my other interests	**Leadership**	To motivate others to achieve goals
Challenge	To be involved in interesting work; to solve a variety of problems	**Passion**	To care deeply about my work; commitment to a cause
Community	To be part of a group; to support community activities	**Recognition**	To earn the respect and recognition of others
Contribution	To contribute to society; to have an impact on people's lives	**Security**	To achieve a stable work and financial situation
Creativity	To be original; to express myself	**Self-expression**	To be able to act in a way consistent with my values and beliefs; to be able to express my ideas
Expertise	To be respected for my competence; to be known as an expert in my field	**Spirituality**	To be at peace with myself; to achieve inner harmony
Friendship	To develop friendships at work; to have time for friends	**Structure**	To have order and a predictable work environment
Fun	To have fun; to enjoy my life and work	**Teamwork**	To accomplish goals as a member of a team
Growth	To develop personally and professionally	**Trust**	To work in an environment in which people trust each other
Health/wellness	To be physically and emotionally healthy	**Work independently**	To be responsible for my own accomplishments

Instructions: In the left-hand column, place your top 10 values, ranking them from most to least important. Place the value most important to you in the top cell and move down the column in order of preference. Then think about the industry or profession you are considering. How well do you think this value will be satisfied in that work? For example, if you think there is strong compatibility between the work and the value, place a check mark in the circle labeled High.

Value	High	Medium	Low
1	○	○	○
2	○	○	○
3	○	○	○
4	○	○	○
5	○	○	○
6	○	○	○
7	○	○	○
8	○	○	○
9	○	○	○
10	○	○	○

If you need more information about the career you're considering, check out these Web sites:

THESE SITES: for more info about industries:

www.bls.gov/oco
www.online.onetcenter.org
www.collegegrad.com
www.wetfeet.com
www.rileyguide.com

My Career Journal

At the end of every chapter in Brand You, *you'll find an area like this one. It's a place to write your thoughts as you're reading and thinking about your future. First, some questions are provided to prompt your thinking. On the last page, you'll find space to record random thoughts as they occur to you.*

Do you know of any positions that might be of interest to you? Why?

_____

_____

_____

What other career fields have you been considering?

_____

_____

_____

_____

Look at your list of top 10 values from Activity 1.1. With those in mind, imagine a typical workday that reflects those values. Write a few sentences to describe your day.

_____

_____

_____

_____

Now that you've determined your values, does that change your thinking about possible career fields to consider?

_____

_____

_____

_____

When you think about your top value, what comes to mind?

_____

_____

_____

Notes to **Myself**

2

Planning Your Career:
Setting Your Direction

You've probably heard that the current economic situation might make it difficult for students to find internships and new graduates to find jobs. Don't be discouraged! Companies are still looking for and hiring great people. Your biggest challenge is to establish what makes **you** different from all of the other candidates. That's where personal branding comes in. **Your personal brand defines you and what makes you unique and compelling; it's what gives you direction and confidence.**

Great brands like Google, Red Bull, and Amazon.com don't just happen overnight. In fact, it takes time, research, and consideration to create a compelling brand. This is true for products, places, and people. Rachael Ray didn't become an overnight success. When she was working in a grocery store, she wanted to sell more canned goods, so she tried something different and unique—she did in-store demonstrations to show customers how to create a meal in 30 minutes. Her simple approach to cooking made her stand out and became the basis of her famous personal brand.

If you want to increase your chances of success when you are looking for an internship or full-time job, start planning *NOW*. **Leaving your career decisions until your senior year is risky.** Without a clear sense of direction, you'll miss important opportunities to find mentors among your professors, internships with companies that might hire you, or contacts that could lead to job offers.

Whether you are the type of person who plans or one who leaves things to the last minute, career planning is essential. And there's no better time to start than right now. As CEO of your own personal brand, you want to speak in a clear voice so that employers (your customers) understand who you are and what you have to offer. **This is the whole point of developing your own personal brand.**

Brand You Checklist

✓ Learn the importance of career planning.

✓ Create your personal mission statement.

✓ Identify your professional strengths and weaknesses.

✓ Understand how to see career opportunities in trends.

Success

It's not just doing your job—it's caring about it, the people you work with, and the results you achieve. Success requires a large dose of self-discovery to find what you really care about.

Planning crystallizes your dreams. Your career ideas are transformed from a blur of vague possibilities to a clear vision of what you intend to accomplish. Creating a career plan is a series of decisions, starting with your personal mission statement and culminating in specific career goals. But career plans, like business plans, require action to become reality. To achieve your goals, you'll need to drill down from the big picture of your career plan to the details—the actions you'll need to take to make your plan reality. With each step in the process, your career choice will take shape and become clearer. As you work out the details, you'll get a good view of what it will be like to do the work. Then, one of two things will happen. Either you'll be more confident about your choice, or you'll realize you need to research a different profession or industry. The latter outcome can be frustrating—but it's better to find it out during the planning stages than after you've accepted a job!

Your Personal Strategic Plan

Businesses deliberately choose a time frame of five years for their strategic plans. In today's rapidly changing world, longer views usually prove to be meaningless. The probability of accurately forecasting developments in technology, business practices, and customer expectations beyond five years is very low. A relatively short time frame gives businesses the flexibility to adapt to changes as they occur. A five-year plan for your career is about the right length of time, too. You also need a plan that is flexible enough to adapt to changes in the workplace. Beyond five years, it's hard to predict what may happen in your job, your company, your profession, or your industry. In addition, your own personal interests and needs are likely to change over your lifetime. There will be times when your career is front and center, and times when it may take a back seat to raising a family, getting an advanced degree, or some other interest.

Although businesses look at five-year time frames for their strategic plans, they actually review and revise them every year. **You should review your career plan every year, too.** That way you'll be able to make incremental changes to your plan. It's much easier to make minor adjustments than to discover too late that your skills are obsolete and you have to start in an entirely new career direction.

We often hear people ask, "What do I want to be when I grow up?" If they're changing careers, the question is modified slightly to "What do I want to be *this time* when I grow up?" Career planning isn't about *being* anything—you're already a real live human being. It's about *doing*. Rephrase the question to **"What do I want to do with my skills and knowledge now?"** With this question in mind, you'll be able to create a flexible plan that allows you to adapt to changes in the workplace—and there will be many!

real people, **Real Brands**

Janée
Burkhalter's Brand

Janée Burkhalter, Ph.D. teaches marketing at Saint Joseph's University in Philadelphia. Her area of specialty is product placement.

See Janée's video profile at www.mypearsonmarketinglab.com.

▼ Q & A with Janée Burhalter, Ph.D., Associate Professor at Saint Joseph's University

Janée's Profile

Undergraduate and graduate school: Florida A&M University

Major: MBA, Business Administration

Doctorate: Georgia State University

Degree: Ph.D. (Marketing)

Topic of dissertation: The focus of my research was brands in music videos and how consumers respond.

Current profession: Professor

First job: Financial services marketing

How I got my first job: I was offered a full-time job as a result of one of my internships.

Brand key word: Random. I'm interested in so many unrelated topics.

My favorite quote: "Random, it's what I do." To me, random means flexibility, which means I don't have to do the same thing all the time.

Description of my personal brand image: I am an individual who is passionate about what she does and what she believes in. I also care greatly about the impact I can have on other people.

My passion: My passion is learning, as corny as it sounds. All of the different things that I do teach me.

Janée's Advice

Favorite advice about job searching: You have to be willing to do the research to find out what you really like to do.

What impresses me about a young person: Confidence and humility. I notice people who are confident enough in who they are and are humble enough to ask questions that you need to ask to learn about a particular career and learn as a person.

What *not* to do on an interview: Don't dress inappropriately. Always dress professionally and conservatively on any job interview. Even if the people with whom you are interviewing dress casually, dress in business attire. You can always dress casually once you get the job.

What I wish I had known about the real world: You need to be able to separate a person's role from his personality. You should always respect someone's role, even if you don't like him personally. Find out a way to work together to achieve a common goal.

Favorite job searching tip: Use informational interviews. You can talk to somebody who has the job that you think you want and you can learn about his or her experiences.

Define Your Mission

The Right Question
Students often start their career planning by asking the question, *"What do I want to be when I grow up?"* A question that fits our changing times better is, *"What do I want to do now?"* This keeps you open to exciting possibilities that will develop.

Organizations start their strategic plans with a mission statement. The mission defines the organization's overall purpose and what it hopes to achieve in terms of its customers, products, and resources. Like an organization's mission statement, your mission statement defines your purpose. It should be narrow enough to give you a sense of focus, but broad enough to adapt to future opportunities. **A mission statement that expresses your overall purpose and what you hope to achieve will help guide your search for a career choice now and in the future.**

Real People, Real Advice ... About Your Mission Statement

"As far as a personal mission statement that I come back to every day, I don't have one, but in the back of my mind, I know I need to get one."

—*Amanda Burd, student, Saint Joseph's University*

"Things that I did to help me (write my personal mission statement): I wrote down (what) my favorite words were, words that I just liked, words that I thought were cool, words that I thought described me, words that other people had used to describe me. I wrote down favorite quotes, I wrote down favorite Bible verses . . . it gives you something to work with. Your personal mission statement doesn't just come to you."

—*Janée Burkhalter, Ph.D. Associate Professor, Saint Joseph's University*

Hear some helpful tips from Janée Burkhalter, Ph.D. about how to start and refine your personal mission statement at www.mypearsonmarketinglab.com.

Your mission statement can serve as your inner career compass, guiding your decisions now and in the future. Lynn Perez-Hewitt says she belongs to the Pinball Wizard School of Career Planning. A glance at her résumé reveals seemingly disconnected work. Among other things, she's worked as a stockbroker, marketing consultant, and an executive for a nonprofit organization. But Lynn has an inner compass, a passion to **"live life fully, love fully, and share fully."** Lynn says she follows opportunities that appeal to her, as long as they fit her mission. There is also an underlying theme to her choices:

Through her work, she influences people in a positive way. She tackles every project with enthusiasm and shares her knowledge and creative ideas with colleagues, friends, and college students. While at first glance it looks as though Lynn bounces from one thing to another, a closer look reveals there's a mission below the surface.

As you develop your personal mission statement, your top values will give you some clues about a mission that describes your purpose for working. (*Hint:* Refer to Activity 1.1.) For example, if your top value is community, you might try a mission statement similar to this: **"To support community activities that sustain our environment."** That would give you many options, such as working for the Environmental Protection Agency (EPA), starting a community garden in a low-income neighborhood, promoting a new technology to reduce pollution, or implementing new forest management practices. As varied as these options are, each is aligned with the mission.

To Develop Your Mission, Think About:

- What's important to you
- Who you are
- What you stand for
- What you like to do
- Why you want to do it

Student Profile—Amanda

Amanda doesn't have a mission statement, but she realizes that it will be helpful to guide her as she begins to make career choices. She is passionate about a career in marketing, but she is not sure about which area of marketing she wants to pursue. She realizes that writing a personal mission statement doesn't happen in just one sitting. She began this important project with a three-step approach.

Amanda's Mission Statement—Step 1

Amanda started writing her personal mission statement by identifying the things that she really enjoyed. She used bullet points because she found it was easier to focus on who she is and what she wants (and avoid getting caught up in wordsmithing).

- Solving challenging strategic problems
- Working with data to make fact-based decisions
- Interacting with people
- Helping people

- Persuading people to see a different or new point of view
- Exciting customers about new products, especially products that can make their lives easier
- Working on major marketing projects and delivering results
- Working for an industry-leading corporation that cares about its employees and society
- Giving back to the community

Amanda's Mission Statement—Step 2

After a few weeks of creating and fine-tuning her list (above), she crafted the key points into a few sentences that would become the foundation of her mission statement.

> I enjoy working with people and using data to solve complex marketing challenges. I think it would be good to start my career at a large corporation so I can be exposed to and learn as much as I can about marketing and bringing new products to market. I would ultimately like to be in a leadership role in marketing. It's important to me that the company I choose to work for is community-minded and gives back to society in some way.

Amanda's Mission Statement—Step 3

Amanda reviewed her mission statement again after thinking about it for a few weeks. Although it captured who she is and what she wants to do, she felt that it was a bit long and wasn't yet memorable. She eventually evolved her mission statement into the one below.

> To connect consumers with brands that provide positive value or utility and give back to the community.

This concise statement summarizes Amanda's passion for marketing and her focus on community service. Based on this mission statement, she could pursue a career in a variety of industries. It also gives her flexibility to work for an established company or even start her own firm. Yet, this mission statement gives her a clear framework by which to make her career decisions.

Tricks of the Trade
Writing Your Mission Statement

It's a good idea to take the time to put your mission statement on paper. That way, you will really spend the time to formulate your direction. Here are some points that will make it easier to write your mission statement.

- Make it memorable.
- Focus on a single theme; don't try to be all things to all people.
- Make it clear and concise (it should fit on the back of your business card).
- It should energize you and rally you to action.
- It should serve to guide you as you make career decisions.

But don't get overwhelmed. Write your mission statement, and then re-visit it at a later date. You'll be surprised how much easier it will be to fine-tune it and make it shorter, more focused, and memorable. Keep in mind that writing your personal mission statement is a process that takes place over the course of time.

Watch a short video that includes some tips from Janée Burkhalter, Ph.D. about writing your personal mission statement at www.mypearsonmarketinglab.com.

It's true that some people work in order to live (as compared to those who live to work), and you may be one of them. **However, this mission statement should focus on your work purpose, not on a generic goal such as "To find a balance between work and family."** Although aiming for balance is a healthy aspiration, it doesn't guide your career choices, which is what your mission statement should do.

Real Questions, *Real Answers*

Q. How is a mission statement different from values and objectives?

A. Values reflect your personal beliefs, so qualities like honesty, integrity, family, teamwork, service to others, are all examples of values. Your values provide the foundation of your mission statement. For example, your mission statement might include some type of community service, if service to others is one of your key values. Objectives are more specific than a mission statement. Objectives help you measure your progress and identify key milestones that you want to achieve within a specific timeframe.

ACTIVITY 2.1 Write Your Mission Statement

Instructions: Write your personal mission statement in the space below. You may want to work on your mission statement over the course of time, then fine-tune it to be short and memorable.

_____

_____

_____

Now What?

Organizations and businesses don't hide their mission statement. You'll often see it displayed on a wall, in brochures, on Web sites, and even on coffee cups. Executives want employees to be aware of the company mission and to use it as a guide for decisions they make on behalf of the organization. **Find a way to display your mission statement. It will help you stay focused on your career goals and guide your decisions.** Here are some ideas to consider: Print it on the back of your business card; type it on your computer's desktop; post it on your Web site; hang it on the wall where you'll see it every day.

Your Internal Analysis

The next step in planning is conducting an internal analysis, which includes identifying your strengths and weaknesses. For a business, this is a complex activity that evaluates its technologies, physical assets, human assets, financial stability, and other elements that influence how well the firm operates.

For career planning, your internal analysis doesn't need to include so many elements, but it does require a large dose of self-discovery to uncover your strengths and preferences. In our busy lives governed by to-do lists, we rarely take time to look inside ourselves and discover our own wants and needs. But without this self-knowledge, how can you make informed decisions? How will you know what work is right for you?

Your internal analysis begins with uncovering your skills and talents. Skills are the basic building blocks of work. Read any job description and you will see a list of roles, activities, and tasks to be performed. If you broke these down further, you would see that skills make the performance possible. You can break down a job into these components as shown in Figure 2.1.

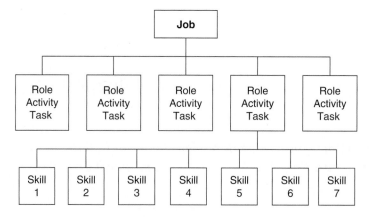

Figure 2.1 Job Skills

In the next exercise, you will determine your portable skills. **These are skills you can take with you and apply in a broad range of situations and settings—that's why they're called portable.** Consider a skill such as resolving conflict. This skill is valuable whether you're working as a mediator, customer service rep, or manager.

Your inventory of skills will help you in several ways. If you are looking for a career direction, research careers to find out which ones rely on the skills you enjoy. If you already have a career in mind, your skills inventory will increase your confidence that this is the right choice—provided the career is built on the skills you like to use. Finally, your inventory will help you clearly describe your skills so employers will know what you have to offer.

Real People, Real Advice ... About Skills Inventories

 "Skills inventories helped me to identify the fact that I love art . . . knowing what my strengths were helped me analyze some of the (career) possibilities that were presented to me later."

—*Janée Burkhalter, Ph.D., Associate Professor,*
Saint Joseph's University

Hear how Janée Burkhalter, Ph.D. used skills inventories and her personal SWOT to choose her career direction at www.mypearsonmarketinglab.com.

Skills Inventory

Instructions: To evaluate each skill, recall a time when you demonstrated the skill, whether at work, in school, or in any other area of your life.

Read each skill and rate your enjoyment of using the skill as follows:

V = Very High   H = High   M = Medium   L = Low

Then rate how effectively you use the skill in the Degree of Skill column. If you're not sure whether you have the skill, think about how others would describe you.

Skill	Enjoyment	Degree of Skill
Communication		
• Speaking persuasively	_____	_____
• Resolving conflicts, building consensus	_____	_____
• Giving effective presentations	_____	_____
• Developing compelling sales approaches	_____	_____
• Listening effectively	_____	_____
• Writing concisely and clearly	_____	_____
• Interviewing for information	_____	_____
• Giving advice or counseling	_____	_____
• Collaborating with team members	_____	_____
• Instructing, training people to perform new tasks	_____	_____
• Explaining complex ideas in everyday language	_____	_____
Using Information		
• Gathering information, doing research	_____	_____
• Synthesizing complex information	_____	_____
• Programming computers	_____	_____
• Classifying information, devising classification systems	_____	_____
• Evaluating data	_____	_____
• Observing and identifying data	_____	_____
• Solving problems using information	_____	_____
• Creating useful reports of information	_____	_____

Continues on the next page . . .

Skill	Enjoyment	Degree of Skill
Managing/Leading		
• Motivating, inspiring others to achieve goals	_____	_____
• Developing and communicating a compelling vision	_____	_____
• Managing multiple projects	_____	_____
• Coordinating, organizing work teams	_____	_____
• Mentoring	_____	_____
• Initiating and executing a plan, task, or idea	_____	_____
• Building trust	_____	_____
• Initiating change	_____	_____
• Coaching, developing employees' skills	_____	_____
• Leading individuals and groups to accomplish goals, objectives	_____	_____
Planning		
• Creating effective solutions to problems	_____	_____
• Developing strategies to achieve goals	_____	_____
• Estimating, reviewing project schedules	_____	_____
• Preparing budgets, computing costs	_____	_____
• Establishing cost controls	_____	_____
Creativity		
• Conceptualizing new or creative ideas, methods, structures	_____	_____
• Inventing/designing a new product, object, process, or art	_____	_____
• Generating innovative ideas	_____	_____
• Using intuition	_____	_____
• Visualizing concepts	_____	_____
• Using your imagination	_____	_____
Customer Service		
• Focusing on customer, client needs	_____	_____
• Building and maintaining relationships	_____	_____
Business Development		
• Generating income	_____	_____
• Identifying and capitalizing on opportunities	_____	_____

List your strongest skills here:

List skills you want to develop here:

Student Profile—Amanda

When Amanda completed the Skills Inventory, she learned her favorite skills were in the areas of creativity, communication, and using information. A nice fit for a marketing person!

Your External Analysis

One reason businesses conduct external analyses is to see how they stack up against the competition. Another reason they scan the external environment is to look for new opportunities. Changes in the economy, regulations, consumers, competitors, and popular culture can have a profound impact on a firm's fortunes. Business leaders know it's imperative to identify these shifts and adapt to them.

Your career success will also depend on frequently scanning the external environment. Here are a few of the recent changes that have affected people's employability: technology that replaced human labor, the crash of the dot .coms, outsourcing of manufacturing and administrative functions, restructuring firms to reduce management layers, and offshoring jobs to third-world countries. People who didn't foresee these events were stranded and often spent long periods looking for comparable work.

At the same time, it's important to remember that the world is full of new opportunities. Ever since scientists broke the genetic code, biotechnology has been growing exponentially. The advent of global terrorism has fueled the growth of security products and services. The retirement of baby boomers, the largest generation in history, will create many jobs related to leisure activities and antiaging products. New interconnected devices continue to find their way into the marketplace and affect the way we work and communicate. It's also comforting to note that it will be a long time before computers can replace jobs that require human interaction and creativity.

Savvy careerists scan the environment, searching for new opportunities to use their skills. They also stay up to date with trends in their industry and profession. They constantly develop relationships with colleagues outside their company and stay in touch. Industries and professions are more stable than individual jobs, and they change more gradually.

The next activity, *Finding Opportunities in Trends*, shows one way to scratch below the surface of a trend and see how it might impact your career field and provide new work opportunities for you. You might just discover an opportunity on the cutting edge that excites you.

Resources for Discovering Trends:
www.bls.gov: U.S. Bureau of Labor Statistics
www.bls.gov/oco: *The Occupational Outlook Handbook*
www.economist.com: weekly journal from England about world and national economics
www.fastcompany.com: career articles geared toward young executives
www.wfs.org: World Future Society
www.cnn.com: current events and business news
www.npr.org: National Public Radio often carries features about careers
www.rileyguide.com: comprehensive site for linking to good career sites
www.salary.com: career information including salary
Business magazines, newspapers such as *BusinessWeek, Wall Street Journal*

ACTIVITY 2.3 Finding Opportunities in Trends

Instructions: Choose four trends that could affect the career field you're considering. Then decide what the impact of each trend might be. Finally, brainstorm career opportunities that might result. This exercise is fun to do with friends or classmates, and a group helps generate more ideas.

Trend	Impact	Possible Career Opportunity
Males between the ages of 18 and 34 are watching less TV. They're spending more leisure time with TiVo and video games.	This prime marketing target is viewing fewer TV ads.	Create and sell advertising in new media; e.g., TiVo, video games, online game sites.

Strengths and Weaknesses

When you are completing your personal SWOT analysis, ask your friends and professionals to give you feedback about your strengths and weaknesses. You'll get an honest assessment of your weaknesses, and you might be pleasantly surprised to learn about some attributes that you didn't realize you have.

Opportunities and Threats

Unlike your strengths and weaknesses, opportunities and threats are elements in the environment that you can't control, but that have an influence on your career.

Your Career SWOT

Now that you've identified your mission and your strengths (skills), and you've discovered some trends that may impact your career, you're ready to try out your personal SWOT analysis.

Amanda's SWOT analysis is shown below. **Strengths and Weaknesses are areas that are within her control. Opportunities and Threats are areas that are outside of her control, but still have influence on her.** Amanda used her Skills Inventory and work experiences to identify her strengths. She read several articles about marketing to identify threats and opportunities.

Real People, Real Advice ... About Personal Branding

 "I think that doing a personal SWOT would help you know what you need to work on and also where you can go with your skill set so you can be relevant in your career."

—*Amanda Burd, student, Saint Joseph's University*

 "It's an interesting process to go through to develop a SWOT analysis, because you can engage other people, so you can make this a team project . . . you might find out things about yourself that you never really even considered, or things that you didn't know that people noticed, or you never really thought, 'This is a strength.'"

—*Janée Burkhalter, Ph.D., Associate Professor, Saint Joseph's University*

See a short video clip featuring Janée Burkhalter discussing how to do a personal SWOT analysis at www.mypearsonmarketinglab.com.

 "The Strengths and Weaknesses are about you . . . who are you, what are your skills, what are your interests, what knowledge do you have. The Opportunities and Threats are . . . the things going on around you that either you can leverage, which would be Opportunities, or the things that are going to present challenges, which are Threats."

—*Janée Burkhalter, Ph.D., Associate Professor, Saint Joseph's University*

Get more tips from Janée Burkhalter about how to think about Opportunities and Threats at www.mypearsonmarketinglab.com.

Your SWOT analysis is one of the most valuable exercises you will complete in this book. Your SWOT analysis will help guide your career direction and help you craft your personal brand message in the form of your cover letter, résumé, and even on your job interviews.

Student Profile—Amanda

Strengths
- Favorite skills: creativity, communication, and using information
- Great organizational skills—able to see the big picture and then figure out how the details relate
- Leadership ability—often asked to lead study groups, also leader in two campus organizations
- Good negotiator—solve interpersonal conflicts in study groups and at work
- Persuader—often get people to agree with my point of view
- Enthusiastic, creative
- Learning marketing theory, strategies
- Good connector—understand how to communicate with people

Weaknesses
- Sometimes impatient waiting for people to catch up to my ideas
- Could be a better listener
- Have so many interests, it's hard to focus on a goal

Opportunities
- Large number of people retiring
- Knowledge of social media and interactive marketing is valued by many employers
- More businesses realizing the value of marketing

Threats
- Challenging economic situation
- Interactive marketing is a popular field—competition for jobs
- Rapidly changing environment can make skills outdated

SWOT Analysis

Instructions: Complete each section of the SWOT analysis. When describing your strengths, use your Skills Inventory and any personal characteristics that will be an asset in the workplace. You may need to do a little research into your career field to identify opportunities and threats.

Internal

Strengths
Weaknesses

External

Opportunities
Threats

Career Objectives

Now that you have your SWOT analysis, it's time to write your career objectives. Objectives are specific goals that you want to achieve by a given time. For example, one of your career objectives might be:

Obtain an accounting internship at a major corporation by January 2011.

Note that this objective is simple and straightforward. And it is **SMART— Specific, *Measurable, Attainable, Realistic,* and *Timebound.*** SMART objectives provide a means of measurement so that you know if the objective has been achieved. In other words, an objective can't be general in nature. For example, the following career objective is not a good career objective because it is not specific enough (how will you know when you have achieved your objective?):

Obtain a position in sales.

When that objective is modified as shown below, it becomes a better way to measure success.

Obtain a sales position at a food marketing company by June, 2011.

Student Profile—Amanda

Amanda wrote the following career objectives:

- To obtain an internship in marketing at a major corporation before graduation.
- To work for an organization with annual sales in excess of $100 million within 3 years of graduation.
- To participate in an industry conference within 6 months on the job.
- To obtain a leadership position within the corporation within 5 years after graduation.
- To earn at least $40,000 within 18 months of graduation.

Career Objectives

Just like a business, you're now ready to set objectives that broadly define what you hope to accomplish within the time frame of your career plan. A useful time line might be five years after your graduation. Your objectives should be a direct outgrowth of your mission.

To be effective, your objectives should be specific, measurable (so you'll know whether you've achieved them), and attainable, realistic, and timebound. Attainability is especially important—otherwise you're setting yourself up for a feeling of defeat. Ask yourself, what can you realistically attain within five years?

Your objectives may relate to revenue, your esteem in your profession, types of work you'd like to do, where you might like to live, and so on.

Your Turn

Write your objectives in the box below. You don't need many objectives, but be sure that the objectives you create are SMART (specific, measurable, actionable, realistic, and timebound).

My Career Objectives

My Career Journal

Forget job titles and asking "What do I want to be when I grow up?" Instead, ask "What do I want to do with my talents?"

Work on a team that _____

_____

_____

Solve this problem _____

_____

_____

Use the following skills _____

_____

_____

Follow my talent in order to _____

_____

_____

Do you think the career(s) you are considering are consistent with your mission? Explain.

_____

_____

_____

_____

_____

Your mission should be broad enough to cover future possibilities. Read your mission statement again. Then quickly brainstorm a list of work options related to your mission. If you don't have a career direction yet, keep adding to this list.

_____

_____

_____

_____

_____

_____

_____

Notes to Myself

3

Choosing the Right Work Environment:

How to Find the Right "Fit"

You probably remember when you were making your decision about which college to attend. You may have visited a few different campuses. While you may have liked most of them, each probably "felt" very different. There were only one or two at which you felt comfortable; they were the schools at which you could imagine yourself being a part of the student body. You probably liked the people you met and what the school stood for. It's most likely one of the reasons you chose to attend your school—you've experienced the impact of the culture of an organization. **Just as you chose a school at which you felt comfortable, you will go through the same process when you are looking for a job.**

Organizational Culture

Values are deeply held beliefs about the right and wrong way to live. These values dictate specific rules about right and wrong and shape the behaviors of people living in a society. You identified your personal values in Activity 1.1.

Organizations also have strongly held values, including beliefs about the right and wrong way to run a business. These beliefs are strongly influenced by the values of the founders, and often survive long after the founder has placed the reins of the business in someone else's hands. Over time, these beliefs become assumptions that nearly everyone in the organization takes for granted. These beliefs and assumptions are so strongly held that it is difficult to change them. In fact, many companies hire organizational consultants to flush out these assumptions (often hidden from consciousness). A company's

Brand You Checklist

✓ Recognize which industry is the best fit for your style.

✓ Discover which work environment is best for you.

✓ Learn how to research different industries.

✓ Understand options to consider an international career.

collective assumptions must change before it is able to make major changes in the way it does business. In other words, these assumptions, if they are no longer viable, can be the downfall of any company trying to change its business plan, marketing strategy, or financial base.

You can think of an organization's culture as "the way we do things." You will find that many organizations have deeply ingrained ways of behaving, including everything from dress codes to managing the supply chain. In very structured organizations, new ideas often have to run up the appropriate chain of command and receive approval before they can be implemented. In less structured organizations, employees have more freedom to try out a new idea and see how it works.

With practice, you'll be able to recognize differences between company cultures in an interview. **You'll receive two benefits from paying attention to corporate culture: (1) You'll be able to decide if this is the right place for you; and (2) you'll be able to tailor your interview responses.** If the culture seems cutting-edge, fast-paced, and innovative, you can emphasize staying current,

---

What I Wish I Knew . . . *About Company Culture*

What's the difference between working for two companies? It could be more than you think . . . and more than just money. Carol, a marketing professional, didn't realize that there could be such a big difference between companies.

Carol had worked in various marketing positions for an established toy manufacturer. She honed her skills as a market researcher/analyst for several of its product lines. She sometimes suggested new marketing strategies, but people above her resisted untested ideas. After three years with the same employer, Carol used time during maternity leave to assess her work and reexamine her career goals. First, she wanted a shorter commute. Second, she realized she had learned just about all she could from her current employer and was ready for a change. A colleague suggested she apply for a marketing management position for a large restaurant chain. Even during her job interview, Carol noticed a difference in culture. She was introduced to people she passed in hallways, who were friendly and smiling and appeared enthusiastic. People talked about their personal lives as well as their work. Carol accepted the position and realized right away that people at the firm worked hard, but they had fun while doing it. This was very different from the serious, traditional, and analytical environment of her former employer. Today she is much happier in this new culture, able to implement new ideas and let her personality shine.

Carol's advice? Observe the culture while you are on every job interview. It's the small things that you see (or don't see) that can tell you so much about the organization's culture and how it operates.

---

real people, **Real Brands**

Brian
Wiggins's Brand

The Philadelphia Business Journal *is the number one source for business news in the Philadelphia region. Brian is responsible for all of the activities to deliver the publication to readers every week.*
See Brian's video profile at www.mypearsonmarketinglab.com.

▼ **Q** & **A** with Brian Wiggins, Director of Circulation, *Philadelphia Business Journal*

Brian's Profile

College: LaSalle University

Major: Communication and English (double major)

Graduate School: Strayer University

Major: MBA, Management

Current profession: Circulation marketing in publishing

First job: Business development and operations for my fraternity

How I got my first job: I got my first job through networking.

Brand key word: Impulsive. I like to gather facts and make decisions quickly.

Description of my personal brand image: I'm very customer focused. Everything I do is all about the customer.

Value I bring to my clients: I have passion for what I do and I manage by facts.

Brian's Advice

Favorite advice about job searching: Don't wait for your dream internship or job to come to you; research the industry and go after it. Whatever position you are pursuing, do something different to stand out from the crowd—be creative about how you present yourself.

Favorite advice about your career: Don't be afraid to take risks. You're at the beginning of your career; if you are going to take a risk, now is the time to do it.

What impresses me about a young person: When a candidate does his or her homework before he or she comes in for an interview. I expect someone to know about the product, the company, and the person with whom he or she is interviewing. Researching the company should include Google searches as well as searches on trade publications, local business journals (such as the *Philadelphia Business Journal*), visits to the company Web site, and use of the company's product or service . . . be the customer and experience the product or service as the customer does.

What *not* to do on an interview: Don't be arrogant. No matter how much you know, the people with whom you are interviewing know more about the business. Come in ready to roll up your shirtsleeves and do whatever job it takes to learn the business.

Favorite job searching tip: Find a person to send your résumé to. Avoid sending your cover letter and résumé "To Whom It May Concern." Show that you have the attention to detail to research the name of the hiring manager and find out something about him or her.

Real Questions, *Real Answers*

Q. Is it appropriate to ask about the company culture during an interview?

A. Yes, it's a very good idea to ask about the company culture during every job interview. Questions like, "How would you describe the company culture?", "What words would your employees use to describe the company culture?", and "Describe an average work day," are all good questions that can help you get a feel for the culture of the organization. In addition, it's always a good idea to ask the same questions of each person with whom you interview to see if you get consistent responses. And always look around to get visual cues such as the work environment, mood of the people, and professionalism of the interviewer.

learning new skills, and being creative. On the other hand, if the company is well established, the culture seems formal, and everyone is well organized, you can discuss fitting in, following guidelines, and being a team player.

Comparing Cultures

The culture of the organization and the temperament of the people who work there have a strong influence on the nature of the workplace. Here are some factors that influence organizational culture:

- **The location of the business** as well as the look of the building and the design of its workspaces. Does everyone have a cubicle or office, or are workspaces open and configured around a hub?
- **The occupation and personality of key players.** Does the company revere its scientists, or its dealmakers?
- **The management philosophy and style.** Do managers micromanage every detail, or do they set goals and then step aside so employees can accomplish them?
- **The history of the company.** What are the values of company heroes? Do people cite lessons learned from past successes and failures?
- **The organization's size.** Is work performed in well-defined silos or do employees have broad responsibilities because the organization is small?
- **Risk-taking.** Does the company take risks, or is it financially conservative? What are the consequences if an employee makes a mistake?
- **Ethics.** Does the company have a code of ethics? Do employees follow the code?
- **Social responsibility.** Does the organization contribute to the public good? Is it a good citizen in its community?
- **Ownership.** Is it publicly traded, or privately held?

Characteristics	Established *Fortune 100* Firm	Start-Up Biotech Firm
Types of workers	Stability seekers	Autonomy seekers
Employment contract	Long-term employment Good benefits and pay	High turnover Lower pay, some benefits, and good stock options
Education	Moderate, with extensive training opportunities	High, with little investment in employee training and development
Predictability	Established guidelines	Continuous change
Emotional tone	Calm	Sometimes frantic
Business strategy	Invest for the future	Stay on the leading edge, take risks, innovate
Accountability	Productivity is measured	Too busy building an enterprise to measure
Management style	Mentoring and coaching	You're on your own

While the culture of each company is different, it might be helpful to compare some characteristics of the culture of an established company compared to that of a start-up company.

Cracking the Code of Organization Culture

Some clues are evident in interviews, but it pays to research a company's culture beforehand. To find a great fit, think about what's important to you. Do you care about social responsibility? How important are the firm's ethics? What makes a company great in your eyes?

The Buzz
To find out what employees say about their employer, go to **www.vault.com**.

There are several ways to investigate a company's culture:

Company Web sites. You may be able to get a glimpse of a firm's culture by browsing its Web site. Is the site devoted entirely to products and services, or does it also feature employee contributions? Does it depict a diverse workforce? Is there any mention of ethics or social responsibility? What company characteristics does it promote as it tries to recruit you?

Research. Business magazines, LexisNexis, and trade journals are excellent resources. A trade journal is a publication or Web site that is dedicated solely to business-to-business news about a specific industry. For example, *Nation's Restaurant News* is a trade journal for the restaurant industry, while *Advertising Age* is one for the advertising and communications industry. Articles may not describe the culture directly, but with a little analyzing, you may be able to infer something about a company's culture.

Figure 3.1 *Philadelphia Business Journal Book of Lists*

There are several other resources that can give you insight about industries and companies. For example, each year *Fortune* magazine publishes the following lists: 100 Best Companies to Work For (based on benefits, salaries, training budgets, work/life balance, and stock performance), America's Most Admired Companies, Best Companies for Minorities, and Global Most Admired Companies. In addition, *American City Business Journals* publishes the *Book of Lists* for over 60 cities. It is an excellent resource to indentify and research companies and non-profit organizations in your local city. Ask your school librarian about the *Book of Lists* for your local city or find it at www.bizjournals.com and enter "Book of Lists" in the search box. *The Philadelphia Business Journal Book of Lists* is shown in Figure 3.1.

Network with an insider. One of the best resources for the inside scoop is to talk to someone who works at a company you are considering. The time to do this is before you interview—that's when people will be more candid about what it's like to work there. In later chapters, we'll discuss the power of networking.

Observe the culture when you interview. If more than one person interviews you, this is probably a team

---

Real People, Real Advice ... About Company Culture

"When you are looking to determine a company's culture, it's important to look at the people themselves. A lot of companies have mission statements and lots of text on recruiting pamphlets and everything like that. But I've always had really good luck determining a (company's) culture by looking at the employees themselves."

—*Amanda Burd, student, Saint Joseph's University*

"Every industry has a trade journal. . . . The first thing is, go to your library and find out (ask the librarian) what the trade journal is for the industry you are interested in. . . . You definitely want to read because you'll get an idea about what's going on . . . if you do a subject search for that trade industry and read the articles for the past year, you're going to learn about what the trend has been."

—*Brian Wiggins, Director of Circulation*, Philadelphia Business Journal

Watch short videos with Amanda Burd and Brian Wiggins providing tips about researching companies at www.mypearsonmarketinglab.com.

Tricks of the Trade
Generational Differences in the WorkPlace

You're probably used to being around people your own age. Chances are, you are a millennial (generally described as born after 1980). You are tech savvy and grew up in a 24/7 world. You look at the world differently than the other generations before you that you will also find in the workplace. Generation X (generally described as those born during the years 1960–1980) has been in the workforce for several years and many are now at different levels of leadership in many companies. They are flexible and independent. Baby Boomers (generally born during the years 1946–1964) tend to be more structured with work processes. They had to learn technology rather than grow up with it; some Boomers embrace it, while others avoid it.

What's the best way to navigate the differences in the workplace? Listen, communicate, adapt, and learn.

---

environment. Ask for a brief tour. Notice people's dress and how their workspaces are decorated. See if you can sense the general atmosphere, noting whether people seem calm or tense. Are people working together, engaged in conversations, or working alone? After your interview, spend time imagining what it would be like to work in this environment.

Finding your Place in 10 Industry Sectors

Culture is specific to each company. In many cases, the culture of the company is influenced by the culture of the industry. Learning about different industries will help you identify an area of interest and help you understand the best environment for you. Following are general descriptions for 10 major industries. Keep in mind that factors such as size, management philosophy, and style of the CEO influence an individual company's culture. But it's a good idea to start your research on a broad or macro level, then narrow it down to identify your target companies within an industry. One industry isn't better than another; it's a matter of which culture matches your personality and work preferences. As you read the descriptions that follow, consider:

- What words appeal to you? What turns you off?
- Think about how well the culture matches your talents, work style, and personality. Ask yourself, "Would I fit in here?"

 **THESE SITES:** for more information about industries:

www.bls.gov/oco
www.online.onetcenter.org
www.hoovers.com

Note: www.hoovers.com requires a subscription; ask your school librarian if your school has one.

• Examine how work functions and industries combine to form different environments. For example, compare a marketing position in a high-tech firm with one in a retail chain. Marketing departments tend to have a distinct culture, but that environment is influenced by the industry where they reside. You will also find it helpful to conduct research on your own to learn about different industries.

Agriculture, Mining, and Construction

Examples: *agribusiness, petrochemical, forestry, aquaculture, residential/commercial construction, and global military installations*

Do you enjoy seeing concrete results? Do you enjoy working outdoors and being physically active? These industries are populated with practical people who take pride in their skills and accomplishments. Once relying on time-honored techniques, workers now face challenges created by new materials and methods. This sector consists mainly of small, family-owned businesses, but global conglomerates such as Archer Daniels Midland (ADM), Bechtel, and Halliburton offer opportunities for world travel. College grads can find work in project management, finance, marketing, and sales. In small firms, managers often wear several hats.

Manufacturing/Research and Development

Examples: *automotive, aerospace, clothing, pharmaceuticals, computers*

Whether it's process, chemical, electrical, or computer engineering, are you a math or science whiz who thrives on developing logical solutions to complex problems? If you aren't bound for engineering, do you enjoy working with analytical, logical personalities? Engineers and research scientists are often the stars in these firms, sometimes earning as much as a vice president because of a breakthrough in technology. In these environments, all work is expected to meet strict time lines, tight budgets, and quality-control standards. The mantra in these organizations is "Do more with less." This sector is a fit for detail-oriented, levelheaded problem-solvers. Employment is fairly stable, although downsizings occur with fluctuations in the economy. If you're looking for a stable environment with opportunities for advancement, this sector might fit you. Organizational cultures vary within this sector, depending on whether the firm is a small start-up or a mature operation with a large investment in machinery and equipment.

Sales/Marketing

Examples: *autos, clothing, food, retail stores and Web-based sellers, cosmetics*

Do you enjoy knowing a product or brand inside and out? Do you have the quantitative and analytical skills necessary to measure the effectiveness of marketing campaigns? Do you want an opportunity to express your creativity? Work includes deciding how and to whom to sell products, improving the supply chain, and creating a "brand experience." For salespeople and marketers, performance and profitability are the name of the game. There is intense competition in the marketplace and within the organization. The Internet plays a significant role in building brands and relationships with consumers. Firms frequently restructure, and employees must be flexible and ready to re-tool themselves at a moment's notice. There is little tolerance for failure. This sector is a good match for high achievers with creative ideas and high energy. If you thrive in a fast-paced, fluid environment, this may be the sector for you.

Information/Media/Entertainment

Examples: *publishing, mass media, software publishing, telecommunications, advertising, public relations, film*

Do you enjoy expressing your ideas and participating in creative activities? Do you like working with words, ideas, and images? People in the creative end of these firms prefer practicing their craft to amassing financial rewards. They identify strongly with their work and derive their status from being recognized for their creative contributions. Their ambition is to rise to more prestigious outlets or high-profile assignments, rather than management. They're interested in "the buzz" and are always up on the latest trends and technologies, especially the Internet. Although creativity and fresh ideas are important, technical skills like editing, researching, and reporting are the building blocks of these professions. Entry positions are usually in these areas—once you pay your dues, you can move on to more creative work. This sector is extremely mobile—people frequently move from one media outlet to another, and much of the work is freelance or project-based. Most people identify with their profession, not their employer.

Finance/Insurance

Examples: *banking, commercial real estate, insurance, securities, venture capitalists*

Do you have a detailed mind and a full understanding of the financial world? This sector requires personal integrity and self-confidence, because you will be entrusted with large sums of money and proprietary information. Your image is important—you must look the part. Be prepared for some long hours and perhaps sleepless nights. For agents and brokers, this is a fast-paced, demanding world, where the next deal is everything. Quieter types usually work behind the scenes as analysts, auditors, or actuaries, or in more sedate environments like insurance or retail banking.

Professional and Business Services

Examples: *computer systems design, employment services, benefits consultants, management, scientific, and technical consulting, public accounting and legal firms, client services organizations*

Do you enjoy selling your expertise and knowledge? Can you uncover client needs and design solutions to their problems? Do you have excellent communication skills? Work environments in this sector are very professional, for reputation is critical. Success is determined by leading-edge technical skills, a talent for building client relationships, and internal self-management.

The cultures of firms vary, usually dependent on their size and the managing partner's style. Many firms rely on large pools of knowledgeable workers to fill rank-and-file positions. They often work long hours to meet individual client needs. It can take several years to move into partner status, when you are rewarded with prestigious clients and shorter hours. Some consultants work in teams at the client's place of business for several weeks or months. Large public accounting and human resource consulting firms house many specialties under one roof, providing opportunities for lateral moves. Many young professionals move from a consulting firm to a staff position in a client organization.

Education and Health Services

Examples: *edutainment (video, e-learning), psychological and social services, educational institutions, hospitals, clinics, fitness trainers, nutritionists*

Are you looking for work that makes a difference in the lives of those you serve? People in this sector work with their hearts as well as their minds. Expertise and skills are paramount and continuous learning is required to stay current with new methods and technology. Organizations in this sector set high professional standards. Most people are not motivated primarily by money, but by a calling to improve people's lives. If you are compassionate, dedicated, and able to keep your spirits up, this sector might fit you best.

Leisure/Hospitality/Culture

Examples: *restaurants, hotels, resorts, recreational facilities, parks, entertainment, museums, art galleries*

Do you like serving people or helping them enjoy their time off? Can you accommodate guests with grace and provide great customer service? When things go wrong, you'll have to stay cool under pressure. Many jobs in this sector are low paying and routine, yet many people enjoy this work and the fact that they don't have to take it home with them. Most establishments create a fun, casual atmosphere, and people enjoy the camaraderie with fellow workers and guests. Employees often have flexible work schedules, making this an ideal environment for people with **composite careers**—artists, authors, and entrepreneurs who need steady income while building their creative enterprise.

Government/Nonprofits/Nongovernmental Organizations

Examples: *federal, state, and local agencies, politicians, city managers, planners, foundations, nonprofit organizations, charities, and service organizations*

Do you enjoy setting policy and improving your community? Is there a social or environmental cause you want to support? This sector is home to activists who like the challenge of working to solve complex issues. These are collegial environments, where cultural diversity is embraced and individual differences are respected. This sector is changing dramatically as government agencies move into the role of contract administration and policy generation, while direct services are provided by contractors, third-party providers, non-profits, and community-based organizations. Historically, most people who work in this sector haven't been paid as well as those in the private sector, though fringe benefits may be richer. This pay gap is narrowing, especially in large government agencies and well-funded nonprofits. As the population ages, we'll see greater demand for recreational programs, meal deliveries, and home health care. People who seek friendly work environments, stability, professional challenges, and meaningful work are attracted to this sector.

Transportation and Utilities

Examples: *trucking firms, expediters, airlines, electric companies, alternative fuels*

Does the challenge of efficiently moving goods (or power) to customers and consumers interest you? Can you balance the sometimes conflicting goals of customer service and profitability? These organizations rely on people with professional skills, sensitivity to customer needs, and the ability to implement business plans. These industries are introducing new technologies that speed the delivery of products and output to customers. Once protected monopolies, utility companies are facing the challenge of greater competition. As a result, they are rethinking their organizational structure and culture. People who seek collegial work environments, challenges, and service to others are attracted to this sector.

Work Environment

Instructions: Read each pair of options and place a check mark in front of the statement that best expresses your preferences regarding work environment.

I prefer:		Or:
○ To work indoors	OR	○ To work outdoors
○ To work alone	OR	○ To work as part of a team
○ To travel most of the time	OR	○ To work at one location
○ Ever-changing activities	OR	○ Predictability and routine work
○ Unstructured workplace and autonomy	OR	○ Structured workplace with clear rules and procedures
○ Private workspace	OR	○ Shared workspace
○ To manage people or projects	OR	○ To manage myself
○ To work with specific deadlines	OR	○ To work with broad goals
○ Work that is precise and methodical	OR	○ Work that is creative and enterprising
○ Taking initiative	OR	○ Being responsive and practical
○ Using my social skills	OR	○ Using my technical skills
○ A large, established company	OR	○ A small, entrepreneurial firm
○ A fast-paced, challenging atmosphere	OR	○ A relaxed environment
○ Influencing others	OR	○ Supporting others
○ Specializing in one set of skills	OR	○ Using multiple skills and expertise
○ Compensation based on performance	OR	○ A set salary
○ Working for myself	OR	○ Working for others
○ Achieving financial goals	OR	○ Working for the good of society

Review the preferences you chose. Keep these in mind as you identify your target companies in Chapter 12. Also, refer to these preferences when you are applying for internships or full-time jobs.

Ideal Work Setting

Instructions: If you've been completing the activities so far, you know your skills and what industry sectors exist. It's time to sum up the results. Write a three- or four-sentence description of the industry sector and culture you are looking for. It's fine to have two or three possibilities, but make each one as specific as possible. Write your ideal situation(s) in the space below. It's a good idea to refer back to Activity 1.1 about your values and Activity 2.2 for your skills inventory.

For example: My ideal opportunity is an accounting position with a health care firm on the West Coast. The atmosphere in this admired facility is caring and professional. People enjoy working together to meet patient needs and run a profitable company. Or, My ideal opportunity is to have my own art studio in a small town in New England where I can be a part of the community and develop my specialty of painting landscapes.

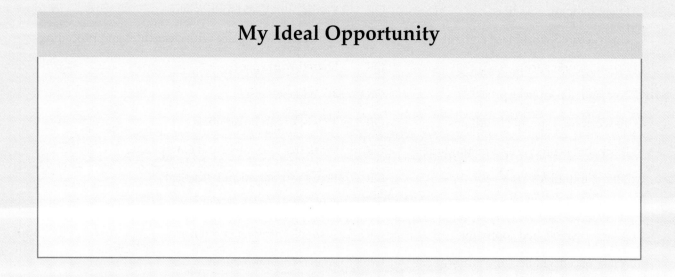

My Ideal Opportunity

Landing a Job Overseas

With the growing dominance of the global economy, uncertainty about off-shoring, and a desire for adventure, many college students are interested in pursuing international careers. Many of the same job-hunting skills apply, but there are some differences. If this is your goal, be sure to check out the Web sites cited in the margin.

Many companies have discovered that they need to strengthen their corporate identity and business processes when they move operations to other countries. In order to do this, they have been sending people on short-term assignments for three to six months. There are many reasons to seek these positions besides a change of place. The learning experience is invaluable. Most corporations with a global presence are looking for people with international experience for their management and executive positions. Being able to do

⊘ THESE SITES:
to increase your international savvy:

www.quintcareers.com
www.monster.com/geo/
siteselection.asp
www.studyabroad.com
www.rileyguide.com/
internat.html

business on the international stage and working successfully with other cultures can't be learned in the classroom.

Generally, it is easier to find these jobs from home. **The best option is to find a job with a multinational corporation in your own country and develop a special area of focus.** Become an expert in a field that has global impact. Examples include quality control, supply-chain management, accounting and financial systems, security, contract administration, and other areas that require global coordination and decision making. Once you have acquired these skills and gained some job experience, then you'll be ready to apply for a transfer to a branch in a different country. Of course, along the way, you'll need to pick up language fluency skills.

One way you can increase your marketability in the global job market is to study abroad while working on your degree. While you're there, combine your studies with an internship, teaching, or volunteer work. Professors in your department or your college career center may have information about work-study student exchanges. Ask the coordinators of the program about available opportunities and applying for a work permit.

Your campus is another vital source of information. **Most colleges actively recruit international students—the same people who sign them up can help you make inroads with their overseas connections.** You can also connect with faculty and counselors in the Department of International Studies. Of course, it's a good idea to take at least a few courses from the department, but even if you don't, the faculty and counselors will share resources and have contacts who can help you.

Of course, not everyone breaks into the international market through a local company with global connections. International exchange organizations, such as the Council on International Educational Exchange, the Association for International Practical Training, and the British Universities North America Club facilitate work exchanges. You can also apply directly to companies in other countries that appeal to you. Experts agree that the strategies we'll be discussing later, such as developing contacts and networking, are even more critical in a global job search. In addition, you'll need to tailor your résumé to the country where you're applying—several Web sites give information on how to do that.

My Career Journal

What did you learn when you studied the 10 industry sectors?

_____

_____

_____

_____

_____

_____

_____

_____

_____

_____

Reality check: Refer back to Activity 3.1, Work Environment and compare it to the industry sector you prefer. Is there a match between your work preferences and the industry environment? Where is there a mismatch? Can you live with the industry after all?

_____

_____

_____

_____

_____

Do you think working overseas is important for your career? If so, what resources do you plan to explore?

_____

_____

_____

_____

_____

_____

Notes to **Myself**

Step 2 Researching the Market

(Chapters 4–7)

Whether you are looking for an internship or a full-time job, you will need to do some research to determine which industry or industries you want to pursue and which companies will be on your target list.

Are you wondering where to start your research? Chapters 4–7 provide valuable information, including the best Web sites for your research. You'll be surprised to learn about many interesting companies and what they have to offer. And you'll learn how the hiring process works so you can anticipate and be prepared for each step.

Chapter 4, "Career Information and Research," is especially helpful because it contains specific information about how to use both online and off-line resources for your job search. It includes Gathering Information Online—11 Tips for Finding the Right Web Sites. In addition, the *Brand You* **Toolkit** includes a listing of recommended Web sites with general job boards as well as industry-specific sites and professional organizations. The chapter also includes Off-line Resources You Shouldn't Skip—6 Places to Explore in Person.

You have learned how to do a research paper for your classes; now learn how to do research for your future. The roadmap and resources are in the next four chapters.

Research has its rewards. ➤

4
Career Information and Research:
Know Where to Look

How does Apple know that consumers want an iPad, even before it is created? How does Nike know that consumers want to design their own athletic shoes before the option is even available online? How does Doritos know just what flavor of chips to offer next? All of these great brands do their homework—before they create any new products, they conduct marketing research to understand consumer needs and wants. Marketing research helps them anticipate consumers' likes and keeps them as the brand of choice. So before any products are created or any marketing is developed, marketing research helps guide the decisions of great brands. Research can do the same thing for your brand.

Know What You Want

If you dread hearing the question, "So what do you want to do when you graduate?" this chapter is especially important. Even though you may not know exactly what you want to do with your life or your career, this is the perfect time to use the resources available to you and find your path. While that's easier said than done, it's an ongoing project you should take on during your academic career. What's the best way to do it? Research!

Too often college students can't get where they want to go (a meaningful job) because they don't know what that is or where to find it. They think they are ready to job hunt, when actually they are ready to explore careers. Recruiters can easily spot job seekers like this—they are unclear about how they want to apply their skills and knowledge, so of course they can't express real enthusiasm for the job at hand. Because so much career information is available at your fingertips, employers lose patience with applicants who don't know what they want. When it comes to job hunting, knowledge is definitely power.

In this chapter, you can learn about tools that will help you avoid being a "lost" student. What these job seekers lack is the *information* needed to make good career decisions. You can get a jump-start on your career by sharpening your focus now. **Take the time to thoroughly research careers and drill down to data that will be relevant to your eventual search for work.** When you reach the end of your college days, you'll know where you want to go and how to get there.

Researching Like a Futurist

Marketing: Real People, Real Choices states that "some marketing researchers, known as *futurists*, specialize in predicting consumer trends to come. They try to forecast changes in lifestyles that will affect the wants and needs of customers in the coming years. Futurists try to imagine different scenarios, or possible future situations, that might occur." When you do your career research, act like a futurist. **Go beyond discovering what's already happened; find out where the profession and industry is headed.**

Real People, Real Advice ... About Thinking Like a Futurist

"(Futurist) It's a vocabulary word that I haven't heard before. I would guess it means how can you be relevant in the years ahead."

—*Amanda Burd, student, Saint Joseph's University*

"If you want to find the jobs, look where the momentum is . . . look at where the trends are . . . and anticipate where these trends might lead, then you give yourself good odds of going into an area where your skill sets are going to carry a premium."

—*Marc Brownstein, President and CEO, Brownstein Group*

Watch videos featuring Amanda Burd and Marc Brownstein discussing job trends at www.mypearsonmarketinglab.com.

Until recently, there was little need to scan the future to decide on a career. When change happened slowly over a lifetime, examining the way things were done in the past was enough. Researching a career field was a simple process. You could read publications that described the skills and abilities needed or you could talk to someone working in the field. Although these are still good methods to begin researching a career, **today you must also know about the future.**

In Chapter 1, you learned about some of the ways work is changing. There is relentless pressure for faster product innovation, the emergence of a global playing field, the new capabilities in a networked world, and the development of more work options. Broad changes like these will affect nearly everyone in the world of work. Other changes will be specific to a particular industry. For example, some futurists predict that by the year 2019, personal virtual realities will be taking market share away from TV, radio, films, and other media. What impact would that have on your career if you were producing content for one of the traditional media formats?

How Futurist Research Can Help

Research into future trends is essential to ensure that changes won't catch you by surprise. Although you can't predict precisely what changes the future holds, you can be sure that no matter what career you're researching, it will change and evolve. **Follow Wayne Gretsky's advice and look ahead so you're ready when the future arrives.** Futurist research can help you in the following ways:

The Gretsky Principle
"Don't skate to where the puck is; skate to where the puck will be."

- **Improve decision making.** When you're aware of potential opportunities or challenges that the future may bring, you can make an informed decision about whether the field is a good fit for you.
- **Create career resilience.** Examining how your career will change ensures that the career you are choosing and the education you are pursuing will continue to provide you with a viable living.
- **Uncover different ideas.** Good research uncovers various viewpoints to help you in considering the impact of trends and opportunities. It's easy to find information about a new technology; it's more difficult to stretch your thinking to forecast the impact it might have in the marketplace.

Keys to the Right Information

Whether you are considering an internship or a full-time job, the foundation of your search for great work is great research. The goal is to identify a career option or, if you have a career in mind, confirm that you have an accurate picture of that career. Knowing how to research career options is a valuable skill. Undoubtedly, there will be times in the future, either because of your own development or changes in the workplace, when you'll use these skills again.

The best place to begin is with good research strategies. Four strategies will help you gather and evaluate career information:

Focus on the big picture.
Discover possibilities.
Evaluate your assumptions.
Ask the right questions.

real people, **Real Brands**

Marc

Brownstein's Brand

Brownstein Group is a full-service advertising agency with a diverse portfolio of clients including IKEA, Microsoft, and Sony Style/Comcast Labs.

See Marc's video profile at www.mypearsonmarketinglab.com.

▼ Q & A with Marc Brownstein, President and CEO, Brownstein Group.

Marc's Profile

College: Penn State University

Major: Advertising

Current profession: President and CEO of a full-service advertising agency

First job: I was a junior account manager (at age 3).

How I got my first job: I worked in the family business (advertising agency), but my first job was at an agency in New York. My dad wanted me to learn the ropes before I came to Brownstein Group, the advertising agency he founded.

Brand key word: Connector. I like to connect people to each other.

Description of my personal brand image: Intensity laced with equal doses of accountability and compassion; I'm the rudder and the spark plug in the company—I chart the vision for the company and I also like to shake things up.

Marc's Advice

Favorite advice about job searching: Cut your teeth on the business . . . get internships, read trade publications, practice the craft, understand the rigors of the business.

Favorite advice about your career: Look at what you do well and how that fills a need in the marketplace. Play to your strengths. I believe that people who market themselves well are going to be more successful in finding the right opportunities for their career.

What impresses me about a young person: When someone "gets it." When you've done your homework, when you really understand the business and know what you're talking about.

What *not* to do on an interview: Don't come in and say, "I'm a people person." Everyone's a people person. That doesn't differentiate one candidate from another.

My favorite interview question: Tell me your story . . . I want to hear it from the beginning . . . I want to hear about the path you took. I listen to determine if things happened to you, or if you made things happen.

Focus on the Big Picture

Begin your research by examining industries and professions rather than specific job titles. Industries and professions are stable—many have survived for centuries. We may use new fuels in the future or rely less on personal cars, but we'll still need a way to get from one place to another. If you're interested in transportation, the right question may be, what alternatives are on the drawing boards?

Professions and industries exist to meet basic needs. For instance, human beings have always had a need to know what's going on in the world. We've evolved from town criers to newspaper journalists to TV reporters to bloggers. The job titles and media have changed, but the need remains constant.

Generally, jobs change more frequently than industries or professions do. However, technology can have a big impact on a profession. Not so long ago, a staff accountant's primary responsibility was entering data into a ledger and calculating debits and credits. Today, an accountant uses a computerized system and delegates data entry to an assistant. The main function of the job now is advisory—collaborating with operations managers to find ways to reduce costs and increase profits for their area. With these changes, accountants have had to learn both technical and interpersonal skills to adapt to their new role.

As you research an industry or profession, think about the need it fulfills. Considering the changes that you read about, will the need still exist in 10 years? How will work in the industry change? In the future, will it still fit with your preferred skills? For example, some accountants are much more comfortable crunching numbers than advising business leaders. They have moved into tax accounting or other fields in which they can still rely on their computational skills.

The Big Picture
Instead of saying, "I want to be a copywriter," it's more useful to say, for instance, "I want to use words to tell a story or influence public opinion." This way of thinking increases your options and your marketability.

Discover Possibilities

In Chapter 2, you completed an activity in which you identified some trends, thought about their impact, and considered opportunities that might result. Continue this kind of inquiry as you research an industry or profession. Be on the lookout for trends that will affect the field. Think about new jobs that will emerge. For example, as online learning becomes more widespread, what will be its impact on education? Some predict fewer teachers will be needed, and those in the classroom will act as learning guides on the side rather than as experts at the front of the room. On the other hand, think of the possibilities for people who develop educational content, graphics, and connectivity. Many predict that education will morph into edutainment.

Evaluate Your Assumptions

We all have ideas about what certain jobs are like. Your tentative career choice is based on your exposure to work, viewpoints you've heard, and things you've read or seen in the media. You may think you know a great deal about the field already (and perhaps you do), but you have probably filled in information gaps with assumptions. One goal of your research is to determine whether the facts support the opinions you've heard and the assumptions you've made.

As you conduct your research, find out what it's really like to do the work—day in and day out. To gain accurate information, it's important to recognize and put aside your assumptions. The following questions will help you:

- **What assumptions am I making about working in this field?**
- **Are my assumptions based on fact?**
- **What questions can I ask to test my assumptions?**

When our marketing student, Amanda Burd, thought about it, she realized she had assumed she would immediately be developing creative marketing ideas. When Amanda decided she wanted to work in an established consumer products company, she realized she wouldn't be *the* marketing department—she'd be the junior member of a marketing team. She decided to find out the typical assignments for new hires. Amanda also realized she needed to learn about the consumer products industry. She wanted to find out which products were expected to do well in the future and learn about trends that might affect people's buying habits.

Ask the Right Questions

Good research requires planning and organization. Just like a marketing professional doing research, your first task is to define the problem and specify your research objectives. What is it you want to know about the industry or profession you are researching?

As you plan your research, look for resources that will tell you things you don't already know. The resources listed in this chapter are a good starting point. A good research strategy will help you discover what a particular career field is like. You'll also want to learn what people are saying about its future.

Your research questions will be unique, depending on the field you are investigating, the amount of information you already know, and your own curiosity. Listed below are some general questions to consider asking as you do your research.

The Nature of the Work
- What are the types of tasks and responsibilities people have?
- What market needs does the work fulfill?
- What kinds of people tend to do well in this field?
- What are some examples of typical projects?
- What kinds of problems do people solve?

Getting Started

- What type of education is generally required to enter this field?
- What college majors are suggested?
- What type of experience is helpful for entering this field?

Values

- Compensation and benefits are not the only things to consider when choosing a career. Also research the internal rewards—the reasons people say they like working in this field. Then return to Activity 1.1 in Chapter 1 to see if these rewards match your own values.
- What is the typical starting salary in this field?
- What is the salary range for people with five years of experience?
- Is there an opportunity to learn new skills?
- What is the work environment like?

Future Opportunities

- How is technology changing this field?
- What changes are anticipated in the way work is performed?
- What factors influence advancement in this field?

Futurist Research Involves

- Focusing on the big picture
- Discovering possibilities
- Evaluating your assumptions
- Asking the right questions

Research Resources—The Best Places to Research Your Career Direction

You have learned how to do research for a paper. Now you are going to apply those skills to researching the direction you want to take for your career.

Whenever you are conducting research, use the following guiding principles:

- **Search from general to specific.** That means that first you should research industries such as the ones discussed in Chapter 3. After you identify one or two industries that are interesting to you, drill down and begin to research specialties (which are discussed in Chapter 5), then drill down again to research companies, and finally research jobs. It might sound like a lot of work, but if you keep your research focused, it will be easier and more informative to help you guide your decisions.

- **Gather information from multiple sources.** You will be investigating many areas and you want to be sure that you get the full picture. For example, if you are interested in advertising, you will most likely find some sources that talk about the excitement and creativity of the industry, and you will also find some that discuss the high-risk nature of the industry. You should be aware of both sides so you can make your evaluation with complete information.

Learn the Ins and Outs

Get the inside story on what works . . . and what to avoid online. Read the Do's and Don'ts of Online Job Searching in the **Brand You** Toolkit.

What's a Business Journal?

Most major cities have a business journal that reports on every local business from health care to nonprofit organizations. Visit your campus library to read a copy of your local business journal or visit **www.bizjournals.com** and choose the link for the appropriate city. The *Philadelphia Business Journal* Web site is shown in Figure 4.2.

Gathering Information Online—11 Tips for Finding the Right Web Sites

You know your way around the Internet, but do you know where to start to make your career direction decision? Here is a guide to help you identify which Web sites are worth researching. Use this framework to begin your research. Don't limit your research to only these Web sites. This should be a starting point for you. Search and find the Web sites that will help you in your research. Bookmark your favorite Web sites on your computer so you can go back to them. Right now, you are gathering information. You will learn in Chapter 12 how to use this information to create a communication plan.

Figure 4.2 *Philadelphia Business Journal* Web Site

11 Tips for Finding the Right Web Sites

Tip #	Topic	What to Look For	Some Suggested Web Sites
1	Industry Research	News, trends, and general information by industry	**www.hoovers.com** **www.bls.gov/oco** **www.online.onetcenter.org**
2	Career Planning	Articles, tips, advice on how to consider a career direction	Your campus career center and Web site. Your campus library may have subscriptions to many paid Web sites such as **ww.hoovers.com**, **www.lexisnexis.com**, etc. Also review Web sites listed in the *Brand You Toolkit* including sites such as **www.career-advice.monster.com www.rileyguide.com www.salary.com**
3	Professional Trade Organizations	National, regional, and local organizations and associations in the industry or discipline in which you are interested, which include industry news, events, articles about influential people and recently promoted people. Professional organization Web sites are an excellent source for internship and full-time job listings.	Visit **www.associationjobboards.com** to find a listing of many professional organizations. Also visit the organization's home page as well as the job board. Also see Recommended Web sites in **Brand You Toolkit** (at the back of the book) for a comprehensive list of Web sites. TIP: Also do an online search for local professional organizations such as the local city advertising club, accounting society, professional teacher's organization, or musician trade group.
4	Industry Trade Journals	E-mail, online, and hard copy publications, which include news, events, and jobs. Most trade publications offer free e-mail newsletters and many offer free circulation of their magazine.	Ask a professor which are the best trade publications to read in the industry in which you are interested. Go to the campus library or public library and ask about the trade publications for your industry. Do an online search for trade publications in your industry.
5	Local Business Journals and Newspaper Web sites	News, key industry people, and financial performance of local businesses. Local job listings are also available.	Visit **www.bizjournals.com** to find the business journal Web site for the city nearest you. Visit your local newspaper's Web site and read the business section regularly.

Continues on the next page . . .

11 Tips for Finding the Right Web Sites

Tip #	Topic	What to Look For	Some Suggested Web Sites
6	Business Lists	Lists of top businesses in a variety of categories, such as Top Public Accounting Firms, Top Advertising Agencies, Top Public Relations Agencies, Fastest Growing Companies, Best Companies to Work For, Top Companies to Start Your Career, Top Companies for Women, Top Companies for Minorities, Top Companies for Families, etc.	National lists are available from national business publications such as **www.businessweek.com**, **www.wsj.com**, **CNNmoney.com/fortune.** Local and regional lists are usually available from the Web site of your local newspaper, **www.bizjournals.com**, and local professional organizations and trade publications.
7	Business Directories	Directories with company listings, financial information, number of employees, key contact people in the industry, and/or geographic area of your preference.	Check your campus library for business directories in your industry. The library may have a subscription to some paid directories such as the Directory of Corporate Affiliations, Advertising Red Books, etc. Also check professional organization Web sites for business directories. For example, on the American Marketing Association Web site you can find as many as eight different directories of companies in the marketing industry by visiting **www.marketingresourcedirectory .marketingpower.com.**
8	Company Web Sites	Use the business lists and directories to help identify your target companies. Check the company websites regularly for internships and full-time jobs.	Various
9	Professional Social Networks	Use Web sites that are focused on business networking where you can learn about a specific industry, talk to small business owners, and create a network of people to ask questions and make contacts.	**www.linkedin.com** **www.ryze.com** **www.ecademy.com** **www.womanowned.com** **www.ziggs.com** **www.jobster.com**
10	Job Boards	Use a mix of large, specialized, and industry-specific job boards.	See Recommended Web sites in *Brand You Toolkit*.
11	Recruiting and Employment Companies	Look for companies that don't charge a fee to search for jobs or post your résumé.	Search for employment agencies at **www .superpages.com**. They are listed by city. You can also narrow your search to your industry.

Offline Resources You Shouldn't Skip—6 Places to Explore in Person

Don't limit your research to the Internet. There are excellent resources that are best used in person. Don't wait until you're a senior to get to know these people and places.

Tip #	Where to Go	Why to Go There
1	Campus Career Center	Your campus career center offers more resources than you think. Make an appointment and meet with a counselor to understand everything that is available. Many offer seminars and how-to clinics, job fairs, mock interviews, résumé and cover letter critiques, research resources, and general advice and guidance. You can find help for career planning, internships, and full-time jobs. Don't just scan the Web site, go check it out.
2	Campus or Public Library	Like the campus career center, the library is an excellent resource. Make an appointment with a librarian and learn about all the tools that are available for your research. Ask about which Web sites, databases, and business directories you can access through the library.
3	Campus Alumni Association	Make an appointment to meet with someone in the alumni association or the office that handles alumni affairs. Look up on your campus Web site which office handles this. Meet with the person and find out the best way to network with alumni that are currently working in the industry or industries you would like to pursue. Alumni are usually very receptive to helping undergraduates or new graduates find an internship or full-time job.
4	Networking	If you want to do effective networking, pick up the phone. Yes, you will probably follow up via e-mail, but your initial contact should be personal. See Chapter 14 for a complete look at how to network.
5	Professional Organizations	Many professional organizations have collegiate chapters or affiliations with colleges and universities. Go to the department of your major and find out what professional organizations are on campus. Go to a meeting, event, seminar, conference, or other activity sponsored by the organization. It's a great way to get exposure to the industry and meet people who can give you more insight. Most professional organizations have reduced membership and/or event fees for students. And, if you become a member, it's a great addition to your résumé.
6	Informational Interviews	You can ask someone who is currently working in the industry if you can meet with him or her to get some insight into the industry. This is a perfect opportunity to learn and ask questions. Ask friends, professors, the alumni association, career center, or professional organization for a contact. People want to help you succeed. Take the opportunity to explore as much as you can. A word of caution: If someone agrees to meet with you, consider it a fact-finding visit. It's not the time to ask for a job.

Ask for the Informational Interview

While informational interviews may be new to you, most professionals are aware of them and are willing to share their experience. Ask a professional in person, by phone, or via e-mail if you can meet him or her for 20 minutes to learn more about what the person does and how he or she got into the industry. You'll be surprised that most people are happy to help you (and flattered that you asked).

Informational Interviews . . . A Powerful Resource

It's worth noting that informational interviews are one of the best ways to learn about an industry, company, or job. An informational interview is different from a job interview. It is an opportunity to meet with someone in the industry who does what you want to do. Professionals in all areas from business to the arts are usually willing to spend 30 minutes or so to meet with you and tell you more about the industry.

The secret to informational interviews is to ask for them. And ask as many people as possible for informational interviews. It's a great way to get different perspectives, which will help you choose your own path.

You might be thinking that you don't know anyone with whom you can do an informational interview. Chances are, you know several people with whom you can meet. Follow up with guest speakers in class, visit your career services center, talk to your professors and parents about people they know that might be in an industry you may want to consider. Go on as many informational interviews as possible. It's a good way to learn first-hand about what you might want to do . . . as well as what you might *not* want to do.

The best way to approach these people is to simply ask them. For example,

"I'm thinking of pursuing a career in public relations. I know you have been in the business for several years. I was wondering if I might be able to come in

Real People, Real Advice ... About Informational Interviews

"An informational interview is when you go in and talk to someone about their job. . . . You kind of sit down one-on-one to gain feedback and insight about how they got to where they are and just connect in an informal, informational kind of way. . . . Having the one-on-one connection with someone can help you narrow down your job search and see through their eyes what they do every day."

—*Amanda Burd, student, Saint Joseph's University*

"Talk to people . . . it's the best way to learn about the industry."

—*Marc Brownstein, President and CEO, Brownstein Group*

Watch short videos featuring Amanda Burd and Marc Brownstein to learn more about informational interviews and how to research different industries at www.mypearsonmarketinglab.com.

and talk to you to learn more about how you made your career choice. Do you have some time next week?"

Or, you might consider using this type of approach:

"I'd really like to get into sales, but I'm not really sure if it's the right career for me. Do you have just 20 minutes or so next week so I can meet with you to learn more about what it takes to be successful in sales?"

When you meet with someone for an informational interview, treat it as if it were a regular interview. That means you should:

- **Dress** in appropriate interview attire.
- **Prepare** before the interview so you know what questions you want to ask.
- **Learn** as much as possible about the company and the interviewer as possible before your meeting (check out your interviewer's profile on LinkedIn so you know his or her background).

Real Questions, *Real Answers*

Q. What types of questions are appropriate to ask on an informational interview?

A. When you go on an informational interview, it's important to be prepared with the questions you want to get answered. Questions about the industry and the background of the person are appropriate; asking for a job is not appropriate. Your role is to learn and gather information to determine if this might be a career path you might want to pursue. Some questions you might consider for an informational interview are:

- What was your first job out of school?
- How did you make the choice to get into this industry?
- What do you do on a day-to-day basis?
- What skills does it take to be successful in this industry?
- What do you like about the industry?
- What don't you like about the industry?
- What piece of advice do you wish you knew before you entered the industry?
- What advice can you give me about getting into the industry?
- **Can you recommend other people I could talk to about work in this field? (Always, always ask this question.)**

Build on the information you gather, **and follow up with your contacts to keep them posted on your progress.** Check the validity of ideas you've heard by asking others about them. For example: "Jasmine Brown at Epstein Partners suggested I start by working through a temporary agency. What do you think? What agency does your company use?"

Planning Your Research

Instructions: Use the following worksheet to plan your research. Write down the questions you want to answer. Review the list of questions noted earlier in this chapter and add your own. Then fill in the last column and you're ready to start searching for information.

Which industry sector(s) or profession(s) will you research? If you need to, review the industry sectors in Chapter 3. Write your choice(s) here:

_____

_____

My Questions	Resources I'll Use
_____	_____
_____	_____
_____	_____
_____	_____
_____	_____
_____	_____
_____	_____

Prepare for each interview by developing a list of questions to ask. Summarize your background by using your value proposition. It is fine to have your questions written down and to take notes during the meeting—it will create a professional impression.

While your first objective is to learn about the industry, an informational interview is the perfect way to make a positive impression and build an ongoing relationship. See Chapter 14 for more details about how to use informational interviews for networking.

A Word of Caution about Informational Interviews

An informational interview is *not* an appropriate time to ask for a job. The person will feel used and he or she won't want to help you at all. If there are openings at the company for which you qualify, he or she will let you know. However, an informational interview is a perfect time to make a positive impression and stand out in the interviewer's mind. He or she will be more likely to call you when there is an opening if you make a good impression, follow up with a thank-you note after the interview, and keep in touch (remember, the rules of networking apply . . . build your network by keeping in touch).

ACTIVITY 4.2 # Conduct an Informational Interview

Identify a professional who does what you want to do. Ask that person if you can meet with him or her for an informational interview. Complete the following steps to prepare for the interview and to follow-up afterwards.

Requesting an Informational Interview

List at least two professionals in the area you are considering for a career.

1. _____
2. _____

Ask at least one of the professionals listed above for an informational interview. Record the following information about the informational interview.

Name of person with whom I am interviewing: _____

E-mail address: _____

Title: _____

Company: _____

Company address, city, state, zip code: _____

Phone number: _____

Date of informational interview: _____

Time of informational interview: _____

Location of informational interview: _____

Make a list of the questions you will ask during your informational interview.

_____

_____

_____

_____

_____

_____

_____

_____

Follow-up from an Informational Interview

Send a thank-you e-mail *and* handwritten thank-you note within 24 hours of your interview. See the *Brand You* Toolkit at the back of the book for sample thank-you notes.

ACTIVITY 4.3

ACTIVITY 4.3

Analyzing Your Results

Instructions: List below the advantages (+) and disadvantages (–) of the field you researched. In doing so, consider how well it matches your preferred skills, values, and work environment.

+	−
_____	_____
_____	_____
_____	_____
_____	_____
_____	_____
_____	_____
_____	_____
_____	_____
_____	_____
_____	_____
_____	_____
_____	_____

The bottom line: If the disadvantages outweigh the advantages, choose another field to research!

Future Possibilities

Instructions: Use the following worksheet to write down trends that may affect this career, or possibilities that may emerge in the future. Place a check mark beside the trends that you want to continue tracking.

Future Possibilities	✓

My Career Journal

How well does your tentative career choice fit with your interests, skills, and values? Explain.

_____

_____

_____

_____

_____

_____

Will you keep it as one of your possibilities?

_____

_____

_____

What do you still want to learn about this career? How will you gather that information? When will you do it?

Research To Do List	Date

What other careers still interest you?

_____

_____

_____

_____

_____

Notes to **Myself**

5

Why Employers Buy:
How to Build Your Brand Based on Employers' Needs

Brand You Checklist

✓ Learn how to create your own personal brand.

✓ Discover which organizational specialties are common.

✓ Identify how to determine which specialty is best for you.

✓ Understand that you might change your mind about your career path.

✓ Explore whether you should focus on what you want or on "hot" careers.

Have you ever thought of an employer as a customer before? Probably not. But now that you are thinking about yourself as a brand, it makes sense that the customer is your prospective employer. Your ultimate goal as a brand is to have a prospective employer "buy" or hire you. To be a successful brand, you need to consider what each prospective employer is looking for and determine how you can meet his or her needs. **Getting a job is not about *you*, it's about what the company (or client) needs.** If a company is looking for a finance person who thrives in a fast-paced environment, you should be ready to tell your story of how you worked on an IPO during your internship. If a client wants someone who can meet deadlines, share the story of how you helped organize the Susan G. Komen Race for the Cure in time for Mother's Day with only four weeks' lead time, and had the most participants in campus history. **While your brand is all about *you*, the way you tell your story should be all about how you and your experience can bring *value* to the company or client.**

Real Questions, *Real Answers*

Q. It seems as if having a personal brand is like being a fake. You just say what you think someone wants to hear in an interview. Is this true?

A. There should be nothing fake or phony about your personal brand. A great brand is authentic and consistent in every respect. Think about ads for Coke . . . it doesn't try to be the mixer for drinks, it's consistently presented as the soft drink that provides refreshment. And a Coke always looks the same with the red and white logo, no matter where you buy it. Great brands are authentic. Think about Harley-Davidson, Red Bull, and Mercedes-Benz . . . each is genuine and doesn't try to be something it's not. Personal branding provides the same type of authenticity and consistency. It isn't a method for being something that you're not. Rather, it's a process that helps you have clarity about what you have to offer and how it can help a prospective employer or client. Branding is a process that creates value. Think of your personal brand as the way you deliver value to a prospective employer.

What motivates an employer to "buy" a new employee? The decision-making process to hire a new employee is not much different from the one that you use to make a major purchase. Generally, there are five steps to the decision-making process. It's a good idea to think about each one and the role you can play as a qualified candidate.

1. **Problem recognition** occurs whenever the decision maker (in this case, the employer) sees a significant difference between her current state and some desired state. For example, when a school has an increased enrollment and needs an additional math teacher, the administration determines that it needs an additional teacher.

2. **Information search** can be aligned with posting of the position. In this step, the school is seeking a number of qualified candidates in order to choose one to fill the position.

3. **Evaluation of alternatives** is the part of the process when the administrator at the school reviews the résumés and decides which of the candidates to consider. The interview process and reference checks are part of this step to help the employer, the school administrator, accurately evaluate the options on a variety of elements.

4. **Product choice** takes place with the decision to extend an offer to one of the qualified candidates. You can see that the prospective employer (in this case, the school) goes through a lengthy decision-making process before deciding on the ultimate candidate.

5. **Postpurchase evaluation** occurs only after the newly hired candidate begins working. There is usually an evaluation time frame for new employees (three to six months), at the end of which, the employee receives initial feedback from the employer.

If you think about the same process you go through before you make a major purchase, such as rent an apartment, buy a computer, or lease a car, you will have a better understanding of the steps that a prospective employer takes before hiring a new employee. In some cases, these steps can be completed in a matter of weeks, while other times it may take several months, even years, to complete the process. To be successful, always have your brand fine-tuned and your brand story ready to be told. You never know when an employer is starting the decision-making process, so you should always be ready.

real people, **Real Brands**

Vince
Giannini's Brand

WPHL 17 is a television station in Philadelphia that broadcasts the baseball games of the World Champion Philadelphia Phillies. Vince Giannini is the Vice President and General Manager responsible for all of the station's programming and profitability.
See Vince's video profile at www.mypearsonmarketinglab.com.

▼ **Q & A** with Vince Giannini, Vice President and General Manager, WPHL 17.

Vince's Profile

College: University of Illinois

Major: Accounting

Current profession: Television executive

First job: My first job was as an auditor for one of the (then) big eight accounting firms.

How I got my first job: I went to an on-campus recruiting interview.

Brand key word: Hard working

Description of my personal brand image: I would say integrity, judgment, competitive, and analytical. I have a positive outlook and keep things in perspective.

Vince's Advice

Favorite advice about job searching: Get experience in any way you can from internships to extracurricular activities. Being able to talk about your experiences on an interview can help you get the job.

Favorite advice about your career: You can't be a yes-man or a yes-woman; learn how to speak your mind, tactfully, then once a decision is made—get behind it.

What do you look for in an intern or entry-level candidate: Tell me how you can help us get to the next level . . . sell yourself.

Favorite interviewing tip: Go on every interview and be sure the company wants to hire you at the end of it, even if it may not be the job you want. You should be the one in control of the hiring decision.

The *worst* thing someone can do on an interview: Don't take out your electronic device or allow it to ring. Turn it off and put it away *before* the interview starts.

Create Your Own Personal Brand

Through the work you've been doing and will continue to do in future chapters, you are creating your brand. Perhaps now is a good time to explain exactly what a personal brand is and what it does for your career. It's also helpful to preview the process of creating a brand. Once you see the process, you'll realize you're already well on your way to creating Brand You.

Branding is the process of determining who you are. You do this so that you can differentiate yourself from all the other college grads seeking work. In this process, you're discovering your strengths, your values, and your passions. **The result of all of this effort is your brand (developed to keep a consistent focus on your benefits)—the value you add to an organization.**

You're not creating your brand as much as you are constantly building and projecting it. Having a personal brand is *not* about being phony. You're determining who you are, not inventing a new persona. Branding is deeper than manipulating other people's perceptions; it's a process of understanding your values.

Your Task in Developing Your Brand Is to Think Like the Hiring Manager

Imagine a job opening in which you are interested. If you were the boss, what kind of person would you select to fill the position? What skills and knowledge would you want a new employee to have? What kinds of problems will this person need to solve? When you have enough information to answer these questions, you'll be able to market yourself to the employer's needs.

Steps for Creating Your Brand

Complete your self-assessment.   Review your mission statement, skills inventory, and SWOT analysis. Distill all this information to decide your core competency—the thing you do best. Your core competency creates the value you add to an organization.

Decide on a target market.   What industry sector? What function within the organization? Learn as much as you can about the employers in this niche. What are their needs? What benefit do they want from the person they hire?

Develop a brand message.   Emphasize the benefit you add. A great brand should be able to answer the question, "What are three things that make you unique and bring value to a prospective employer?" If you can't answer that question in two or three sentences, you will need to work on this and fine-tune your message.

Develop strategies to achieve your goals.   How will you communicate your brand message? How will you connect with your target market? You'll need to proactively plan to get the internship or job you want.

We've already touched on a few of these steps; the rest will be explained in subsequent chapters.

Build Your Brand

As a college student, you have many demands on your time. However, finding short periods to read the latest news in the field you've chosen will pay off. It will open your eyes to a variety of possibilities and alert you to actions you can take while you're in school to further your career. Remember, employers prefer new grads that have relevant work experience, either as an intern or an employee.

Make a commitment to yourself to build your brand while you're in school. As they say, you're worth it. Continue to learn as much as you can about what employers in your field are looking for in new hires. Then find ways to provide the evidence that you can meet those needs.

During your job search, whether it's while you're in school, during your senior year, or after you graduate, you're going to be asking a lot of people for help. At different times, you'll be requesting networking contacts, résumé advice, and finally, you'll be asking for a job. Most people—especially your friends and family—want to help with your job search. However, no one can help unless you're clear about what you need. **The more focused your request, the more likely people are to respond.** If someone says, "I'd like to help you with your search," be sure to say, "As a matter of fact, you can!" Instead of asking, "Do you know anyone who's hiring?" be specific: "I'm really interested in interactive marketing for a consumer products company. Do you know anyone at one of the agencies here in town?"

Brand Strategy
Start with your target customer and work backward. What does he or she need, and how can you show you can fill the need?

Organizational Specialties

In Chapter 3, you learned about 10 industries and their cultures. Another way to think about where you might fit in the job market is to think about specialties within an organization. Whatever the industry, even in government and nonprofit sectors, most of these specialties exist. The size of the firm is a major factor in determining whether work is organized into specialties. Entrepreneurs often start with a few employees and slowly add more people when the volume of business justifies the additional cost. Initially, everyone pitches in and performs a variety of tasks. As the business grows, the need for structure and specialization increases.

Because this is how organizations are structured, employers are looking for people to fill openings in each specialty. **Employers expect you to know**

which specialty fits your skills and interests and why you've chosen to work in it.

But it might seem daunting to make a decision to choose a major and then choose a career in that major. While it's important to choose a major in an area of study that you enjoy, you might be surprised to learn that your college education is a flexible foundation—you can use your education in virtually any major to do whatever you want to do.

The most common specialties are listed in Activity 5.1. Each specialty adds value to an enterprise in distinctive ways. Each one solves different kinds of problems and faces different challenges. As you read about the specialties, pay attention to your reaction. What words appeal to you? What turns you off?

Real People, Real Advice ... About Choosing an Industry

"(About choosing an industry) I think it's more about coming back to culture that you like and people that you connect with. . . . If it came between me having access to a company I loved and really fit in with, I'd probably take a job that wasn't necessarily in my discipline, just so I could be a part of that company and part of that culture."

—*Amanda Burd, student, Saint Joseph's University*

"I love baseball . . . I miss it, I need it, I want it . . ." (about how he integrated his passion for baseball into his job).

—*Vince Giannini, Vice President and General Manager, WPHL 17*

Watch short video clips featuring Amanda Burd and Vince Giannini discussing how to position your brand to meet employers' needs at www.mypearsonmarketinglab .com.

Preparing for a Specialty

You'll need more information in order to decide if a particular specialty is really the right one for you. Many of the same resources you found while researching industries will help you learn more about a specialty. You'll find that career sites on the Web, discussion groups, job descriptions, and articles in professional journals will provide a wealth of information about any specialty you're considering.

Specialties exist to meet an organizational need. You'll want to uncover enough information so you can decide if meeting this need seems like an interesting challenge to you. **Be sure to think like a futurist, and find information about how the specialty is likely to change**. Will it be meeting the same needs, or will it evolve into meeting new challenges? Many specialties are revamping to meet the demands of the new economy; the evolution of accounting that we described in the last chapter is just one example.

Here are some good questions to ask about specialties:

- What kind of person does well in this area?
- To succeed in this field, what skills should a person have?
- Am I working toward the right degree for this field?
- How do I see this field evolving in the future?

Yes, But I Want to Go into Management

If management is your major or minor, you will want to consider a specific specialty that you would like to pursue. While the focus of your education is in management, there is not a "Management Department" in any company. Management can be found in virtually every area of the company, in positions such as sales manager, account manager, accounting manager, human resources manager, and others. While it may seem a bit confusing, you will probably not be able to start at an organization in management. You will most likely need to gain some experience in a particular specialty such as sales, human resources, accounting, procurement, or project management. After you gain some practical experience, then you will be able to move into managing people within that specialty.

Some large- and medium-sized organizations have management training or leadership training programs geared to "high-potential" employees. Companies who provide this training are hoping to retain talented, committed employees. In addition, they often draw from this pool of employees to appoint team leaders as well as managers.

Leadership or management training programs can be a good path to a leadership or management role in a company. But the bottom line is, you will need to gain some hands-on experience in a particular specialty before you will become a manager.

Tricks of the Trade
Learning the Ropes

It's a good idea to avoid saying, "I want to be in management" during an interview. Many interviewers perceive that a person who says this as someone who doesn't want to "get their hands dirty" to gain experience or expects to start at the top. A better approach is to say something like, "I want to be in sales. Then, after I have some field experience, I want to be a sales manager." That lets someone know that you are willing to learn. And, when you get hired, be willing to take on any job that needs to be done. That's how you set yourself apart and demonstrate that you are willing to do what it takes to help the company and get the job done.

Organizational Specialties

Instructions: Read the descriptions carefully. Circle the specialties that appeal to you the most. Highlight the words within the descriptions that you find most appealing.

Specialty	Typical Activities
Finance	Manage the organization's money. Prepare and analyze financial reports, invest and borrow money for the company, and prepare budgets and balance sheets.
Accounting	Track the flow of the company's money including money spent and money to be received.
Administrative Services	Provide support services such as facilities management, security, and secretarial and administrative assistance.
Human Resources	Develop and implement systems and procedures to hire, train, promote, and evaluate employees. Write job descriptions, conduct salary surveys, and recommend salaries and benefits for each position. Forecast the labor pool needed to meet strategic plans. Train employees in classrooms and via e-learning.
Marketing	Enhance the organization's brand by planning and executing the conception, pricing, promotion, and distribution of products or services. Conduct market research, determine pricing strategies, plan promotions, and develop distribution channels.
Sales	Persuade potential customers to purchase products or services by building relationships with customers. In some companies, sales are directed to consumers; in others, they are directed to businesses. Sales administration, customer support, and supervising special accounts are other roles within the sales function.
Marketing, Public Relations, Communication	Communicate with employees, stockholders, government, and the public. Write press releases and handle the media. Plan and execute events to promote the company and its products.
Information Systems	Operate and maintain an organization's computer system, including hardware and software. Manage information systems (like the Marketing Information System) that help managers make effective decisions. Advise management on technology purchases or design systems to capture the data needed to run the business efficiently. Maintain the company Web site(s).
Operations	Oversee the activities necessary to create products and services. Operations include the following functions: research and development, production planning, quality control, purchasing, inventory control, and scheduling production.

Once you've researched the specialty, review the values and skills you identified in Activity 1.1 in Chapter 1 and Activity 2.2 in Chapter 2. How well do your preferences fit the specialty? Activity 5.2 will help you analyze the information you've gathered.

Analyzing the Match

Instructions: After you've completed your research, answer the following questions. Then decide if you're on the right track or if you need to rethink your choice.

In which industry sectors have you identified the most positive characteristics with the fewest negatives? (Review your choices in Activity 3.3)

_____

_____

_____

_____

Which specialties might be a good match for you? Consider your values and favorite skills.

_____

_____

_____

_____

Characteristics that appeal to me:

_____

_____

_____

_____

_____

_____

_____

Characteristics that don't appeal to me:

_____

_____

_____

_____

_____

_____

_____

Who can you talk to who would have the "inside scoop" on the industry sectors and organizational specialties that appeal to you?

_____

_____

_____

_____

Top 10 Demand Occupations—Why They May Not Matter

Most college students want to know the future demand for their career field. Many lists of "hot careers" are published every year. These projections are based on past statistical trends and the opinions of industry insiders—who always want their field to look promising, whether the facts bear it out or not. Often, they don't consider the impact of new technologies or the global economy. It's interesting to compare several lists and see how they differ. Remember, demand today is no guarantee for the future. Don't choose a career solely on projections, because they may change. Just ask the people who studied computer science in the 1990s! Talking to people who work in the field can give you a more accurate picture of the demand for an occupation in your geographic area.

Don't dismiss a career option because demand seems low. Demand for specific skills is constantly changing. While the job market was flooded with IT experts during the 1990s, now there is a shortage of skilled people in this field. People who choose occupations based on their passions and interests are usually able to discover a successful niche and develop winning strategies to achieve their dream.

What If You Change Your Mind?

If you are a few years away from graduation, you are likely to discover new information as you take additional courses and learn about new career opportunities. As a result, you may decide that you want to take a second look at your career plan. That's okay—in fact, it's the right thing to do. For instance, in this course you are learning a good deal about what a career in marketing would be like. You may decide you're intrigued by the challenges and opportunities in this field. Taking additional courses in marketing will help confirm that choice—or change your mind.

Your experiences in various classes are a good barometer of future career satisfaction. If you enjoy learning about a subject, you're likely to enjoy work that is related to it. **Remember, your career plan should be flexible, and that sometimes means changing your goal**. Many college students feel pressure to choose a career and a major very early in their college days. That is understandable, considering the high cost of education. At the same time, don't discount your own reactions to information that you gather while you're in school.

So, change your mind if a different field fits your personality and career goals better than your first choice. You might not have to change your major just because you change your career choice. Many successful people have

Real Fact
There are no mistakes! Make the best decision you can based on the information you have at the time. So get the facts and decide well.

college majors entirely unrelated to their career field. The important thing is to get a degree!

If you do change your goal, be sure you do the same thorough research recommended throughout *Brand You*. You'll still need to develop your brand—it may require retooling your message for a different type of consumer, but it still needs to be done.

Real People, Real Advice ... About Changing Your Mind

"I think there's a point in every student's life where you really question what are you doing, what's going on with your life and your major, and where are you going. . . . I think people put limits on themselves and have preconceived ideas of what they can and can't do without trying something."

—*Amanda Burd, student, Saint Joseph's University*

"I don't think it's hard (to change your discipline or career path). It just depends on what stage of your life you are at . . . what responsibility level are you at. . . . I'm surely not doing anything accounting-related today in my life . . . but the background helped me immensely."

—*Vince Giannini, Vice President and General Manager, WPHL 17*

Hear more about changing your mind in short video clips with Amanda Burd and Vince Giannini at www.mypearsonmarketinglab.com.

ACTIVITY 5.3

My Career Journal

What specialties interest you the most? Why?

_____
_____
_____
_____
_____
_____

Reality check: Does the specialty you're considering match your values and skills? How?

_____
_____
_____
_____
_____
_____

How do you think a personal brand can help you achieve your goals?

_____
_____
_____
_____
_____
_____

Notes to **Myself**

6

Meeting Employers' Needs:
How the Hiring Process Works

It might be hard to know exactly what is going to happen during the interview process for an internship or job. Depending on the position for which you are interviewing and the company or client or organization, the process might feel very different. Even if you are interviewing for the same type of position, the process can vary from place to place. And, in some cases, the process can be completed in just a few weeks, whereas in other cases, it could take months.

Some things are the same no matter where you are interviewing. To anticipate and be prepared for all of the steps in the process, this chapter reviews some key things you will find helpful during the candidate selection process. By the way, when you are interviewing for any internship or full-time position, you and others who are interviewing are referred to as **candidates**.

Brand You Checklist

✓ Learn how employers decide whom to interview and ultimately hire.

✓ Identify the role of the human resources department and outside executive recruiters.

✓ Understand what to expect during the interview process.

✓ Recognize how to decode a job description.

Tricks of the Trade
Play to Your Strengths

There are many things that new grads do better than those who have been working for many years. Use these to your advantage in your brand communications.

1. Relate to college students
2. Travel
3. Perform routine tasks—they aren't boring yet
4. Spend more time researching and preparing for interviews
5. Provide a fresh perspective
6. Know the latest technology
7. Bring a flexible approach
8. Cost less
9. Show enthusiasm
10. Do activities others dislike

The Role of Human Resources in the Hiring Process

The size of the company or organization has an impact on the role of human resources. Small companies or organizations probably don't even have a human resources specialist. The managers may do their own hiring, or the company may rely on outside recruiters, also referred to as executive recruiters or headhunters, to find qualified candidates for their company. If a company hires a recruiter, it is the recruiter who does the preliminary interviewing and presents a few qualified candidates to the human resources manager and/or hiring manager. But the final hiring decision is up to the hiring manager, or the owner of the company.

The human resources department plays a critical role in the hiring process, but it's important to note that it is rarely the human resources manager who makes the ultimate hiring decision. The final decision as to which candidate to hire is usually made by the hiring manager, the person for whom you will work. The human resources representative will usually screen résumés and then conduct phone or in-person screening interviews to determine basic skills and to evaluate a candidate's cultural fit within the organization. The hiring manager (e.g., accounting manager, marketing manager, creative director, operations manager) will usually evaluate the candidate's technical skills in the discipline (e.g., fluency in computer programming languages, experience in creating and implementing marketing plans, financial planning skills, etc.). The final decision whether a candidate is hired is usually up to the hiring manager. Human resources has influence over which candidate is hired. In other words, the human resources department doesn't say "yes," but it can say "no."

Sometimes you will meet with several people in an organization, including someone from human resources, the hiring manager, as well as other people with whom you will be working. It's important to share your brand story and make an impression on each one of the people with whom you meet during the interview process. While not all are decision makers in the process, all probably have influence on the decision to hire you or not to hire you. All of the feedback from multiple interviews usually channels through human resources to the hiring manager before the final decision is made.

Your Digital Brand

Employers and recruiters may check out your brand online . . . even before they call you. Be sure your social networking pages don't include anything you wouldn't want a prospective employer to see.

Watch a short video featuring Karen Carroll discussing how employers and recruiters use social networking to research candidates at www.mypearsonmarketinglab.com.

What I Wish I Knew . . . *About Headhunters*

If you think that a recruiter or headhunter will find you a job, think again. Recruiters or headhunters work for and get paid by clients; they don't work for *you*. Recruiters and headhunters are paid a percentage (as much as 30 percent) of a candidate's starting salary when they place someone in a job.

Just because recruiters and headhunters don't work for you doesn't mean you shouldn't work *with* them. It's a good idea to build and develop relationships with as many recruiters and headhunters as possible. While you might not be the perfect candidate for a job they are looking to fill today, you might be the ideal candidate for a job in the future. Keep in touch with recruiters and headhunters, even if you go on an interview and didn't get the job. You never know when the perfect job will come along. If you keep in touch, you'll be on top of their mind for future opportunities.

Real Questions, *Real Answers*

Q. Is it better to deal with a recruiter or work directly with the company?

A. It depends on the situation. Many companies hire outside recruiters, sometimes referred to as **executive recruiters or headhunters**, to identify and screen candidates for a particular position. Other times, the company hires without the use of an outside recruiter. In some cases, the company has an internal recruiter, someone in the human resources department who focuses exclusively on identifying new talent for the company.

There is no single way of working that is best. It's a good idea to create relationships with as many people as possible including executive recruiters, internal company recruiters, and hiring managers. The more people you know, the greater your chances are for getting an interview.

Role of the Recruiter in the Hiring Process

A recruiter, or headhunter, is a broker. His or her role is to find the perfect candidate and present him or her to the hiring manager. Recruiters are in the business of finding people who meet the skills and background for the job their clients want to fill. While it might sound like a glamorous job, it's very hard work. It means that recruiters are constantly looking for people because they need to find the right fit in both skills and personality to meet their clients' needs.

When you work with a recruiter, you have the opportunity for the recruiter to be an advocate for you. Clients that hire outside recruiters (and have internal recruiters) rely on their knowledge of people and the marketplace to provide the best of the best for each open position. Although the recruiter does not make the final hiring decision, like the human resources manager, he or she has influence over which candidate is hired.

Not every job is filled using a recruiter. Sometimes, hiring managers work directly with candidates or with their human resources department to identify and interview candidates. Whether you are working with a recruiter or dealing directly with the hiring company, building relationships and telling your brand story is equally important. Recruiters don't usually work on filling internships, but it's never too early to make contact and build relationships with recruiters. And, because recruiters fill many different jobs all the time, it's a good idea to keep in touch. You never know when the next opportunity may come knocking.

Real People, Real Advice ... About the Hiring Process

"It's kind of a mysterious process.... I don't think you can know everything about the hiring process."

—*Amanda Burd, student, Saint Joseph's University*

"Typically, a candidate finds us on our Web site or from some other places where we have posted. They would send their résumé via e-mail . . . and if it looks like they are worth talking to, I would schedule an interview for them to come in."

—*Karen Carroll, Executive Recruiter, Blue Plate Minds*

Learn more about the hiring process from Karen Carroll by watching the video clips at www.mypearsonmarketinglab.com.

How the Hiring Process Works

Interviewing for a professional position, an internship or entry-level job, is more involved than interviewing for a part-time job. Many companies interview candidates three or four times and may take several weeks to extend an offer.

1. **Screening interview.**   Your first interview may be over the phone with a recruiter from the human resources department. The purpose of this interview is to determine whether you meet the basic qualifications for the job. If you do, you will likely be asked to interview in person.

2. **Company-fit interview.** The first in-person interview determines whether your personality, skills, and attitudes match the company culture. It may take place on campus or at the company's place of business. Usually, a recruiter or human resources representative conducts the interview and screens out candidates who don't seem to fit. For example, a company may be looking for people who work well in teams, deliver excellent customer service, or solve problems independently. **Successful candidates will be referred to the hiring manager**.

3. **Hiring manager interview.** Your second in-person interview will probably be with the **hiring manager—the person for whom you will work**. Usually the hiring manager interviews 3 to 5 candidates to evaluate skills and experience related to the specific work that has to be done. For an internship, you may only have one interview, whereas for a full-time position, you may be asked to come back for two or three interviews and meet with several people during each time.

4. **Final selection interview.** The top two or three candidates are sometimes asked to come back for another interview, which might be a panel of co-workers. **Making a good impression with the panel is just as important as impressing the manager**. Many managers will reject a candidate if co-workers don't think the person will fit in with the team.

Interviewing and selecting candidates is not a science. Sometimes you will be interviewed by experienced people who know how to make you comfortable and ask questions that bring out your best. You will also meet interviewers who are inexperienced and end up doing most of the talking. **Preparation and practice will help you find ways to interject relevant information to sell yourself**. If an interview goes poorly, it might have more to do with the interviewer than you.

real people, **Real Brands**

Karen
Carroll's Brand

Blue Plate Minds is an executive recruiting firm. Karen is an executive recruiter with over 20 years of experience.
See Karen's video profile at www.mypearsonmarketinglab.com.

▼ **Q** and **A** with Karen Carroll, Executive Recruiter, Blue Plate Minds.

Karen's Profile

College: Penn State University

Major: Marketing

Current profession: Job Swami at an executive recruiting company (look up Karen Carroll on LinkedIn.com and you will see her official title of Job Swami!)

First job: I was a recruiter. I started in the profession I am still in today.

How I got my first job: I was recruited.

Brand key word: Can-do

Description of my personal brand image: Personable. I like to put people at ease, be casual, be open. I like people to feel like they can open up and talk and not have any kind of barriers.

My passion: My passion is helping people.

Karen's Advice

Favorite advice about job searching: Be confident in yourself. You're not showing up for a different part, you're showing up for your part, so you don't have to have the script for someone else's part, just your own.

Favorite advice about résumés: Don't assume there's a magic genie that will decipher the highlights of your background and experience in your résumé. Don't make me work hard to find out who you are . . . always send a professional and well-written cover letter with your résumé to tell me who you are and what I'm about to read.

Favorite interviewing tip: Somebody who is going to make my client's job easier is going to get my support as an advocate.

The *worst* thing someone can do on an interview: Don't say, "I need a job." That's just not a good thing to say on an interview. Focus on talking about why this job is right for you and what you can bring to the company.

Figure 6.1 The Hiring Process at a Glance

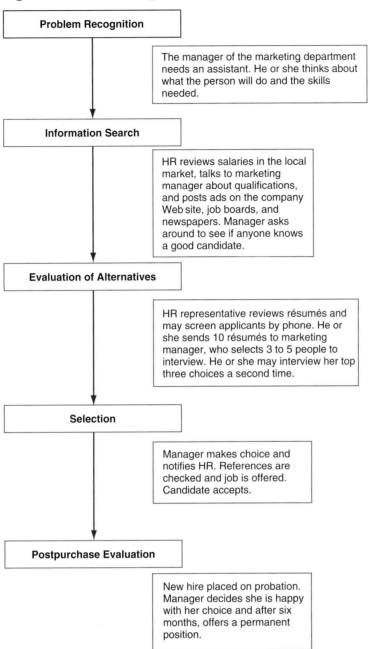

| Problem Recognition |
| The manager of the marketing department needs an assistant. He or she thinks about what the person will do and the skills needed. |

| Information Search |
| HR reviews salaries in the local market, talks to marketing manager about qualifications, and posts ads on the company Web site, job boards, and newspapers. Manager asks around to see if anyone knows a good candidate. |

| Evaluation of Alternatives |
| HR representative reviews résumés and may screen applicants by phone. He or she sends 10 résumés to marketing manager, who selects 3 to 5 people to interview. He or she may interview her top three choices a second time. |

| Selection |
| Manager makes choice and notifies HR. References are checked and job is offered. Candidate accepts. |

| Postpurchase Evaluation |
| New hire placed on probation. Manager decides she is happy with her choice and after six months, offers a permanent position. |

Human resources professionals and hiring managers know that résumés and interviews are only two ways to evaluate candidates. Now that almost everyone has learned slick answers to tricky questions, many companies administer tests, request work samples, and examine portfolios.

Selection Tests

Many employers, ranging from consulting firms to manufacturers, use pre-employment tests to help decide which candidates to hire. Current estimates suggest that as many as 30 percent of *Fortune* 500 companies use some type of testing to match candidates to openings. The smaller the company, the less likely you will be tested.

In competitive fields for which finding enough qualified candidates is difficult (health care, engineering, and technical positions), professional certification is used instead of testing. In industries in which customer service is critical (service firms, retail, and hospitality), the use of tests is increasing. You may not encounter pre-employment testing as a new college grad, but you are likely to face testing sometime during your career.

Testing is controversial. Because many people are concerned that tests are culturally biased, federal and state legislation has been enacted to ensure that tests are administered equally to all candidates. Any company using tests for selection must show that the criteria used to evaluate test results are relevant to the job.

Tests allow employers to ask more questions in a shorter amount of time and to ensure consistency among all applicants. **Several types of pre-employment tests are used: personality tests, task-oriented tests, problem-solving tests, and honesty tests**.

The goal of **personality tests** is to help identify candidates who match the corporate culture. Too often, people try to ace the test, but this may give a false impression. You may be doing yourself a disservice by presenting yourself inaccurately. If you present yourself as someone you are not, you may be selected for the position and find yourself in a job that doesn't fit your personality. The employer may, for example, expect you to be more outgoing than you are, if that's how you responded to the test. Honesty is the best policy. Be yourself and be realistic about your strengths. There are no right or wrong answers to the questions, so answer what is true for you regarding your beliefs and attitudes about work.

Task-oriented tests evaluate your technical knowledge and skills. You may be asked to demonstrate computer literacy, programming, or other technical skills required in the position. Your scores will be compared to those of employees working in the position. These scores are only part of the selection process. A company will often hire candidates with lower test scores if, overall, their response to questions is positive.

Problem-solving assessments present a variety of situations that the candidate may encounter on the job. You may be asked to role-play a situation (like dealing with a difficult customer) or solve a particular problem. Some companies use assessment centers, where an observer watches you complete a variety of tasks. In all these situations, your analysis of the problem and the way you go about solving it are more important than whether you arrive at a perfect solution.

Employers who hire people for work that involves direct access to money often administer **honesty tests** to help screen out applicants who may be dishonest. These multiple-choice tests ask the same questions several times to test the consistency of your answers and your honesty. They are often worded in a way that makes it sound as if everyone is dishonest. Don't be offended. There is no way to prepare for these tests. Just answer them truthfully.

References

Before a final decision is made to hire a candidate, references are usually checked. **A reference is someone who will speak on your behalf about your character, work ethic, skills, and personality.** There are two types of references—**personal references** are people who know you personally, such as a family member or friend; **professional references** are people with whom you have worked at a job or volunteer activity, such as a professor, supervisor, team leader, or internship mentor.

Professional references are usually required for full-time positions. It's a good idea to keep in mind that you will need at least three professional references after you graduate, so continue to keep in touch with professors and past supervisors so you can ask them to be references when you need to provide them.

There's more about how and when to provide references in the *Brand You* Toolkit in the back of the book.

References
Avoid putting "references available upon request" on your résumé. It's assumed that prospective employers will check your references. Be prepared; read about references in the ***Brand You Toolkit*** at the back of the book.

Tricks of the Trade
What Employers Want

Are you wondering what employers look for? Here are the top 10 attributes. How many do you have?

1. Communication skills (verbal and written)
2. Honesty/integrity
3. Teamwork skills (works well with others)
4. Interpersonal skills (relates well with others)
5. Strong work ethic
6. Motivation and initiative
7. Flexibility and adaptability
8. Analytical skills, solves problems well
9. Computer skills
10. Organizational skills

Hear Karen Carroll, Executive Recruiter at Blue Plate Minds, discuss what she looks for in a candidate at www.mypearsonmarketinglab.com.

Demonstrate Your Skills
College helps you to expand the characteristics listed here. As CEO of Brand You, it's your job to provide the proof that you have them.

Demonstrating the Personal Characteristics Employers Want

An important aspect of building your brand is demonstrating the personal characteristics for which employers look. Following are 10 characteristics sought after in today's job market and some tips and suggestions from recruiters.

Communication

Interviewers look for written, verbal, and electronic communication skills. **Your résumé and cover letter demonstrate your writing ability**. The interview shows whether you can clearly express your ideas verbally. Speak like a professional. Know your industry, learn the right language, and use the right buzzwords. Don't use academic jargon and talk in generalities. Discover the key words and phrases used by insiders. If you don't understand what an interviewer is asking, don't be afraid to ask questions for clarification. It is much better to ask than to assume incorrectly.

If you feel that you could improve your writing skills, make an appointment to go to the campus writing center. To be sure your interviewing skills are well honed, go to your campus career center and set up several mock interviews. It will be worth your time.

Honesty/Integrity

The recruiters we interviewed said that even if they don't ask direct questions about honesty, they rate candidates on ethics. If you can back up information on your résumé with more specific information, you'll be considered honest. **Some interviewers ask for examples of situations or projects in which you have faced personal dilemmas and then ask for details on how you handled the situation**. They look for the level of match between what you describe and what they would expect of an employee confronting a parallel situation. Most employers confirm dates, employers, and degrees listed on your résumé. Some employers conduct extensive background checks, including researching criminal records and credit ratings.

Teamwork

Most companies use teams to complete projects or solve problems. Whether they're looking for programmers, accountants, or customer service reps, they want people who can work with others. One manager told us, "I look for a person who can bring balance to our team. I discuss their skills and accomplishments to find what value they can add." **Describe how you participated in study groups, activity committees, and work teams**. What did you contribute? What was your role? What did you do to help the team stay focused on the task?

Skills

Do you get along with a variety of personality types? Do you adjust your communication style to that of other people? Do you resolve conflicts or create them? Saying you are a "people person" is not adequate. **Employers want work-related examples that show how you successfully worked with a difficult teammate or calmed an angry customer**.

Strong Work Ethic

Employers want workers who will do more than simply show up on time. They want employees who will complete their projects on time and care about the quality of their work. **Pointing out that you worked or completed an internship while attending school and/or maintained a high grade point average are great ways to show evidence of a strong work ethic.**

Motivation and Initiative

Employers want candidates who have demonstrated initiative by gaining experience in the industry while in college. **A recruiter for a *Fortune* 500 company said that internships are key**. He doesn't consider candidates without intern or co-op experience. You can also show initiative in the interview by being prepared. Research the company and ask good questions. Show the interviewer that you have invested the time to learn about the company and this position.

Flexibility and Adaptability

Interviewers say flexibility is important in today's workplace as organizations continuously strive to improve the way they do things. **Share experiences that demonstrate your ability to manage change**—moving to a new city, changing colleges with good reason, adapting to a new boss, trying new approaches to solve a problem, and so on.

Analytical Skills, Solving Problems

As a knowledge worker, you will be expected to be able to gather information through various media and keep it organized. People who are good analyzers know how to ask and answer the right questions, evaluate information, and apply this knowledge to workplace challenges. In many positions, you'll also need to use quantitative tools, such as statistics, graphs, or spreadsheets. No matter what industry or specialty you choose, you'll be involved in solving problems. **Be prepared to discuss how you go about identifying problems, develop a range of possible solutions, and then launch the solution**. Most of your college courses provide ample opportunity to apply these skills.

Computer Skills

No matter what your major, you would be wise to take a few computer courses, if needed, so you are **fluent in Microsoft Word, Excel, and Power-Point**. Even though you may take it for granted that you have computer skills, be sure to include them on your résumé because recruiters and hiring managers want to be sure you are fluent with the current technology.

Organizational Skills

With the premium on time so prevalent in today's workplace, being organized is a top priority. This means more than keeping your workspace neat, although that's one aspect. You'll need to organize and present information you've gathered about a topic in a logical sequence. You'll also need to organize multiple projects and meet every deadline. In today's workplace, multitasking rules!

If you feel that your organizational skills need improvement, check to see if your school offers time management seminars. You will be surprised at how much it will help you in all areas of your life.

Analyzing Your Strengths

Instructions: Look over the 10 characteristics just described as the ones employers look for in a job candidate. Then answer the following questions. You have ability in all these areas, but be honest with yourself. Everyone can improve.

Characteristics that are your strengths:

_____

_____

_____

_____

Characteristics you want to improve:

_____

_____

_____

_____

List below activities that will help you develop the characteristics you want to strengthen. Choose things you'll really do and keep your commitment to yourself.

_____

_____

_____

_____

Sample Activities to Strengthen Your Skills

Take a communication course	Volunteer for a community service organization
Work on a group project	Join a professional association as a student member
Join a campus club and run for an office	Travel to a foreign country
Take a speech course	Take computer courses
Make oral presentations in class	Take a creative- or business-writing course
Practice listening	Set a personal goal and achieve it
Work at a job that involves contact with the public	Invest in an electronic or paper organizer
Keep a journal	Take a research methods course
Take a time-management class	When you intern, ask if you can work on a team
Visit the writing center at your school	Write a blog

Getting Down to Specifics

One of the best ways to determine the specific skills a particular employer is looking for is from the job description. Notices you see on the Web are a brief synopsis of the qualifications the company wants the candidate to have.

It's a good idea to explore various job descriptions now so you can prepare for the position you're likely to want in the future. **Highlight the employer's needs, including skills, and personal characteristics**. Skills are either action verbs or words that end in "ing." Characteristics are adjectives like detail-oriented or highly motivated. Here is a sample job description for a medical supply sales rep. Notice that the key employer needs are highlighted.

Medical Supply Sales Rep

We're Health52, a leading provider of cardiovascular products for hospital use. We are currently seeking a highly motivated sales rep. Selected candidate will be responsible for a geographic area to generate sales and meet quarterly sales goals. Position requires daily interaction with customers, including decision makers in hospitals and health care facilities. Candidate should have demonstrated results in a sales organization, preferably in B2B sales, must be able to work independently and should have proven leadership skills. Focus on customer service, follow-up, and customer satisfaction is key. Reports to the Regional Manager and will be a part of the Southwestern Regional Team.

Requires a bachelor's degree in business or 1 to 3 years applicable sales experience. Knowledge of MS Excel is essential. Health52 offers an excellent compensation and benefits package, a leading-edge work environment, and opportunities for professional growth. We invite qualified candidates to send or fax a résumé to. . . .

Developing the Right Skills

Instructions: Visit a job board like www.monster.com, www.collegegrad.com, or www.wetfeet.com. Find a job description that interests you. Highlight the skills and characteristics the employer is seeking. Write the skills and your development plan in the space below.

Skills Listed in the Ad:	My Development Plan

My Career Journal

Now that you've looked at some job descriptions that appeal to you, what do you like best about these kinds of work?

_____

_____

_____

_____

_____

How well do the skills in these job descriptions match the skills you like using (refer to Activity 2.2, Skills Inventory)?

_____

_____

_____

_____

_____

Review the list of 10 characteristics employers seek in this chapter. Which three are your strongest assets? What activities have you done that show these are your strongest skills? How can you capitalize on them as you market yourself? What are some specific tactics you can use?

_____

_____

_____

_____

_____

_____

_____

_____

_____

Notes to **Myself**

7

Sharpening Your Focus:
How to Use Target Marketing in Your Search for Work

Brand You Checklist

✓ Learn why you should target your job search.

✓ Decide which segment of the job market to target.

✓ Determine how to position your personal brand to influence potential employers.

✓ Understand how to bring your personal brand to life.

Early in his senior year, Dennis Kruchek wisely started his search for work. Active in several campus organizations, he assumed his self-confidence, popularity, and the good sense of recruiters would help him land his first professional job. Dennis was sure that after talking to him, recruiters would know just where he would fit into their organization. Dennis signed up for fall interviews on campus. With résumé in hand, he talked to recruiters from many kinds of companies. He was enthusiastic about his abilities and Dennis let recruiters know he was open to considering whatever vacancies they had. When it was all over, Dennis was shocked when he didn't hear from recruiters again. What did Dennis do wrong?

Real People, Real Advice...About Targeting Your Job Search

"At some point you need to zone in on something specific that you are looking for."

—*Amanda Burd, student, Saint Joseph's University*

"It does hurt a job-seeker when they're not focused. . . . Companies are looking for the person who wants to be there (in the specific job) and who wants the job."

—*Kristin Kane, Director of Social Networking and Recruiting, Kane Partners Staffing Solutions*

Watch a short video featuring Kristin Kane discussing how to target your job search if you don't know what you want to do at www.mypearsonmarketinglab .com.

Many job seekers approach their job search just like Dennis. Instead of targeting their search, they want to keep their options open. Perhaps, they reason, there's an employer or job out there that would be perfect. They're afraid they'll miss it if they target their search for work toward one segment of the job market. What these unfocused job seekers don't realize is that recruiters can't suggest additional options unless you can explain to them your strengths and the type of work that interests you. It's a fact—people who are unfocused have more difficulty finding work than those who have particular goals in mind.

One problem with an unfocused approach is that you lack direction. That makes it hard to know whom to contact or what to say once you do. Walmart can have an undifferentiated market because it can afford mass media advertising. You, on the other hand, probably can't. Also, unless you tune in to the needs of a particular market segment, you won't know how to develop your own personal brand—a clear, consistent message about the value you have to offer. You won't know what to emphasize among all your skills, talents, and experiences. This makes it difficult to write a résumé or develop dynamic answers to interview questions.

Just as individuals are not all alike, neither are business consumers. As we've said many times, every business wants to hire employees who will create value and satisfy its particular needs. You'll find that using target marketing strategies will make your work search efforts easier, and you'll actually find a job more quickly.

Real Questions, *Real Answers*

Q. If I target my job search and I don't really know what I want to do, won't I be missing out on some opportunities?

A. Sometimes less is more . . . less of a scattershot approach and more focus will definitely lead you to the internship or full-time job that you want. Although it's hard to make decisions about what you want to do when you are in college, it's far better to have a targeted approach than an unfocused approach. Think about your class schedule . . . you carefully chose which courses you would take each semester based on your year in school, your schedule, and your preferences. Imagine if you just randomly chose courses. You might end up with electives in premed, theatre, and accounting . . . that wouldn't really make much sense. The same is true for your job search. You wouldn't be very successful if you applied for a job as an X-ray technician, a role on Broadway, and a marketing assistant. Focus and targeting are key to getting the job you want.

Kristin
Kane's Brand

Kane Partners is a full-service staffing firm concentrating on technology clients, especially information technology (IT), engineering, and manufacturing.

▼ **Q** and **A** with Kristin Kane, Director of Social Networking and Recruiting, Kane Partners Staffing Solutions

Kristin's Profile

College: Fairfield University

Major: Double major—Classical Studies and Studio Art; Minor—Marine Biology

Current profession: Recruiter

First job: Recruiter

Brand key word: Energized. I'm always going like the Energizer Bunny. I'm very focused, passionate, and enthusiastic about what I do.

Description of my personal brand image: My focus is being the "go-to" person. I'm willing to do whatever it takes to get the job done, even if it's outside the standard job description.

The greatest value I bring to my clients: My work ethic and willingness to do what it takes sets me apart and defines the value I bring to my clients.

My passion: Helping people. Whether it's helping a client find a candidate or helping a candidate find a job, I'm passionate about helping people.

Kristin's Advice

Why having a personal brand is important: You have to sell yourself. Having a personal brand is like putting together marketing materials for yourself. It gives you an opportunity to identify and showcase your skills, experience, and passion.

What I wish I knew about job searching: Reach out to alumni as early as possible. They can be a huge resource to learn about the industry and help you choose your path. They are also an excellent source for networking. I wish I had taken advantage of the alumni network and career services when I was in school.

Favorite advice for student job seekers: Millennials need to embrace the work ethic of the company. Students should avoid falling into the "Millennial mode" and learn the appropriate business etiquette and what the expectations are in the workplace. It's not appropriate to text at work, use improper grammar, wear flip-flops, or expect that you will be given a job when you graduate. You have to work for what you want.

Favorite interviewing tips: First impressions are key. Be sure to dress the part. Be confident. It makes a big difference. When you meet someone for the first time, it's the confidence he or she has that allows him or her to stand out immediately. Be prepared. Go into every interview with in-depth knowledge about the company, the interviewer, and why you want that job.

The worst thing someone can do when they are looking for a job: Don't rely only on the Internet. Really put your heart and soul into what you want to do. If you don't have the passion, you're going to find yourself job hopping and just lost.

Target Marketing

Target marketing is necessary in today's world because people have diverse interests and backgrounds. Businesses are diverse, too. For instance, a high-tech manufacturer has very different reasons for forming an enterprise than a school. Instead of trying to sell your skills to everyone, it makes sense to target a particular segment of the job market. That will also make it easier to demonstrate the value you can bring to a specific company, rather than simply generically talking about yourself.

The target marketing process includes three steps:

1. **Segmentation.** This is the process of dividing the market (companies or organizations within an industry) into groups. For example, you may be interested in the hospitality industry. Within the industry, there are restaurants, hotels and resorts, and casinos. Identifying the segments or groups within an industry will help you fine-tune your focus and help you determine which segments you want to pursue . . . and which you don't want to pursue.

2. **Targeting.** This step includes choosing the segments that you want to pursue. For example, you may want to work for a large restaurant group, but you may not be interested in working for a casino or gaming company. Targeting helps you identify where you will focus your efforts.

3. **Positioning.** Based on the segmentation and targeting, this should help you determine what position you want your brand to have. **Positioning is the place you have in your customer's mind relative to the competition.** Remember that your customer is your prospective employer and your competition is the other candidates for the job. **The bottom line is that positioning helps you determine what makes your brand unique and has value to your prospective employers.**

Going through these steps will help you get more clarity for your brand and help you establish the unique value you can bring to employers.

Segmentation

Segmentation is the process of dividing the total market into different segments based on meaningful, shared characteristics. In the case of the job market, this segmentation has already been done for you. In Chapter 3, they are called "industry sectors," and there are 10 different ones described. It's a good idea to research these 10 sectors and decided which one(s) you prefer. Through your research, you should also know something about the sector's characteristics.

One way you can learn about the characteristics of a sector is by studying the corporate cultures of companies within that sector. As you saw in Chapter 3, usually there is quite a bit of similarity among firms in one sector. Articles

Targeting Works
When you speak clearly to your target audience, your message is crystal clear and makes it easy for an employer to understand your brand message. When you try to appeal to everyone, your message gets diluted.

Targeting
Evaluate the industry sector, and then choose the one that's right for you.

in trade magazines and professional journals often describe the interests and motivations of organizations.

The table on the next page compares a few of the characteristics of the education sector and the high-tech industry sector. These two sectors have different interests, but, both want to achieve their missions. Therefore, they have different needs they want employees to fulfill. When you compare sectors in this way, you can see the difference in the way you would want to develop your brand, depending on which type of employer you are targeting.

Education Sector	High-Tech Industry Sector
Use communication skills	Use analytical skills
Provide learning opportunities	Provide solutions to problems
Values doing good for society	Values innovation, speed to market
Values expertise	Values customer/supplier relationships
Motivated by ideals	Motivated by achievement
Expects compassion	Expects results

Targeting

Target for Success
If you want to target more than one industry sector, write a different cover letter for companies in each sector.

Targeting is the process of evaluating the attractiveness of each potential segment and deciding which of these groups is worth spending resources on to turn into a customer. The group becomes the **target market.** In your search for work, you will be using resources too—your time and energy. Zeroing in on a target allows you to put your resources where they'll have the greatest effect. **You can have more than one target market, but you'll want to fine-tune your messages (your résumé, cover letter, and interview responses) to appeal to each market.**

Developing Sector Profiles

It is helpful to generate a profile of "typical" companies in the sector that you want to target. This is a more detailed look than the previous exercise, in which you were looking at the characteristics of an industry sector. In this phase, you are drilling down to really understand the companies within the sector in which you might want to work. This profile will really help you zoom into the organizations' needs and look for employment opportunities. **Within a sector, you may be interested in several subgroups.** For example, within the manufacturing sector, you might be interested in high-tech, aerospace, and pharmaceuticals. In that case, you should develop a profile for each group or segment.

Characteristics of My Preferred Sector

Instructions: Place the name of your preferred industry sector in the top row of the box below. Then list all the characteristics you've learned about that sector from your research. Consider their business interests, organizational culture, and their needs.

Sector That Interests Me:

You may be considering more than one sector at this point. If so, complete the box below in the same way. Comparing the differences will help you prioritize your choice.

Sector That Interests Me:

Amanda Burd, the student we've been following, decided to write a profile of consumer products companies. Her description highlights the characteristics of the firms she researched. She wrote down what she thinks they are looking for in employees. She also created a list of potential employers and wrote down the demographic information (size of the firm, number of employees, location, and number of marketing employees) she thought would be useful when she started searching for work.

Targeting Tip
Visit www.bizjournals.com to learn about companies, organizations, and trends in the city in which you live or want to live. Even if you're not pursuing a career in business, the local business journal can give you valuable insight for targeting your job search.

Choosing a Targeting Strategy

Should you go after one sector or several? That depends. How sure are you about the sector you've selected? How large is the segment? If your first choice seems to have plenty of potential employers, one sector is all you need. However, if there are few employers in your geographic area, you may want to look at several types of firms within the sector, as Amanda did. **If you decide you want to target more than one sector, write a profile for each sector.**

Tricks of the Trade
Evaluating Industry Sectors

Here are some questions to help you evaluate industry sectors:

- Why does this sector appeal to you?
- Do your values match the values of the companies in this sector?
- Is the sector large enough, that is, are there enough potential employers?
- Do companies in this sector exist in the geographical area where you want to live? If not, are you willing to move to a different location?
- Do you have the knowledge to serve the market?
- Do you have the expertise and experience they seek? If not, do you have the means and motivation to acquire it through coursework, internships, or other activities before you graduate?
- The bottom line: Is this a realistic target?

Student Profile—Amanda

Amanda decided to target with the following:

Company demographics: consumer products firms in northeastern United States with $100 million or more in annual sales.

Amanda's preferences: products that appeal to age group 25–49. Possible products: athletic clothing, cosmetics, food, health or fitness products.

Company characteristics: strong brand strategies, conduct extensive market research, emphasize supply chain management, and customer relationship management. All have Web sites to educate consumers; some not very effective.

Employers are looking for: people who can speak to young adults, stay current on market trends, analyze research data, have innovative ideas, work on project teams, know about brand management, and interact well with people.

Company Profile

Instructions: Research a handful of companies in the industry sector you are considering. List demographic information (domestic or multinational, location, number of employees, total sales), their needs, and the type of skills they are looking for. The more detailed the information, the more this profile will help you when you develop your résumé.

Type of Company That Interests Me:

Company demographics:

Company characteristics:

Employers are looking for:

Company names:

Your best chance for success is to use a concentrated marketing strategy. That is, you'll develop your own personal brand and marketing campaign to appeal to one or two segments of the marketplace.

As you become more adept as a job hunter, you can also take a customized approach. **This involves reworking your résumé, cover letter, and interview responses toward a specific company.** Remember how in the last chapter we looked at job descriptions, and highlighted the skills and knowledge the employer was seeking? Once you have a basic résumé, it isn't difficult to tweak it to meet the specific needs of one employer. We'll discuss this in more detail in later chapters when we talk about résumés and cover letters.

What I Wish I Knew . . . *About Targeting*

After spending day after day applying for jobs online, Adam finally realized that he wasn't going to get the job he wanted that way. He contacted a professor that he had for a class last semester and she helped him to refocus his job search efforts. Once he fine-tuned his career direction and identified the fact that he was looking for a job in sales, the professor showed Adam how to use targeting to put together his list of 25 target companies. There are at least three effective ways to target:

- By industry (e.g., pharmaceutical, media, agriculture, etc.)
- By location (city)
- By your interests (sports, environment, technology, etc.)

Adam landed a sales job at a major food manufacturer in the area and uses the same concept of targeting in his current role. He won the "Rookie of the Year" sales award.

Positioning

The more you can position yourself as a person who can provide the skills and competencies that meet an employer's unique needs, the better your chances for being hired. **Positioning is developing a marketing strategy aimed at influencing the person who makes hiring decisions.** To do this, you'll first show how you can add value and satisfy their needs. Then you'll decide the best way to get in touch with the person who has the power to hire you. In the next few chapters, we'll show you exactly how to position your own personal brand.

Evaluating your own personal brand and the way you've positioned it is important. Once you've developed your marketing materials (your résumé and cover letters), evaluate the response you're getting from employers. The purpose of a résumé is to get requests for an interview. If it isn't doing that, you may need a different strategy for contacting employers, or a more effective cover letter and résumé.

Real People, Real Advice ... About Positioning Your Brand

"It's hard to think about it. You know yourself, but then other people see you, and do they see the same thing you see in yourself?"

—*Amanda Burd, student, Saint Joseph's University*

"In terms of positioning, it can be very effective for someone that's fresh out of school because most likely you have several things to offer that may be relevant to different types of industries."

—*Kristin Kane, Director of Social Media and Recruiting, Kane Partners Staffing Solutions*

Watch the short videos to hear Amanda Burd and Kristin Kane talk about positioning your brand at www.mypearsonmarketinglab.com.

Bringing Your Personal Brand to Life

Brands come to life and gain appeal when they seem to have a personality. Marketers do this by creating an image that captures the brand's characteristics and benefits. The image is more than a logo—it's the total impression that will be communicated in every phase of the marketing process. (If you doubt that brands have personality, think about the difference between the Geico gecko and the AFLAC duck.)

To bring your product to life, you don't have to start from scratch like a product marketer does—you already have a personality! Think of your personality as a cluster of characteristics that describe you. We think we know our personality, but sometimes other people are actually better at defining who we are. So to identify your personality characteristics, think about how people you know have described you. Would they say you're outgoing, influencing, and goal-directed? Or perhaps reserved, thoughtful, and thorough in the way that you approach tasks is a better way to describe yourself? The first cluster of characteristics is valuable in positions for which team interaction, leadership, or customer service is important. The second cluster is valuable in positions for which attention to detail, analyzing information, or implementing new ideas is important. In addition, consider how you typically react in various situations. For instance, do you tend to finish one thing before you start another, or do you like to have a variety of things on your plate?

When developing your personal brand, you want to build on your personality, rather than invent a new one. A helpful way to do this is to create a list of personality traits and adjectives you want to incorporate into your brand. You're looking for an identity for the product (you) and you want to show it to your target market. This identity includes the image you want to present, your personality characteristics, your skills, and behaviors that demonstrate what you can accomplish. These things, taken together, are what make you unique; they are the things you'll want to emphasize as you communicate your own personal brand to others.

The professionals interviewed in *Brand You* **mention that it's important to be yourself, show passion, and let your personality come through on the interview.** It's hard to show passion if you're hiding your true personality or trying to invent a new one. It's also hard to show passion if you haven't thought about your values and what is important to you. In creating your own personal brand, you are trying to identify who you are, so that you can find employment that is consistent with your values. When you know who you are and what you want, it's easy to show passion in an interview. **The right attitude to have during a job interview is, "Here I am, here is what I stand for. Here is what I care about. If you want someone like me, I'm ready!"**

Real People, Real Advice ... About Marketing Yourself

"Realize that you are your best marketer. It's your confidence, personality and skills and how you package that in every contact from your résumé and cover letter to an e-mail or interview. Be proud of who you are. Be prepared and show your enthusiasm and excitement about the job on every interview. It will help you find the job of your dreams."

—*Kristin Kane, Director of Social Media and Recruiting,*
Kane Partners Staffing Solutions

Hear Kristen Kane's advice for job searching at www.mypearsonmarketinglab .com.

In the earlier chapter on research, we discussed the benefits of talking to people who work in the field to find out about employers' needs and exactly what professionals do. This is one of the best strategies you can use to bring your personal brand to life. Ask professionals about the specific characteristics employers in this sector look for in job candidates. Armed with this information, you can develop a brand that excites employers!

My Career Journal

Bring your own personal brand to life. List your personality characteristics that appeal to your target market. Don't try to be someone you're not!

_____

_____

_____

_____

_____

_____

_____

How will your personality add value? What do you want to say about yourself when you are job hunting?

_____

_____

_____

_____

_____

After talking with several friends and acquaintances, write down the five words people use to describe you.

_____

_____

_____

_____

Is there anything you'd like to change about the impression you make? What would you change?

_____

_____

_____

_____

_____

Notes to **Myself**

Step 3 Creating Your Value Proposition

(Chapters 8–11)

What do you have to offer to a prospective employer? How do you stand out among all the other students and graduates competing for an internship or full-time job?

Before you begin to write your résumé and cover letter, you need to clearly outline what you have to offer to prospective employers. **Step 3—Creating Your Value Proposition** helps you define what you have to offer to employers and what makes you unique. Chapters 8–11 include information, activities, and insights about how to translate your experience, skills, and passions into a concise statement about your value. You will learn how to use your value proposition to get the internship or full-time job you want or to pursue an alternative career choice such as freelancing, contract, or other flexible work arrangements.

Your value proposition can also help you define your market value or how much you can expect to get paid for your internship or full-time job. You'll find out about the latest in salary trends and resources to learn about up-to-the-minute changes in the market.

Increase your value and you will increase your income. ➤

8
Creating the Product—You:
Identifying Your Value

An iPad, a Mini Cooper, a McDonald's Happy Meal, a Best Buy gift card . . . all are familiar products with familiar brand names. What makes these products so compelling? Each of these products has layers. The concept of product layers recognizes that a product has more to offer than just the physical product that meets the eye. Think about it . . . an iPad has multiple functions including e-mail, photo sharing, and ability to read electronic books (just to name a few). It's sleek and well designed, just like all other Apple products. **These characteristics are part of the actual product.** An iPad provides many benefits including the ability to check your e-mail on the go, opportunities to view, edit, and share photos, and access to thousands of books, newspapers, and magazines in seconds without the weight or bulk of the actual reading materials. These characteristics are called the core product. And, the iPad has the capability to work on a 3G network for even greater speed (the actual service contract is offered through AT&T). **This additional service is called the augmented product.** Now you can see that a product isn't just a product, it's a bundle of features, benefits, and extras that makes that particular product more popular than any of its competitors.

Think about the layers for each of the products mentioned above:

	Actual Product (features)	Core Product (benefits)	Augmented Product (extras)
iPad	Functionality Design	Mobile access	3G service
Mini Cooper	Transportation Design	Energy and space efficient	Financing Service and maintenance
McDonald's Happy Meal	Fuel for the body	Fun to eat	Cool toy
Best Buy gift card	Monetary value	Buying power, choices, flexibility	800 number and Web site to check balance 24/7

This same concept of product layers applies to your personal brand. You are not simply a student who has taken management classes, you are a highly motivated student with interests and experiences in the area of management (*actual product*) who can help your target company increase sales and provide a higher level of customer service (*core product*), and are willing to work flexible hours, put your social networking skills to work to connect with customers, and are willing to move anywhere in the country for the right job (*augmented product*).

Don't sell yourself short. Take the time to develop your features (actual product), benefits (core product), and extras (augmented product) to develop your brand story. **You are the most important product you will ever market, whether you are a marketing major or a math major.** And you have layers to your product, just as an iPad or Mini Cooper has. You may not have thought of yourself in that way, but when you use **the concept of product layers you can easily see what you have to offer a prospective employer.**

Real People, Real Advice ... About Your Product Layers

"I don't mind getting up in the morning, that's rare for a college student. I will come in early in the morning and work on things when maybe no one else would."

—*Amanda Burd, student, Saint Joseph's University*

"You're going to impress more people with what you are willing to learn and what you are willing to do more than with what you think you know."

—*Brian Wiggins, Director of Circulation, Philadelphia Business Journal*

See the complete videos from Amanda Burd and Brian Wiggins about product layers at www.mypearsonmarketinglab.com. See Brian Wiggins's profile in Chapter 3.

Add to Your Product Layers

You're spending time online anyway, why not leverage it? Try one or more of the following ideas, and then mention your achievements on your résumé. You can also describe your contributions and provide samples during an interview. Activities like these demonstrate your initiative, a quality employers are always looking for. If you don't have time during the school year, make at least one of these a project for your summer or semester breaks. Take Brian Wiggins's advice to heart and show your prospective employer what you are willing to learn and what you are willing to do to be the candidate of choice.

- **Contribute to an online brain trust** such as Lilly Company's InnoCentive, Inc. It's a network community of 80,000 independent, self-selected "solvers" who tackle research problems for firms like Boeing, DuPont, and 30 other large companies. Drew Buschhorn, a 21-year-old chemistry grad student at the University of Indiana, participated. He came up with an art-restoration chemical—a compound he identified while helping his mother dye cloth when he was a kid. The "seeker" company paid Drew for his efforts. Says InnoCentive Chairman Darren J. Carroll, "We're trying for the democratization of science."

- **Create digital content** such as contributing to game production for Linden Lab's Second Life, where participants create just about everything from characters to buildings.

- **Volunteer online** by downloading apps such as Catalista onto your mobile device in order to connect with local causes across the country. Choose the day and time that's most convenient for you and give back to your community.

- **Participate in open-source development** such as SugarCRM, Inc., which provides an open-source version of customer-relationship management software. Or consider Black Duck, a start-up providing bundles of open-source software.

- **Write buyers' guides and lists of favorite products** for Amazon.com and other e-retailers. These provide valuable insights for consumers and help position your brand as a subject matter expert.

- **Blog for business.** You can contract with interesting companies to develop a blog on the company Web site that creates buzz for their products and their brand. Or, you might try maintaining your own blog for consumers, perhaps even acquiring sponsorship income.

- **Blog for a job.** Develop a social network for job-hunting students at your campus. Provide leadership and space for people to share networking ideas, discuss job-search strategies, and vent frustrations. Your blog will generate lots of ideas and one just might lead to the perfect job for you!

- **Blog about an interest or experience.** Chances are if you are interested and passionate about a topic, you have a lot to share. Consider your hobbies such as yoga, travel, photography, or cars, or experiences such as travel, as a topic for a blog. Kelly Corcoran, a junior who participated in a Semester at Sea program, blogged about her experience of traveling around the world on a ship. She used her blog as an example of her work for interviews for her internship.

- **Share your work online.** Take your Facebook page to the next level and share your professional videos, photography, and blog. Provide status updates on Twitter, Facebook, and LinkedIn.com so that everyone in your network can see your work. Share your PowerPoint presentations on Slideshare, a slide-sharing Web site. Or put your slide shows to music and create a video to post on YouTube.

- **Create a professional Web site.** Collect highlights of your professional work (from classes, internships, jobs, community service, or other volunteer work) and create a Web site. It's a perfect way to showcase your capabilities to a prospective employer and the URL is an ideal addition to your résumé.

- **Join a professional social network.** Create a profile, make connections, and request introductions at professional social networks such as **www.LinkedIn.com** and **www.Plaxo.com.** See Chapter 14 for specifics about how to use and leverage LinkedIn.com to create and expand your professional networking. Visit www.mypearsonmarketinglab.com for video demonstrations about how to use LinkedIn.com.

Tricks of the Trade
You Have More Experience Than You Think

If you've worked at a restaurant, retail store, bank, or other customer service environment, you have features and benefits that are sought after by companies and clients.

Whether you plan on entering the corporate world, nonprofit, education, or other career path, that experience will serve you well. Jennifer Wolf, Event Manager at the *Philadelphia Business Journal*, says that this type of experience is perfect because it demonstrates that you know how to work under pressure, multitask, and provide excellent customer service. Include training, service awards, sales achievements, and other accomplishments on your résumé.

Defining Your Product Layers

Figure 8.1 shows how Amanda Burd, student from Saint Joseph's University, applied the concept of marketing layers to describe herself. **No matter what field you plan to enter, it's a good idea to define your own product layers.** One benefit of this illustration is that you can see an example of the types of features and benefits you want to emphasize as you are building your brand.

The Core Product—Your Benefits

Benefits Sell

Think about the contributions you have made and the results you have generated to turn your features into benefits. Instead of saying, "I worked at a restaurant during the summers," tell a stronger brand story like, "I have customer service experience. In fact, I was recognized as Employee of the Month three times at Olive Garden."

The core product consists of all the benefits you can provide for your customer. Because you have many skills, a wealth of knowledge, and a history of diverse experiences, you can provide many benefits to employers. The key to exciting your customers (prospective employers) is to zoom in on those benefits that will add value to their enterprise.

Defining benefits is a little more difficult than identifying features (your skills and knowledge). **Benefits are the outcomes or results that occur because of your efforts.** Examples of benefits are higher sales, increased customer satisfaction, improved brand recognition, lower costs, and higher profits. Activity 8.1 will help you pinpoint the benefits you can provide that focus on an employer's needs. These benefits will become critical elements of your value proposition. Knowing the key benefits of your skills and knowledge is the secret to communicating effectively, whether you want to interview for a job or write a dynamic résumé.

Hint: It will be easier to figure out your benefits after you write down your features.

Figure 8.1 Product Layers for Amanda Burd

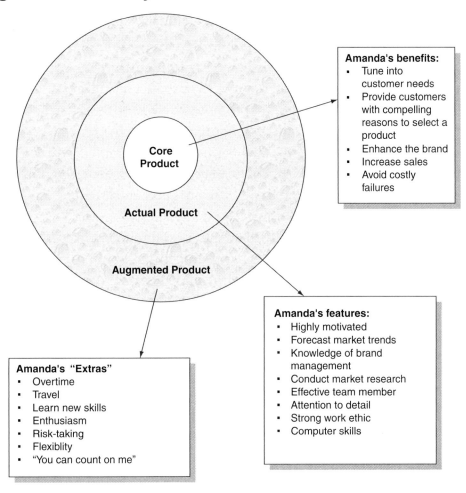

Real Questions, *Real Answers*

Q. I don't have any work experience. How can I create product layers?

A. There are opportunities to enhance your product layers all around you. You don't need work experience to build your brand. Get involved in a campus organization that is of interest to you or volunteer at a local charity or professional organization. Don't just join . . . get involved. The more you do, the more you'll learn. You'll have the opportunity to work with many different kinds of people and even gain leadership experience. Put your skills and interests to work, and you'll be surprised at how impressive your product layers will be.

The Actual Product—Your Features

People buy products and services to receive benefits. But the product or service has to *do* something in order for you to get the benefit. Even when you buy a necklace or a tattoo, there is a benefit and some features. The benefit of your purchase is "bling" (or that's what you hope). The feature—its function—is to decorate your body. Of course, your customer, your next employer, won't be buying bling—he or she wants the genuine product, someone who can function and achieve results. Before they hire you, your customers want to know what you can *do*. **The most important thing you can do to develop your brand and plan your career launch is to identify your features and benefits.** Just as a brand manager knows the product inside and out and decides which features and benefits to promote, you will be much farther ahead if you know yourself and your outstanding strengths.

Most of us take our strengths, talents, and skills for granted, which is why it isn't easy to identify them. However, once you know your strengths—that is, the skills you like using, the things you are good at—it will be much easier to know the profession or industry in which you fit best.

While you are in college, you will be introduced to many learning experiences that are excellent ways to assess your strengths. *And* you'll have to spend time developing skills that you don't particularly like or are particularly good at. This is actually good information for you—your college experiences will help you decide if the assessment you are doing now is on target.

Build on Your Strengths

Don't worry about what other people think you should be good at or what you wish you were good at. Make enjoyment the criterion you use to decide which skills belong in your actual product.

Get Feedback

Most people think they know what they're good at, but they're not always right. As Janée Burkhalter mentioned in Chapter 2 regarding your personal SWOT analysis, it's important to get feedback on your strengths. How do others see you? Are their perceptions about your abilities the same as yours? If anything, most people tend to underestimate their abilities, so it's good to get other viewpoints. Get a reality check by asking people for their opinions (even if they're not your biggest fans). Anyone who knows how you tend to react to different situations can provide important insights. Some possible sources: professors, roommates, classmates (especially if you've worked on a project together), club members, parents, relatives, and if you've held jobs or internships, people with whom you've worked. Here are some questions you can ask them:

- What do you see as my major strengths?
- If you had a problem, what kind of advice would you ask me for?

- Under what circumstances do you think I work best?
- What do you think someone else would say about me?
- How can I improve how others see me?

Your actual product is the work you deliver that supplies the desired benefits. Remember, however, you are a total package, not just the work you perform. **In addition to your skills, potential employers will evaluate your attitudes, your promises, and your presentation.**

Attitude Employers seek a person who is committed to his or her career and to quality job performance. If you've done your homework by researching the company and its products, mission, and culture, you'll be able to convey that you're a determined candidate who takes his or her job search seriously. You can do this by discussing what you've learned about the company and how your skills match its needs.

Before you go on a job interview, put yourself in the shoes of the employer. If you were recruiting someone for this position, what attitudes do you think would be important? For instance, many employers focus a good deal of attention on customer service. In an interview, you could discuss ways in which you'll put the customer first. Other attitudes that might be important: self-confidence, flexibility, a willingness to take on new tasks, a commitment to producing top-quality work, and a desire to continue learning. **After you've identified attitudes that are important to the employers you'll meet, think of things you've done—actions you've taken—that demonstrate those attitudes.** There's a place for these actions on your résumé and in the job interview.

Promises Your own personal brand will have little meaning if you can't deliver the goods you promised in your interview. **This is a key reason why you should never overpromise or exaggerate your abilities.**

Presentation Another major aspect of your package is how you present yourself when job hunting and meeting people. **Your transition from student to young professional requires more than trading in your backpack for a briefcase.** Your first real impression will likely be made in the first few seconds—right about the time you say, "My name is . . . ."

Looking professional takes preparation. Here's the scoop:

- Dress in business attire for interviews. You only have one chance to make a good first impression.
- When in doubt, choose a conservative look. You can't go wrong with neutral colors such as gray, black, or navy. Your clothes don't have to be expensive, but they should fit well.
- Pay attention to details. Scuffed shoes won't cut it.

- Women should avoid too much makeup. Bright over-outlined lips and dark-lined eyes should definitely be avoided.
- Body piercings are better left at home.
- The eyes have it—make eye contact with everyone with whom you interview.
- Leave cell phones and all other electronic devices turned off and out of sight.
- The perfect accessory is a smile—for everyone you encounter, not just the interviewer.

The Augmented Product—Your Extras

If you think about it, the "extras" are often the very things that convince you to buy one product over another. If you've purchased a car, for instance, it may have been the warranty or the interest rate that clinched the deal for you.

What are the "extras" you can offer an employer? If you're willing to travel or work overtime, that might be the offer that tips the scale in your favor. However, don't promise what you're not prepared to deliver.

Other extras may relate specifically to the position being discussed. Perhaps you have a solution to a problem that other candidates aren't likely to have. Some successful candidates offer to take classes or attend training to pick up a skill that would be useful to the employer.

Sometimes giving an employer the opportunity to size up your potential sweetens the deal.

You might offer to work on contract, or work as a temp through an employment agency. Working arrangements like these involve less risk on the part of the employer, and give both of you an opportunity to test the match between you and the position. Other successful candidates have offered to work as an intern. This is another effective way for the employer to test-drive your abilities. Strategies such as these are useful during a tight job market, or if you really want to work for a particular employer. They aren't always necessary.

Extra! Extra!
Spend the time to consider your augmented product. Travel, flexible hours, overtime, and enthusiasm are just a few "extras" you may have to offer.

What I Wish I Knew . . . *About Volunteering*

Phillip Watson, an education major, had a passion for politics. He didn't realize that his volunteer work for a local political campaign was a part of his product layers. He served on several reelection campaigns and took on the leadership role for training new volunteers. He shared his accomplishments on a job interview and landed the teaching job he really wanted.

Your Product Layers

Instructions: Fill in the boxes below with descriptions of your product layers. Refer back to Activity 2.2, Skills Inventory and Activity 2.4, SWOT Analysis for help in identifying your features. Afterward, check your responses with the characteristics you listed in Activity 7.1 and other research you've done. Have you included things your target employers are looking for? This information will come in handy when you write your résumé and prepare for networking and interviews.

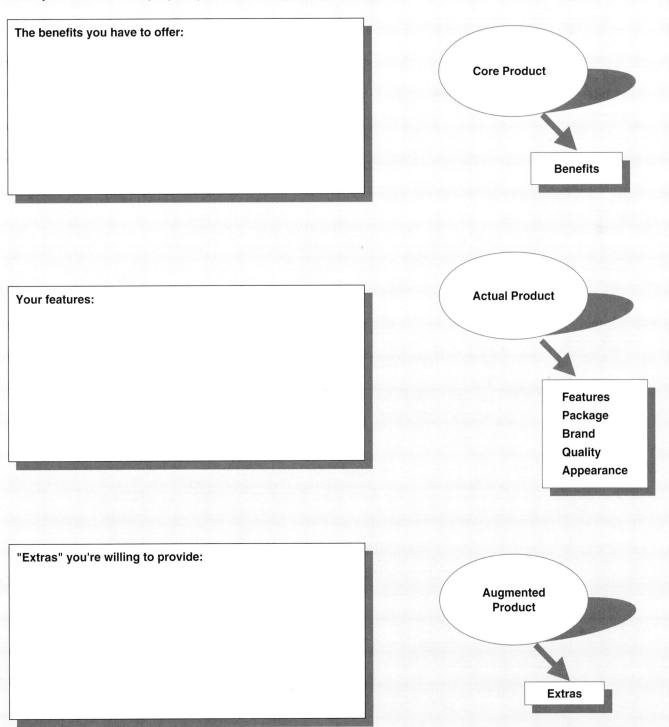

The benefits you have to offer:

Core Product → Benefits

Your features:

Actual Product →
Features
Package
Brand
Quality
Appearance

"Extras" you're willing to provide:

Augmented Product → Extras

My Career Journal

Which of the benefits that describe your core product are in demand by your target employers?

_____

_____

_____

_____

_____

_____

_____

_____

_____

What other skills might you be able to enhance or develop during classes while participating in campus clubs, or while doing volunteer work?

_____

_____

_____

_____

_____

_____

_____

_____

What new areas might you like to pursue to enhance your value?

_____

_____

_____

_____

_____

_____

_____

_____

_____

Notes to **Myself**

9

Managing the Product—You:
Launching and Managing Your Career

Brand You Checklist

✓ Learn the best strategies for launching your career.

✓ Discover how to develop your value proposition.

✓ Understand how an internship can benefit your career launch.

✓ Explore how you manage your career.

You've probably watched the Super Bowl and paid special attention to the commercials. You can most likely name your favorite ones, quickly describe each one, and say exactly why you liked it. Some commercials use humor, others use images, still others use celebrities. Brands as familiar as Coke and as controversial as Focus on the Family tell their story in 30 seconds. No matter what approach each brand uses, the stories are clear, the communication is unmistakable. The commercials that hit the mark have a clear value proposition.

You might be wondering what a Super Bowl commercial has to do with launching and managing your career. Believe it or not, every time you meet someone and talk about what you want to do, it's a Super Bowl commercial for your personal brand. **You have about as long as a Super Bowl commercial to impress the person to whom you are speaking and deliver a compelling value proposition**. What makes you different? What do you have to offer? Why would someone want to hire you instead of someone else? Your value proposition should answer all of these questions in less than a minute.

If you were creating a Super Bowl commercial for your personal brand, what would you say in 30 seconds? If you think that commercials are only for marketing majors, think again. If you are interviewing for a position as a law clerk, special education teacher, research assistant, nurse, videographer, or Web site developer, you need to have your value proposition fine-tuned and ready to deliver in virtually any situation including networking and job interviews.

Ike
Richman's Brand

Comcast-Spectacor is a sports and entertainment firm that owns several sports properties including the Philadelphia Flyers, Philadelphia 76ers, and the home of the two teams, the Wells Fargo Center in Philadelphia. Ike is responsible for all of the Public Relations for all of the sporting events and concerts held at the Wells Fargo Center. See Ike's video profile at www.mypearsonmarketinglab.com.

▼ **Q** and **A** with Ike Richman, Vice President of Public Relations, Comcast-Spectacor.

Ike's Profile

College: University of Maryland

Major: Communications with a minor in Journalism

Current profession: Public Relations

Brand key word: Opportunist. You have to take advantage of opportunities.

Description of my personal brand image: My personal brand image is credible, accessible, creative, all-knowing (or the ability to get the answers). I have to be above the crowd and stand out. I don't wait for the phone to ring, I make it ring.

My passion: Make a difference.

Ike's Advice

Favorite career advice: Ask for help. Tell your professors and other professors what you want to do and ask for help. We're not going to come and find you, you have to come and find us.

Favorite advice for finding a mentor: Find people who do what you want to do, and reach out to them. Meet with them; learn from them. Don't assume that they won't meet with you. People want to help you, they just need to know what you are looking for.

How to get experience: Get an internship or get a temp job. You can learn what you want to do, or what you don't want to do. Network with everyone in the organization to take advantage of opportunities that exist.

How to make the best of your internship: Get noticed. Stand out by doing extra projects, like writing a blog. Make sure everyone knows what you want to do after the internship. Talk to your supervisor and be sure he or she knows what you are looking for. Don't assume that just because you had the internship that the company will hire you for a full-time job. You have to let people know what you want to do. Use your internship to help yourself.

How to get the job you want: Aim high, shoot low. Aim for your absolute dream job, but you need to start somewhere and get the experience, then work your way up to the top tier job.

The worst thing a student can do when looking for an internship or job: The worst thing you can do is *nothing*. Let people know what you want to do, stand out from the rest of the crowd, tell your professors what your ultimate goal is, do an internship . . . *you* have to make a difference. No one is going to do it for you. You have to do it for yourself.

Your Value Proposition—the Key to Success

You've probably been on several interviews where the interviewer starts by saying, "So, tell me about yourself." It can be one of the toughest interview questions to answer, if you're not prepared. What the interviewer means when he or she says that is, give me your "headlines" so I know where to start the conversation. That's when your value proposition comes in. When you get one of those open questions like "So, tell me about yourself," or "What do you want to do?" on a job interview, at a networking event, or even from a friend of the family, your value proposition is the perfect reply. From there, you can tell your brand story based on what you said in your value proposition statement.

Your value proposition is a short, simple statement that includes four key pieces of information:

- Who you are
- What you have accomplished
- What makes you unique and how you bring value
- What you want to do

Your value proposition is a summary of the information you created about your product layers—your features, benefits, and extras—put together in a few simple sentences that you can say in any situation. **In fact, your value proposition is also referred to as your elevator pitch because you should be able to share it with someone in the time it takes for the average elevator ride.**

Going Up!

Your elevator pitch should give someone a summary of your value proposition. It should be no longer than the time it takes for an average elevator ride and should tell someone who you are, what you've done that makes you unique, and what you want to do.

ACTIVITY 9.1

Your Value Proposition

Instructions: Notice the steps Amanda Burd used to develop her value proposition. Then it's your turn to write a memorable value proposition. Refer back to Activity 8.1 to review your features and benefits.

Student Profile—Amanda Burd

What Need Can I Fill?

I can use my marketing research and analysis skills to learn more about customers and develop strategies and ways to help the company grow and build its brand. I can use my creative-writing skills to inform, persuade, or amuse people in innovative ways.

My Features

I can forecast trends and tune in to customer needs. I have experience writing collateral materials that tell a compelling brand story and produce results. I'm very organized and like to focus my efforts on generating results.

Continues on the next page...

My Benefits

My focus and creative approach to marketing sells products and services in unique ways.

Amanda's Value Proposition

"Hi. My name is Amanda Burd. I'm a marketing major with marketing research experience and creative writing skills and I'm really excited about combining these interests. While in school, I completed an internship that gave me the chance to work on building several brands at General Mills. In fact, I worked on projects that helped increase distribution of products in major grocery store chains across the country like ShopRite and Walmart. I'd like the chance to explore entry-level job opportunities with consumer product companies in the Philadelphia area."

How to do it: In Chapter 8, you identified your features and benefits. You can't get all of them into a value proposition that you can say in 30 seconds. So select the top items for each step that will interest someone in you and what you have to offer.

Your Turn

What Need Can You Fill?

_____

_____

_____

Your Features (skills and knowledge)

_____

_____

_____

Your Benefits (my accomplishments and contributions)

_____

_____

_____

Your Value Proposition

_____

_____

_____

_____

_____

Once you have an idea of what you want to say, get out a timer or use the second hand on your watch. **Your value proposition, like a commercial or the average elevator ride, should last about 30 seconds.**

Tricks of the Trade

Practice, practice, practice saying your elevator pitch out loud. Even though you think you know yourself, it's important to be able to say your elevator pitch effortlessly. Try approaching different friends and family and take your elevator pitch for a test drive. Then, visit at least one of your professors, deliver your elevator pitch, and get some honest feedback. Even seasoned professionals practice and constantly refine their elevator pitch. Most people get a little nervous when they are talking about themselves, especially at a networking event or on a job interview. Rehearsal is the best way to deliver your elevator pitch in a crisp and compelling manner.

Launch Your Career with Marketable Skills

A college degree isn't the only ticket you're likely to need to launch your career. **Many recruiters say they don't interview students who haven't shown the effort to get real-world experience through internships, service learning, or cooperative learning programs.**

Real People, Real Advice ...

"I think internships are the best way to really understand what you can honestly expect from a job after graduation."

—*Amanda Burd, student, Saint Joseph's University*

"An internship is a great way to whet your appetite for that career. . . . It's really a 16-week job interview. An internship is an opportunity to gain the knowledge of that company, department, position, but more importantly . . . get noticed. . . . How are you going to stand out and become the next employee?"

—*Ike Richman, Vice President of Public Relations, Comcast-Spectacor*

Watch short videos with more advice from Ike Richman at www.mypearson marketinglab.com.

Internships

Ask any recruiter or hiring manager in any profession and he or she will tell you that the best way to get a job is to have at least one internship or co-op on your résumé. No question about it—internships provide opportunities to gain valuable work-related experience. It's also a great way for you to explore the real work world and decide if this truly is the career for you. With an internship, you are enhancing your academic education with practical career-related experience. The result? You'll gain marketable skills and build your résumé.

Vault.com reported that in a survey of more than 1,000 college seniors nationwide, 86 percent had completed one internship and 69 percent had completed two or more. **With so many students taking advantage of this resource, people without relevant internship or work experience are at a distinct disadvantage.** The numbers also suggest that obtaining an internship is a competitive venture. As internships become more and more competitive, it becomes even more important for you to have a strong set of job-search skills.

Your first step is to decide what you hope to gain from an internship. You might want an internship to help you evaluate your career goal, learn new skills to beef up your résumé, gain networking connections, or all of these. Knowing what you want to accomplish will help you evaluate internship offers. Inevitably, you'll be asked about your goals when you interview. Once you know your purpose, decide where you'd like to do your internship—what industry and specialty would best meet your needs?

If an internship (co-op, student teaching, clerking, etc.) is necessary to get a job, how do you get an internship, you might ask? Fortunately, there are many opportunities for internships, or other ways to gain experience, in virtually every profession. And many employers are willing to give the right candidates a chance to earn on-the-job experience. To get the right internship for you, it's a good idea to know a little bit about your options.

Paid versus Unpaid Internships

While many internships include an hourly rate and/or commission or bonus for reaching a specific goal, some internships are unpaid. It might seem that if you have the opportunity to have a paid internship or an unpaid internship, you would naturally take the paid internship. However, that might not always be the case. **It's best to pursue the internship that you think will give you the best exposure to the real world.** In some cases, that might mean forgoing a paycheck to work for free. Sometimes, those are the best internships. **Keep in mind that your internships are designed to give you experience and help you choose your path.** For example, many television and radio stations offer unpaid internships. Getting production, graphic design, writing, or sales experience for a local station may be far better experience and exposure than a paid internship at which you might primarily be making copies and answering the phone. While your ultimate goal is to make money, your internship is not the time to put the pedal to the metal on earnings . . . focus on getting experience.

Credit versus Noncredit Internships

Some employers offer the opportunity to gain college credit for internships or co-ops. While the number of hours may vary based on industry and area of

THESE SITES: for internship opportunities

www.quintcareers.com
www.wetfeet.com
www.internweb.com
www.vault.com
www.InternshipPrograms.com

study, it is common to be able to earn 3 hours of college credit during a semester- (or summer) long internship. College credit internships come with requirements set out by your school; you can usually find them by visiting your advisor or the head of the department in the area in which you are pursuing a degree. Internship credit requirements may include a minimum number of hours of work per week, job description, on-the-job supervisor, and an offer letter from the company (see Chapter 16 for more information about offer letters). In some cases, the employer pays an hourly wage in addition to offering credit.

Any Internship Is a Good Internship

What if you can get an internship, but it's not in the area in which you want to pursue a career? It's always good to build your résumé with internships, even if they are not in the area of your major or interest. You will learn many things, and the internship may expose you to some opportunities that you didn't know existed. And, if you perform well, it will help you build your network. It's best to keep an open mind when you are considering an internship. What might appear to be the best short-term opportunity might not be what leads you to your long-term career.

Which One Is Best?

How will you know which is the best internship? In many cases, an internship, whether it's paid or unpaid, credit or noncredit, can lead to a career direction, full-time job offer, and life-long professional networks. There are no hard and fast rules to choose the best internship for you. You should write down the pros and cons of each internship before you accept one. **Give extra consideration to the internship that will give you hands-on experience and exposure in the area you want to pursue.** In other words, choose an internship with your future in mind, not just the present.

Temp Jobs

A temporary position is another good way to get experience, learn what you want to do, and meet a lot of people.

Real People, Real Advice ...

"Get a temp job. . . . You'll get experience . . . if you don't like the job, you can request a different position, you can easily go on interviews, and you can network with a lot of people."

—*Ike Richman, Vice President of Public Relations, Comcast-Spectacor*

Watch short videos with more advice from Ike Richman at www.mypearson marketinglab.com.

Volunteering

While internships are an excellent way to gain practical experience, you can learn about yourself and the real world in other ways. Volunteering for a nonprofit, professional organization, or campus organization can help you gain valuable experience while you are making a difference. No matter what profession you want to pursue, volunteering can help you make your mark.

Real Questions, *Real Answers*

Q. What if I'm not sure what I want to do. Should I wait to get an internship?

A. An internship, co-op, student teaching, clerking or other hands-on learning experience is invaluable. Not only does it expose you to the real world and build your résumé, it helps you gain first-hand experience that you can't learn in a class or a textbook. **And, an internship can also be valuable to help you learn what you** *don't* **want to do.** It's okay if you find you don't like the area in which you did your internship. That will help focus you on other areas and help you target your job search. **So don't wait . . . jump in and start as early as you can (freshman year is not too early). Get as many internships as you can throughout your academic career and you will build your résumé, your confidence, and your brand.**

What I Wish I Knew . . . *About Experience*

Students share creative ways they found to get experience in different areas.

- "Foreign exchange programs. Study history in London for a semester or go to a foreign country to practice a new language."
- "Join a campus club, like the sociology or advertising club. An opportunity to network, develop skills, and make connections in school that could lead to work."
- "Enter your artwork for recognition and awards. When you win, it reinforces that you're good and keeps you going. It's a good opportunity to practice new software applications."
- "Complete a project during your internship. Have something concrete to show for your work, like a brochure or a report."

Whatever career you are interested in pursuing, there's a way to get experience while you're still in school.

Mentors—the Key to Success

Navigating the real world alone can be extremely challenging. One of the best ways to find your way is to have a mentor. **A mentor is someone who has more experience than you and is willing to take the time to share his or her experiences and provide support, guidance, and counsel**. You probably have at least one mentor in your life right now: someone who provides guidance, answers questions, and takes you under his or her wing such as a parent or guardian, priest, professor, or friend of the family. When you were choosing which college to attend, your mentor probably helped guide you as you were making the decision. During your years in college, you may have grown close to someone who is older than you who helps you plot your path and make major decisions.

A mentor can help you in the same way in the working world. In fact, most successful people in every profession attribute their success to having great mentors. Your mentor might be someone who works at a corporation, he or she may be an entrepreneur. In either case, this person is willing and able to share his or her experience with you and provide leadership and support. A mentor can help you go through the personal branding process and provide insights about your strengths and weaknesses, provide feedback on your cover letter and résumé, and even help you expand your professional network. A mentor can coach you through career decisions such as which path to follow, how to pursue your passion, and how to stay positive, even if it seems that your dream job isn't right around the corner.

You might be wondering how you can find a mentor. Some organizations have formal mentoring programs, so check with a local professional organization, your college alumni office, or even corporations that are on your target 25 company list. Learn about the requirements of the program and what you need to do to enroll in it.

Or, you can find a mentor on your own. Either way, there are a few things to consider in order to have the best fit for a fruitful mentoring relationship.

- **Identify what you want from a mentor.** If you want to learn specific skills, it's best to find a mentor who has that experience.

- **Find a mentor in the profession you want to pursue.** It's a good idea to find someone who does what you want to do. That way, he or she will be able to help you navigate the profession.

- **Be willing to invest time.** Mentoring is a two-way street. Mentors take young people under their wings for many reasons. Some like to share their experiences, others want to pass on the traditions of the profession, while others find satisfaction in helping young people because they remember when they were new to the industry. No matter what their motivation, all mentors want a committed mentee. That means that you have to be willing to spend time with your mentor and learn the craft. And it's important to keep your mentor in the loop with your job search activities.

- **Find chemistry that works.** One of the benefits of finding a mentor on your own is that you can gravitate toward someone who shares your values and whom you would like to emulate. When you have a connection to your mentor and he or she to you, it's a relationship that can last for a lifetime.

Real People, Real Advice ... About Mentors

"The best thing that ever happened to me in college was just connecting with mentors whom I could turn to for silly questions and serious questions. . . . Those people really guided me through the whole process."

—*Amanda Burd, student, Saint Joseph's University*

"Find somebody that does (what you want to do) and get in touch with them. . . . Ask for help. . . . I want to help students be where they need to be. . . . It's up to you."

—*Ike Richman, Vice President of Public Relations, Comcast-Spectacor*

Watch short video clips including Amanda Burd and Ike Richman talking about mentors at www.mypearsonmarketinglab.com.

Manage Your Career by Remaining Employable

Keeping one's career alive by remaining employable has become *the* critical mission for every working adult. As a senior manager at a major technology company warns, "Time-to-market for new products and services has shrunk dramatically over the past 10 years. Employee skills are now outdated in three to five years, and new jobs will emerge (each year) that involve tasks that don't even exist today."

No matter where you are working, following the Career-Management Strategies (shown in the margin) will ensure that you succeed in today's workplace. As CEO of your own personal brand, plan on using these strategies to thrive in the workplace. By doing so, changing work demands won't leave you stranded, wondering where your next paycheck is coming from.

Career-Management Strategies

- Be resilient.
- Develop flexible plans.
- Expand self-awareness.
- Think like a futurist.
- Communicate your value.
- Be ready for the next opportunity.

Be Resilient

In a normal product life cycle, products reach a peak and then sales start to decline. Marketers use a number of strategies to lengthen the product life cycle as much as possible. A similar phenomenon happens to careers.

Figure 9.1 shows the progression of one's career over time. For most people, their productivity and value to an organization rises in the growth stage of their career. After they reach a peak, productivity begins to fall. This drop can occur because the job becomes routine. More often in today's world, it occurs because the

Figure 9.1 The Career-Resiliency Concept

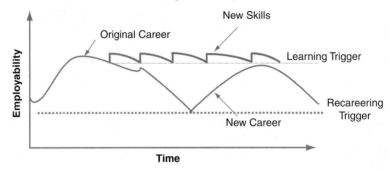

person doesn't keep growing and learning to stay current with new ideas and/or technology. As a result, his or her value to the organization drops dramatically.

Almost everyone can sense when their productivity is falling—they feel bored, dissatisfied, or burned out. Left untended, these feelings worsen, and the person usually ends up recareering, sometimes by his or her own choice and sometimes because he or she is terminated.

Instead of denying these feelings of dissatisfaction, resilient careerists use the information as a trigger to take action. They know they are responsible for keeping their skills up to date. They actively seek new opportunities to stretch their comfort zones by taking on new projects. They continuously learn through company-sponsored training, coursework, professional associations, and reading books and journals.

Resilient people are proactive. They take charge of their careers and make sure they have choices. That way they can bounce back from the impact of changes in the marketplace.

Develop a Flexible Career Plan

Although we can't know exactly what the future holds, we can create flexible plans that allow for uncertainty. **Plan your career to keep up with continuous changes in the world of work.** A flexible plan helps you set targets for achievements and also allows you to take advantage of emerging opportunities. As you add new skills to your portfolio, you'll be ready for challenges you couldn't imagine when you launched your career. Many successful people are surprised by their achievements—they didn't necessarily aspire to their current roles. Their success occurred because they kept on learning and were willing to take risks when opportunity came knocking.

As we mentioned earlier, five years is about the right length of time to look ahead for your career plan. As you approach that milestone, use the same process you've learned here and set new goals for the next three to five years.

Expand Self-Awareness

By following the steps to develop your career plan, you've seen that the cornerstone of good planning is awareness of your strengths and preferences.

As you gain different experiences, learn new skills, and acquire new knowledge, you will develop into a person who can readily handle responsibilities you can barely imagine today.

Most working adults know that in the future they will have five to seven careers. Many people are alarmed by this fact. They think it means they will be adrift in a sea of change without a life preserver. **However, you'll always have a lifeline—your skills and knowledge.** Most of your career changes will be incremental rather than disruptive. The more likely scenario is that you will reconfigure your skills to meet new needs in the marketplace. Rather than moving from banker to physicist, it will look more like an engineer moving into technical sales or a marketing analyst moving into brand management.

Look inside yourself to focus on what you want to do next. It will be a necessity to keep pace with changes in the marketplace. **Periodically take an inventory of your updated skills and preferences and map out new territory for your own personal brand—just as you are doing now.** Recognizing that you have choices will give you the self-confidence to adapt to change.

Think Like a Futurist

Continually scan the work environment to discover emerging trends and needs. **When you hear about an interesting new trend, think about the impact it will have in the marketplace.** You'll discover new opportunities that will keep you interested and engaged. Just as a product gains market share through early arrival into the marketplace, you'll gain prominence in your profession by becoming an early adopter of new career trends.

Your future promises to hold unprecedented opportunities. **As CEO of your own personal brand, it's your job to study the future and prepare your business for tomorrow.**

Communicate Your Value

Marketing *you* is a never-ending process. Keep an eye on the next big work project, company shift, or product innovation, and position yourself to participate in completing the task(s). That means being able to sell yourself.

Once inside a company, learn what the organization values. Ask to see the strategic plan. Look for ways to align your work with your employer's strategic goals. **Anticipate the skills that will be relevant in the future and map out a strategy to develop them.**

Look for ways to gain visibility in the organization. Volunteer for special projects and problem-solving teams. Find a mentor who will help position you for new assignments. Use e-mail to send progress reports to your manager and other key people in the organization. Volunteer for community-service projects sponsored by the company. One team leader told us, "I volunteer for our corporate sponsorship with Habitat for Humanity. The person next to me pounding nails might be a vice president, and I wouldn't even know it unless I asked."

Be Ready for the Next Opportunity

Once you're in the workplace and performing your best, you will see new opportunities. So you always want to be prepared. That means tracking your accomplishments and keeping your résumé current.

Sharpen your job-hunting skills so you can change your position or your career when you're ready for the next opportunity. **One way to keep your value proposition fresh is to join a professional association.** You'll always be meeting new people and telling them what you do. Not only will these contacts help you find new opportunities, the experience of talking about your accomplishments will make job hunting less intimidating.

ACTIVITY 9.2

My Career Journal

Take a look at the value proposition you developed in Activity 9.1. How could you change it for a professional networking event?

_____
_____
_____
_____
_____
_____

How might you change it for a career fair?

_____
_____
_____
_____
_____
_____

Think of some companies or job settings that might be of interest to you in seeking an internship either during the summer or during the school year.

_____
_____
_____
_____
_____
_____

Notes to **Myself**

10

Providing Services as Brand You:

Exploring Entrepreneurship and Other Alternative Ways to Work

Brand You Checklist

- ✓ Understand how to achieve work/life balance.
- ✓ Explore alternatives to working in a corporate environment.
- ✓ Discover what makes a successful entrepreneur.
- ✓ Learn how to create your own path to success using your personal brand.

Be your own boss. What a compelling concept. Once left only to those with means to pursue their dreams, entrepreneurship takes on many different forms in today's diverse working environment. While being on the payroll of a company or organization is a common way to earn a living, it may not be what you aspire to do. In today's work environment, you have many choices about how you want to spend all or part of your career. Sometimes people want to work at established companies to gain some experience so that they may eventually start their own companies. Some would like to pursue their passion immediately and start their own companies right out of school. Others would prefer to work as independent contractors or freelancers and choose the clients with whom they work. Still others would like to own companies that have the power of brands behind them by buying a franchises, while others want to make their marks by starting nonprofit organizations. **Whatever the profession, whatever the working arrangement, being an entrepreneur (or working in a noncorporate environment) can be a rewarding— and challenging—career path.**

Corporate life is not for everyone. In today's highly competitive environment, corporate employees frequently work over 40 hours a week, often placing a strain on their personal lives. Rather than succumb to corporate pressures to perform, you may prefer a lifestyle that gives you more flexibility or provides more balance between work, family, and leisure.

"I think someday I would like to just be my own boss and develop something that no one else has developed yet ... but it's kind of scary to go away from the known world."

—*Amanda Burd, student, Saint Joseph's University*

"I was at a job ... I took the time to really think about what is it I really want to do . . . it became very clear that I needed to leave my job ... it was the impetus to record my first album."

—*Monica McIntyre, Musician and Entrepreneur*

See the video clips including Amanda Burd and Monica McIntyre discussing the opportunities and challenges of being an entrepreneur at www.mypearsonmarketinglab .com.

If you're unsure whether you want to join the corporate world, perhaps it's time to think about other ways of working. You might be motivated by being your own boss, choosing the projects on which you work, bringing a new idea to fruition, or making a difference in the world around you. There are several alternative work arrangements that can allow you to achieve your dreams; you just may find the one that matches your personality and lifestyle preferences.

The number of people working in alternative arrangements has increased dramatically in recent years. Many people started doing so after being laid off, and then found they preferred their new lifestyles. Other people became disenchanted with large companies when their bosses wouldn't accept their ideas for improvement or they were passed over for promotions. These are realities that frequently occur when you work for someone else.

What I Wish I Knew . . . *About Being an Entrepreneur*

Alma Garcia thought she was living her dream. With a marketing degree from the University of Illinois, she moved to New York, started moving up in the marketing department at her new job, and was making good money. There was only one problem: She was miserable. Up at 6 a.m., she would get home just in time to watch the late-night news; she also often worked weekends. "I reached burnout pretty quickly," says the 27-year-old, who yearned for some time for herself. She found it when she moved back to her small Illinois hometown and started her own marketing firm. Now she has plenty of time to enjoy sports, volunteer at a women's shelter, and enjoy her friends and family.

Monica
McIntyre's Brand

Monica is a successful musician, singer, and cellist. After leaving her 9-to-5 job, she struck out on her own to pursue her passion for music.
See Monica's video profile at www.mypearsonmarketinglab.com.

▼ **Q** and **A** with Monica McIntyre, Musician and Entrepreneur.

Monica's Profile

College: Drexel University

Major: Fashion design

Current profession: Musician, songwriter, singer, cellist

First job: My first job was at a fabric store.

Brand key word: Balance. Balance between body, mind, and spirit.

Description of my personal brand image: My personal brand image is a work in progress. My focus is innovation. I'm constantly introducing people to the cello in other ways than they expect.

Monica's Advice

How did you decide to go out on your own: I was laid off from my job. I decided to use my unemployment checks to focus on music full time.

The best thing about being an entrepreneur: It changes with you . . . whatever is most important to you changes and you set the priorities.

The most challenging thing about being an entrepreneur: Deciding how long to stay in something. Because you're so aware of your own present needs, you might not realize that you need to consider longer term things. Finding comfort and structure on your own can be challenging.

What to consider when setting prices for your work: Know your value. Know how much work it will take to do a specific piece of work and assign a value number to that and stick to that value. Understand the value you bring and be comfortable with your unique product.

The most important thing an aspiring entrepreneur can do: Do it. Whatever it is. Your passion or fervor will drive everything, and your ideas will fall into place because you're doing what you love, you're not fighting the natural urge to just do it.

Favorite advice about career searching: Be comfortable in your own skin. Don't be concerned about being different; don't be scared to be different. The "differentness" is what separates you. If you start from that place and refine it, it will only get better.

Favorite career tip: In life as well as in a career, when you are an entrepreneur it seems to be one and the same, I've learned that people will follow your lead, so it's very important that you set a good lead for yourself.

Many experts are predicting that everyone's work lives will be more flexible in the future. Many of us will move from entrepreneurship to full-time jobs in corporations to consulting, and back, full circle. If you are truly in charge of your career, you can leverage many different types of opportunities when they arise. **Of course, to manage this type of career successfully, thinking of yourself as your own personal brand is imperative.**

Myth or Reality?

For generations the prevailing advice for young adults was to "settle down and get a good, steady job." This advice wasn't voiced by mean, uncaring adults. It was the economic imperative of the time. Income statistics proved it was right year after year. In those days, striking out on your own was simply not a viable option for most people.

This conventional wisdom became so entrenched that it is still the basis of many assumptions about the job market today. Assumptions act as filters that affect the information we gather and the way we evaluate it. Assumptions and beliefs can continue to influence decisions even when they are no longer true. For example, most schools still dismiss students in June, even though children no longer spend summers helping out on the family farm.

Outdated assumptions limit possibilities and impact the way you think about your future. If you're like most people, you may have difficulty separating myth from reality. Without realizing it, you may be relying on outdated advice as you plan your future. Check the advice you've heard against the following facts.

Myth: Company loyalty is rewarded with job security and a secure retirement.

Reality: Job security is a thing of the past. Career-savvy employees create financial security by choosing projects and opportunities to help them stay in demand as employees. People who continually develop new skills in their professions and seek new work opportunities earn more than their counterparts who remain loyal to one company.

Myth: A college degree guarantees a good job.

Reality: A college degree doesn't come with any guarantees. A recent business school graduate was complaining that even though the employment rate was improving, she'd had no luck finding a professional job. When asked about the focus of her job search, she responded, "Oh, whatever, I just want to get my foot in the door." When asked if she had developed professional relationships or contacts while in school, she replied, "Not really—I was too busy studying." When asked about relevant work experience or internships, she had none.

Myth: The best jobs are in large corporations.

Reality: Large companies used to offer more advantages, including job security and career advancement opportunities, than small companies. That gap is narrowing. Since 1980, the proportion of the American workforce employed by *Fortune* 500 companies has shrunk significantly. Some of the best opportunities are in small companies. The real growth and opportunities for rapid advancement will come from microbusinesses (those started with fewer than four employees), venture capital– backed start-ups, and entrepreneurial-venture start-ups within large companies.

Myth: Go to work for a good company and move up the career ladder.

Reality: In the past, Americans worked for large companies in which they had opportunities to move up and build careers over a span of 20 or 30 years. New college graduates entered management training programs and followed predictable career paths, with periodic promotions. The career ladders are gone. **Today, the responsibility for career advancement and employability has shifted from the company to the employee.** Although companies may offer assistance through tuition reimbursement and training programs, the clear message is that you are responsible for developing your own career path, including finding ways to identify and learn the skills you'll need for continued employment.

The Dynamic Workplace

Not only have the sheer numbers of companies in the United States increased significantly, but the ways employees contract their services to employers have also increased. Some professionals choose one of these options. Others fall into it when they cannot find suitable full-time work. Out of necessity, many people have tried these new approaches to get work, and now they wouldn't trade them for traditional employment. These new ways of working provide more autonomy and more variety. Keeping track of your intangible skills and qualities is imperative. Many individuals who want continuous employment put more faith in their own marketing ability than in the vacillations of corporate payrolls. Here's a look at some of the new work options that are available.

Core employee. Permanent full-time employees are being referred to as *core employees*. The number of core employees is shrinking as companies increase their reliance on other hiring options. Companies retain core employees whose work is directly involved in the design, testing, production, and distribution of core products. Support and staff positions such as customer service, communications, shipping, product repair, human resources, and accounting are outsourced to smaller firms or "offshored" to cheaper workers in foreign countries.

Contingent worker. Companies hire additional people during peak periods, so the number of employees is contingent upon the amount of work that needs to be done. When the peak period ends, these workers are off to another gig (think movie productions). Entertainment companies are not the only ones who rely on contingent workers—many manufacturers do when they're ramping up a new product. Companies that need seasonal workers, such as hotels and retail stores, also hire contingent workers. All types of nonpermanent employment—such as contract, temporary, and part-time work—fall into this category. Contingent workers may contract directly with employers or they may be paid through temporary agencies, contractors, or consulting firms.

Concurrent worker. Working two or more different careers at the same time is called concurrent work. An example is a computer programmer who writes code on a flex schedule that allows him to spend evenings and weekends pursuing his career as a rock musician.

Independent contractor. Professional sports figures aren't the only ones who consider themselves free agents or independent contractors. Independent contractors are actually a type of entrepreneur who own their own business and contract their skills to other companies or clients. They thrive in many professions, including Web site developer or designer, photographer, event planner, and have the ability to choose their own clients. These are highly skilled freelance workers who are loyal to their profession rather than to a particular employer. Independent contractors look for interesting and challenging work that allows them the freedom to use their knowledge and provides opportunities to improve their skills.

Job sharer. Sometimes the best person for the job is actually two people for the price of one. Some companies have learned that having two people work at the same job, but for only half the work week each, is an economical and productive way to deliver value to the company and the employees. The advantage to the employer—there are two minds instead of one. The advantage to the job sharers—they can choose the part-time work schedule that suits them best. Job sharers include positions such as receptionist, medical assistant, customer service, and human resources. Job sharing is especially popular among working

What Independent Contractors Say

- "Working as a consultant, you have to do your own marketing—that means that you have to allot time to that process as well as put on a different mindset. I personally found that very hard work. I also had to deal with the natural feelings of rejection when speaking to potential clients who didn't buy my services."

- "I must say that I like it. Money and a certain amount of freedom."

- "Typically, there is more variety in assignments."

- "You can have more flexibility in your schedule."

- "There are no buddies to meet in the hallway or bounce an idea off. I've got a network of folks to call now, but it takes a while to set that up."

- "I personally have to discipline myself to get dressed before I go to my basement office, or I find myself in front of my computer at 3:00 p.m. still in my jammies!"

- Companies expect you to be at your best at all times, no ups and downs, because they are paying you premium bucks to be the best. You need to guard your emotions and mood swings so that you are always professional and prepared."

- "Autonomous freedom is wonderful—especially if your previous experience was being micromanaged. On the other hand, you may (and probably will) find yourself working much harder and for longer hours than you ever did for someone else."

mothers as it provides flexible work hours and still gives coverage during the traditional workday.

On-call worker. On-call workers are called into work when needed and aren't guaranteed a set number of hours. Many health care workers, repair technicians, and even wildfire fighters work on call.

Entrepreneur. You may decide to completely strike out on your own and start your own business. While most people think that being your own boss is a motivating force behind starting your own business, most entrepreneurs will tell you that the reason they do it is because of their passion for bringing an idea from concept to reality. Famous entrepreneurs such as Bill Gates, founder of Microsoft; Walt Disney, creator of the Disney empire, including Disneyland, Disney World, and the Disney Studios; Steve Jobs, founder of Apple; Dave Thomas, founder of Wendy's; and Mark Zuckerberg, founder of Facebook, would all tell you that it was the dream of bringing something unique and special to people that motivated them to do what they did. And, while there are many very famous and wealthy entrepreneurs, all would also tell you that it takes a lot of hard work and belief in yourself and your idea to be successful. There are some very talented entrepreneurs who are not successful. It takes a great idea, hard work, and some luck to realize your dreams as an entrepreneur.

Social entrepreneur. Some entrepreneurs believe in investing their time and money in social causes that will have a positive impact on society. **Social entrepreneurs apply entrepreneurial strategies to social problems such as hunger, education, women's rights, and others.** For example, Oprah Winfrey demonstrated social entrepreneurialism when she funded and opened a school for girls in Africa. Nicholas Negroponte started OLPC, One Laptop Per Child, with the vision to build and distribute low-cost laptops to children in every corner of the world. Social entrepreneurs dedicate their careers and focus their efforts and their passion on inspiring others to give time and money to solve the social issue that they have taken on as their cause.

Tricks of the Trade
Free Resources for Entrepreneurs

Being an entrepreneur can be exciting and exhilarating. But it is also challenging, especially plotting a course that will provide you with the income you need to cover your living expenses. Before you decide to go out on your own or start your own business, it's a good idea to use some **free** resources that are available to you.

Entrepreneur Magazine—www.entrepreneur.com—articles and resources
Inc. Magazine—www.inc.com—articles and resources
Small Business Administration and Small Business Development Centers—www.sba.gov—workshops, counselors, and resources to help you plan and start your business

SCORE (Service Corp of Retired Executives) www.score.org—one-on-one counseling with expertise in specific areas to help you plan and start your business.

Trends Driving Alternative Work Options

Affordable Technology

New technology is putting powerful tools once available only to large organizations into the hands of people who are using them to start home-based and other small businesses. Today, with computer and telecommunications technology, you can work virtually from anywhere—in cities, small towns, suburbs, even hilltops or seaside cabins. For a small investment, anyone can have the same capability as a *Fortune* 500 company.

Outsourcing

Organizations have become leaner (and more economical) by sticking to their core businesses. Support departments are disappearing as companies outsource necessary but peripheral tasks. Because of technology, it's often more cost effective for big business to contract with individuals and small firms than it is to hire employees. Outsourcing is so prevalent that even some CEOs are working on contract! These turnaround specialists take on ailing companies, improve their financial operations, and then move on to the next needy client.

Small-Business Services

As the number of small businesses increases, so does the need for services to this sector of the economy. Service businesses are the fastest-growing sector in our economy. They mainly serve other small businesses by meeting essential needs such as accounting, marketing, desktop publishing, Web site maintenance, and newsletters.

Niche Consumer Markets

From nannies to personal shoppers, people are creating niche markets of people-based services to meet the needs of busy two-career couples and single parents. Increasingly pressed for time, consumers need other people to take care of the ordinary chores of living, such as housecleaning, running errands, taking care of pets, and home improvement.

Real Questions, *Real Answers*

Q. I have an idea for a business, but I don't have the money to start it. What can I do?

A. Whether you are planning to be an independent contractor or start your own business, it's important to have a business plan to understand exactly what it's going to take in terms of income and expenses to have a profitable enterprise. Most small businesses fail in the first year because of lack of capitalization. If you need to purchase inventory, real estate, or other assets, or if you just need to get the word out about the services you provide, either way you will need a business plan. A business plan is a comprehensive document that commits to paper the basics about your business—what business you are in, what makes it unique, who the customer is, how much you can sell, what the cost of doing business is. There are several free resources that will help you develop your business plan and provide feedback *before* you take it to prospective investors.

Choosing Alternative Work Styles

When you work for someone else, you have a safety net. Although you don't have a guaranteed job, you do have access to benefits and retirement plans. Your work is usually well defined and predictable. You also have support from co-workers and the satisfaction of inclusion in the organization's community. So why do people choose alternative work styles? Here are some of the reasons they cite:

- More control over their work life. People can choose their clients, schedules, and tasks.
- Combine earning a living and a simpler lifestyle. With telecommunications and computer technology, many young professionals are opting to live in small towns or rural communities.
- See direct results of their efforts. These workers enjoy developing relationships with clients and seeing the results.
- Freedom to do the work they love. In corporations, most professionals spend countless hours in meetings and other required tasks. The self-employed aren't impeded by company politics, bureaucratic systems, or mercurial bosses.

Am I an Entrepreneur?

Instructions: Circle the number that best describes your level of agreement with each statement. Circle 1 if the statement is rarely true; circle 5 if this describes you most of the time.

I prefer working on multiple projects.	1	2	3	4	5
I like getting an assignment and running with it.	1	2	3	4	5
My skills are cutting edge.	1	2	3	4	5
I'm a self-starter.	1	2	3	4	5
I'm good at helping people identify the cause of their problem.	1	2	3	4	5
I create schedules for myself and stick to them.	1	2	3	4	5
I like learning new skills.	1	2	3	4	5
I like to solve problems.	1	2	3	4	5
I enjoy coming up with new ways to do things.	1	2	3	4	5
If I don't know the answer, I know where to look.	1	2	3	4	5
I'm a good communicator and establish good working relationships.	1	2	3	4	5
I've developed my brand and am willing to market my services.	1	2	3	4	5
I'm self-disciplined.	1	2	3	4	5
I can handle rejection.	1	2	3	4	5
I'm motivated by my own goals; I don't need a boss to motivate me.	1	2	3	4	5
I have good project management skills.	1	2	3	4	5
I can manage tracking my time, billing, accounting, and paying taxes.	1	2	3	4	5
I'm well connected in my profession.	1	2	3	4	5
I have a strong network.	1	2	3	4	5
I have excellent references and a portfolio of work samples.	1	2	3	4	5

Scoring: A score of 70 or higher indicates you have the makings for going out on your own. If your score is below 70, you'd better stick with working for someone else, at least for now.

Check It Out

Instructions: As you might imagine, there are many Web sites dedicated to going out on your own. So if you want to know what it takes to get started, check out the following sites:

www.startupjournal.com The Wall Street Journal's Web-based publication for entrepreneurs

www.kauffman.org Kauffman Foundation's Web site puts essential entrepreneurship resources at your fingertips

www.entrepreneur.com Resource for start-ups from Entrepreneur magazine

www.ceoexpress.com Portal to many business tools of interest to entrepreneurs and independent contractors

www.springwise.com Idea database that gives thumbnails of start-up ideas

www.quintcareers.com Has articles about consulting and free agents

www.cehandbook.com Book and newsletter; free with sign-up

www.inc.com Articles of interest from Inc. magazine

www.businessforum.com A forum for ideas and discussion of going out on your own

www.gmarketing.com Guerrilla marketing for small businesses

www.businessownersideacafe.com Conversations among business owners

www.edwardlowe.org Not-for-profit foundation for entrepreneurs

www.workingsolo.com Resources and ideas for independent contractors and people working on their own

www.sologig.com Listing of open projects

www.score.org Free one-on-one counseling for small business owners from retired executives

Use the space below to write your impressions from these Web sites:

Preparing for Going Out on Your Own

Enroll in entrepreneurship courses while you're in college. This is one way to assess your interest as well as to prepare for the realities of setting up shop.

Develop a business plan.

Recognize that you'll have to get really good at marketing—and that it will be an ever-present part of your work life.

You don't have to be a risk-taker (although it helps), but you do have to be self-managing.

Great interpersonal skills are a must. You'll need referrals from clients to succeed, and that will happen only if you can establish positive relationships (and keep your commitments).

My Career Journal

Do you see yourself working in a "typical" 9-to-5 job, or launching an alternative career path upon graduation?

_____

_____

_____

_____

If you would prefer the security and camaraderie of being a core employee, what steps can you take now to achieve that status?

_____

_____

_____

_____

If you would prefer the freedom and uniqueness of an alternative career, what steps can you take now to hone your skills and/or make contacts with others involved in the same type of work?

_____

_____

_____

_____

_____

Notes to **Myself**

11
Pricing the Product:
What Salary Can You Expect?

How much are you worth?

This may a difficult question to answer, especially if you are just entering the workforce. You probably want to make as much money as possible, but how will you know if the job offer you get is competitive?

To understand salary, you need to understand value. For example, would you pay $10.00 to download a song on iTunes? Probably not, since the going price is $0.99 to $1.29 per song; $10.00 would *not* be a good value. The same concept holds true for employers. An employer is not going to offer you a $75,000 annual salary when most other companies are paying $35,000 for a comparable job. Just as you know the going price for a song download, you should know the standard compensation for the job you want to pursue.

In the general marketplace, price is the value that customers exchange to obtain a desired product. **In the job market, your price is your salary, or more specifically, your total compensation. It's the amount of payment in the form of salary, benefits, and perks that an employer is willing to give in exchange for your valuable skills.** Employers, like all consumers, have expectations about what a product (you) is worth. Compensation fluctuates in the same ways as product pricing. Competition, demand, revenues, and the environment impact the salary you can expect. Just as marketers try to come as close to "reasonable" as possible when deciding on price, your chances of obtaining work increase when you set reasonable salary expectations.

Brand You Checklist

✓ Discover how to research what salary and other compensation elements you can expect.

✓ Determine how to calculate the cost of living in different cities.

✓ Learn how to handle salary questions on an interview.

✓ Understand how to calculate your living budget.

Know How to Talk the Talk

You're used to studying vocabulary words for your classes. Believe it or not, there are vocabulary words you need to know in the real world. Some of the most important ones pertain to your income, also called compensation. **It's not enough to get the salary you want, it's better to think in terms of compensation—the total amount that you are paid for performing a job, including all additional elements such as commissions, bonus, benefits, and other perks or extras.** Here's a quick glossary of words you should know in order to maximize your earnings.

- **Base salary**—annual salary on which commissions and bonuses are calculated. (For example, a 5 percent bonus on a $30,000 base salary is $1,500, whereas a 5 percent bonus on a $35,000 base salary is $1,750.)
- **Commission**—(usually applies to sales positions) additional compensation that is paid based on the amount of products or services sold.
- **Bonus**—additional compensation that is paid based on performance or achievement of a prespecified goal.
- **Stock options**—additional compensation in the form of ownership of the company. Usually stock options are shares of stock that may be purchased by the employee.
- **Benefits**—compensation elements that may include insurance (usually medical, dental, optical), vacation and sick days, day care, tuition reimbursement, 401(k), and others; benefits vary by company, so it's best to ask to see the benefits package.
- **Other perks**—some companies include subsidized cafeterias, office services such as a concierge, game tables, free coffee and snacks, flex hours, and other "extras" that help offset your living expenses or make it more attractive to work at the company. In addition, some positions may include a car allowance or other transportation allowance as part of compensation.

It's unlikely that a position will include all of these elements as part of compensation. And there may be others that are offered that are not listed here. This should help you conduct your research and understand that salary is only one part of total compensation.

What I Wish I Knew . . . *About Compensation*

One recent graduate quoted on QuintCareers.com said, "For starters, (I wish I had known not to) take the first offer ever when talking about salaries." That's why it's best to know what you're worth before you even begin the interviewing process. That way, you'll be armed with information and you'll know what to expect in terms of compensation.

Know What You're Worth

Your value, or what a prospective employer is willing to pay you as an annual salary, is part of your personal brand. Just as in every other phase of job searching, compensation is a critical topic for which you should do your research *early* in your personal branding process. In fact, you should do your research about compensation to know what you're worth even *before* you create your résumé.

Begin your compensation research by talking to people you know in the industry including alumni, friends, and recent graduates. While an individual's compensation is a personal matter, people will generally give you an idea of what you can expect given the economy, competition, and your background for the position you are seeking.

But don't stop there. You can find specific facts by going to Web sites that give you details on compensation. Salary.com has a free Salary Wizard that provides information on total compensation for thousands of different positions including base salary, commission, benefits, bonus, and other compensation elements. This salary information is based on ongoing surveys and research that is conducted by employers. This reflects the market value for the position. While some employers may pay slightly more or less for the same position, it would be rare to find compensation that would be significantly higher (or lower) for a similar position within the same geographic area. This compensation information is extremely valuable to help set your expectations when you begin your job search.

If you are considering a position in a city other than where you currently live, you should research the difference in the cost of living. A $28,000 salary in Eugene, Oregon is much different from the same salary in New York, New York. The cost of living varies greatly from city to city, so it's a good idea to know the difference in the cost of living before you begin the interview process. Web sites such as www.BestPlaces.net provide a comparison of the cost of living in your current city compared to the city you are considering. For example, according to www.BestPlaces.net an annual salary of $30,000 in Portland, Maine should increase to $52,724 in San Francisco, California. This is extremely helpful so that you realize that compensation will be higher in certain cities, but that reflects the higher cost of food, housing, and transportation in those cities.

THESE SITES: Web sites that calculate salary, usually based on geographical areas:

www.bls.gov
www.salary.com
www.salaryexpert.com
www.vault.com
www.collegegrad.com
www.careerjournal.com/salaryhiring

Real Fact
More jobs are created in companies with fewer than 100 employees—and there's less competition to get them.

Real Questions, *Real Answers*

Q. **How do I find out the salary for a job if it is not included in the job posting or job description?**

A. While you might want to ask about salary in the interview, it's *not* appropriate to ask about salary during a job interview. Wait until the employer brings up the topic. Then, be ready to answer the question with the salary range that you are seeking.

The bottom line is that it is critical that you do your homework on compensation *before* you begin the interviewing process. If you don't, you may be disappointed with a job offer or be taken by surprise on an interview.

Handling Salary Questions on an Interview

It seems as if it should be straightforward—if you want to know the salary for a specific job, just ask on the interview. Well, it's not quite that simple.

Real People, Real Advice ... About When to Discuss Salary on an Interview

"(About asking about the salary for a position on the interview) I would be afraid to say something that is kind of out of bounds or off limits. You don't want to ruin the good rapport you've built with a company by saying something that's just not acceptable."

—*Amanda Burd, student, Saint Joseph's University*

"Usually I tell people it's not appropriate to talk about salary until the second interview. . . . go through the interview process and when the employer brings it up, and they will, that's when you can state what you are looking for."

—*Karen Carroll, Executive Recruiter, Blue Plate Minds*

Watch Karen Carroll's short video about how to handle the compensation question at www.mypearsonmarketinglab.com. See Chapter 6 for Karen Carroll's profile.

Compensation is a complex issue, and it requires patience and finesse to handle it properly on an interview. Before you even go on an interview, you should conduct your research about compensation. It's important to understand the following:

- What is the compensation range for the position in general (based on your research)?
- What is the minimum salary can you afford to live with (see Determining Your Costs below)?
- What is your desired salary?

From this information, you should develop the salary range you are seeking. This salary range should be slightly higher than your minimum affordable salary and slightly higher than your desired salary. In other words, if you must have at least $25,000 in annual salary in order to meet your expenses, but you would like to earn $28,000, the salary range that you use in a job interview is $30,000–$35,000. This will give you and your prospective employer some room for negotiation. If you tell your prospective employer that you need $25,000, it will be difficult to negotiate up, but if you say $30,000–$35,000, it will be easier to fall back down to $29,000, if need be. You'll learn more about how to negotiate a job offer in Chapter 16, but it's important to set your expected salary range long before you start the interviewing process so that you will be in a good position to negotiate when the time comes.

After you do your research, you are prepared for the compensation conversation on a job interview. But just because you are prepared doesn't mean you should bring up the topic. **In fact, recruiters and hiring managers alike strongly suggest that candidates do _not_ broach the topic of compensation on a job interview.** If you are working with a recruiter, he or she will most likely discuss compensation with you prior to the interview. **A candidate should wait until the prospective employer brings up the topic of compensation.** It is out of place for a candidate to bring up the topic. It's up to the employer to bring up compensation, usually when the employer is interested in moving forward with the candidate. **Even though you may want to ask about compensation, _be patient._** Go through the interview process and let the prospective employer take the lead on the topic.

When you do get asked about compensation, be ready with your answer. In many cases, a prospective employer will ask a question such as, "What are your salary expectations?" **When possible, it's best to avoid giving a specific number.** A response such as, "I'm sure you have a very competitive compensation package," is a very appropriate answer. However, sometimes a prospective employer or recruiter will persistently pursue a specific answer to the question. If that's the case, be ready to share your desired salary range. A response such as, "I'm looking for a base salary between $30,000 and $35,000 with competitive benefits," sets the tone for your expectations. Even if the prospective employer tells you the salary range for the position, it's important to wait until you receive a job offer before you start negotiating. Just because a prospective employer asked you about your salary expectations doesn't mean you have a job offer.

What Is a Good Offer?

Learn how to evaluate a job offer by reading Chapter 16, Evaluating and Finalizing Your Offer.

Real People, Real Advice...About Stating Salary Expectations

"You should have a number in your mind . . . . Don't be afraid to put a number out there because the worst they can do is offer you $2,000 less or $4,000 less. If you come in really low, you'll never get higher than that. If you come in at $25,000, they won't offer you $28,000. So if you want $28,000, you have to say $30,000, but negotiable."

—*Karen Carroll, Executive Recruiter, Blue Plate Minds*

Learn more about compensation in a short video featuring Karen Carroll at www.mypearsonmarketinglab.com.

Determining Your Costs—Setting Your Budget

Calculate Your Budget

Keep a small notebook handy for the next two weeks and jot down every penny you spend. Then double those amounts to estimate your monthly budget. Once you've written everything down, you can mark areas where you can reduce expenses.

Compensation is only half of the story. To determine what is a good compensation package, you will need to determine how much money you need to cover your costs. In fact, you'll need to complete this exercise in order to truly be able to evaluate a compensation package from a prospective employer. There are some realities in life for which you need to put pencil to paper (or fingers to keyboard) . . . a personal budget is one of them. It doesn't matter if you have the skill to discuss and negotiate a job offer; if you can't cover your living expenses, you will be looking for another job in short order.

Here are some things to consider. You'll have some fixed costs, like housing and transportation. You'll also have variable costs, such as food, clothing, and entertainment. The following activity will help you determine your monthly budget.

ACTIVITY 11.1

Your Monthly Budget

Instructions: List the dollar amounts you think you will need in each expense category for an average month. If your plans include moving to another city, you may need to research expenses in that location

Expense	Amount
Housing (rent or mortgage + utilities)	_____
Food (groceries + eating out)	_____
Clothing (purchases + cleaning)	_____
Automobile/transportation (payments + gas)	_____
Insurance	_____
Child care or child support	_____
Education loans or expenses	_____
Bills and debts (credit cards, stores, loans, etc.)	_____
Savings	_____
Amusement/discretionary spending (movies + reading + other entertainment, gifts + vacation)	_____
Total amount you need each month	_____

Ways to Increase Your Value

While there is not as much room to negotiate on an entry-level salary, you can ensure that you are offered the amount on the higher end of the range by increasing the value your brand has to offer. Here are just a few things you can do:

- **Intern.** The best internships are in the area where you hope to work after graduation. You'll learn the problems faced, develop networking contacts, and best of all, have relevant experience to communicate on your résumé and in interviews.

- **Gain work experience.** As college costs rise, more students find it necessary to work at least part time to offset expenses. Any work experience provides the proof that you keep your commitments and can work with others. If it's related to your future career, even better. Getting involved in volunteer activities, professional organizations, or sharing experiences in a blog are excellent ways to improve your value and build your résumé.

- **Give a good impression.** Every phase of the hiring process is important. From your first phone call to your last interview, convey a professional image.

- **Keep in touch.** If you have an internship with a company, consider it a 16-week job interview. Even if a full-time position is not available when you graduate, keep in touch with your manager and other people at the company or organization. Keep yourself top of mind so that when a position is available, you are the first person they think about.

- **Send a thank-you note.** You can't say thank-you enough. After you complete your internship, after a job interview, or after you have an informational interview, be sure to send a thank-you note. It's appropriate to send a thank-you e-mail within 24 hours. In addition, it's a good idea to send a handwritten thank-you note within two days. You can set yourself apart and demonstrate your writing skills with a sincere and well-written thank-you note.

THESE SITES: Web sites that calculate the cost of living for various geographic areas:

www.bestplaces.net/COL/
www.salary.com
www.freeusaguide.com
www.moving.com/real-estate/compare-cities/index.asp

Get a Higher Salary
You can create a competitive advantage in the job market. Communicate the benefits of your qualifications. Show employers you'll give the job performance they want for a price they are willing to pay, and do it better than the competition.

Tricks of the Trade

The best way to ensure that you get the job offer with the best compensation is to impress everyone from the receptionist to the hiring manager when you go on your interviews. When everyone at a company or organization likes your attitude and skills, chances are you will get a good offer. You are establishing your brand value the first time you come in contact with a recruiter or prospective employer.

My Career Journal

After reviewing salary Web sites, how does the salary for the position you are seeking compare to what you thought you'd be making after college? Was this a reality check, or did it simply confirm your expectations?

_____

_____

_____

What is the cost of living in the city in which you work? Research some of the Web sites listed in this chapter to determine the average cost of items such as housing, food, and other regular expenses.

_____

_____

_____

_____

What are some ways that you can increase your value?

_____

_____

_____

_____

_____

_____

Notes to Myself

Step 4 Communicating Your Value Proposition

(Chapters 12–14)

Think of your favorite ad. Think about what makes it great . . . it is the right message for the right product at the right time in the right place?

Now think about your personal brand. Will your advertising be as compelling?

Yes, it will!

Chapters 12–14 will give you the framework to create an integrated marketing communications plan for your brand and powerful advertising (résumé and cover letter) that will help you get interviews at the companies that are on the top of your target list.

Don't make the mistake of only sending out a few résumés to see what response you get. Use the activities and resources in Chapters 12–14 to actually implement your "advertising campaign" by getting out your cover letters and résumés online and off-line. There is no single answer for the best way to get out your cover letter and résumé. But like successful brands, you should use all (not just some) of the methods available to you. Prospective employers can't hire you if they don't know about you.

You're in charge of your career. Get the word out about your brand. ➤

12
Creating Your Communication Plan:
Getting the Word Out about Your Brand

Now that you have defined your brand, it's time to craft your own **integrated marketing communication (IMC)** plan. Think about great brands like McDonald's, Coke, and Verizon. Each of these brands communicates often (you see each ad multiple times), uses multiple media at the same time (TV, magazine, radio, Internet, mobile apps, etc.), and tailors their message for the different segments of their target audience (for example, McDonald's has ads that market salads to health-conscious women, premium sandwiches to working profes-sionals, and Happy Meals to moms and children).

You want to follow the same strategy whether you are look-ing for an internship or your first full-time job. Think of your cover letter and résumé as "advertising" for your brand. You want as many people in your target audience to see it as fre-quently as possible. You may also want to tailor your cover let-ter for each segment of your target audience. You'll learn how to do this in Chapter 13.

Your Integrated Marketing Communication Plan

As part of your IMC plan, you will use a media mix or a mix of different ways to reach your target audience. In Chapter 4, you learned about resources to use to conduct your research. Now you will learn about the following seven "media" you can use to effectively get your résumé to the right people at the right time:

1. Online job boards and recruiting Web sites
2. Social networking Web sites
3. Company Web sites
4. Direct mail
5. Career fairs
6. Networking
7. Follow-up

Increase your chances of getting the internship or full-time job you want by using all of the options you have to get the word out about your brand. You will only get a response from a small percentage of résumés you send out using any of these "media." Use all of these options frequently to increase your chances of success. **Don't make the mistake of only using one or two media.** There's no single method that will give you the results you want. Give yourself every opportunity to have multiple job offers from which to choose. **You can get the job offer you want if you use all of the following media in your integrated marketing communication plan.**

Online Job Boards and Recruiting Sites

Online job boards and recruiting sites should be an ongoing part of your integrated marketing communication plan, but not the focus of it. While there are hundreds of Web sites that have job listings in a variety of industries, it's rare that you will get a call from an online job posting. You've probably read some online job postings that thought you would be a perfect fit for the job, yet you didn't get a call for an interview. That's not uncommon, because many positions are already filled by the time the jobs get posted. In some cases, the job posting is just fulfilling a legal requirement to let the public know about the job. As Brian Wiggins, Director of Circulation at the *Philadelphia Business Journal,* said in the video in Chapter 3, **by the time the job is posted, it's probably too late.** If you rely solely on applying for jobs that are posted on Web sites, you may be disappointed. However, if you use online job boards as one of many approaches to your brand integrated marketing communication plan, you will probably have better results.

One way to be more successful using online job boards is to use a combination of many Web sites. The most popular job boards are important because they have the largest number of jobs. But don't limit yourself to only those sites. There are many sites that have unique listings or aggregate job postings, provide excellent search tools, offer e-mail alerts, and have career planning information.

Because job sites are powered by search tools, it's important to use the right keywords. Make a list of keywords to use in your searches on these sites so that your searches yield relevant job results. You will only see the jobs you want if you take the time to create comprehensive searches with the right keywords.

"I don't really know the best way to get a job. In my opinion, when you apply online, you kind of just throw your résumé out there with a bunch of other résumés and there's not a high likelihood that they'll get a clear idea of who you are."

—*Amanda Burd, student, Saint Joseph's University*

"If you're only relying on the job boards ... then you're selling yourself short. You're only having exposure to a small amount of the available jobs, so we tell candidates that it's only one part, and it's a very small part. Most likely you'll find your next opportunity or your next interview through successful networking, through marketing, and explaining to people what you have to offer and what you're looking for."

—*Kristin Kane, Director of Social Media and Recruiting,*
Kane Partners Staffing Solutions

Hear Kristin Kane's tips about how to get the word out about your brand at www.mypearsonmarketinglab.com. Read Kristin Kane's profile in Chapter 7.

If you want to post your résumé to a job site, take a minute to read the privacy policy of the Web site to be sure your contact information will be protected. Based on the site's privacy policy, you may want to skip posting your résumé and only use the site to search and apply for jobs.

Activity 12.1 will guide you as you create your own list of Web sites you will use for your work search. It's a good idea to review the Recommended Web Sites list in the **Brand You** Toolkit at the back of the book. Don't forget to include local job boards and local professional organizations on your list. Here are some ideas about how you can identify the best online job sites for you.

- **General job boards and recruiting sites.** Web sites such as www.monster .com, www.careerbuilder.com, www.wetfeet.com, and www.experience .com are good places to start. See the Recommended Web Sites in the **Brand You** Toolkit.

- **Job boards and recruiting sites that specialize in your target industry.** For example, if you are looking for a job in Internet marketing, Web sites such as www.marketingsherpa.com and www.sempo.org are excellent resources. See a list of recommended Web sites by industry/specialty in the Recommended Web Sites in the **Brand You** Toolkit (at the back of the book).

Keep It Fresh
Always look for new job boards, recruiter, and company Web sites to add to your target list. New Web sites can give you a fresh perspective on your work search.

• **National, regional, and local professional organizations in your target industry.** Professional associations such as the American Institute of Certified Public Accountants, American Marketing Association, Public Relations Society of America, and others are ideal places to search for information and job postings. A list of key professional organizations is included in Recommended Web Sites in the **Brand You** Toolkit. Or, go to www.associationjobboards.com to find the national associations in your discipline. In addition, research local trade associations such as the local advertising club. Most professional organizations have job listings on their Web sites.

• **National, regional, and local trade publications that serve your target industry.** Go to the Web sites of the publications that serve the industry in which you are interested. Most trade publications also include jobs on their Web sites. If you don't know the name of any trade publications, ask one of your professors. He or she will be happy to give you the names of the best trade publications in your target industry.

In addition, many trade publications have regular e-mail newsletters. This is an excellent way to stay abreast of news in the industry. And many trade publications also offer hard-copy magazines at no charge to subscribers.

Social Networking Web Sites

Social Networking Works
Join professional social networking Web sites to establish connections in your target industry.

www.linkedin.com
www.plaxo.com
www.jobster.com

You are probably comfortable using social Web sites for communication with your friends and classmates. Many companies use sites such as Facebook and MySpace to recruit for internships and entry-level jobs.

In addition, professional social networking Web sites such as www.linkedin.com, www.jobster.com, and www.plaxo.com can help you develop contacts in your target industry and/or at your target companies. Most professional social networking Web sites provide the option for you to create a profile/résumé and many also include a job board. Social networking combined with personal networking can be an extremely effective way to create and develop professional relationships. This important tool for your job search is discussed in detail in Chapter 14.

A word of caution about social networking and job searching . . . you are available to prospective employers 24/7 online. **Be sure your pages, blogs, pictures, videos, and all other communication on ALL social networking pages are appropriate for prospective employers to read at any time.** Don't assume that prospective employers won't search the social networking Web sites to see who you are and how you express yourself. Take the time to review your pages to be sure everything you have posted is appropriate and is an accurate reflection of you.

"If you're not going to say it in front of a prospective employer . . . or if you wouldn't say it in public, or if it's inappropriate, it probably shouldn't be online anyway."

—*Kristin Kane, Director of Social Media and Recruiting, Kane Partners Staffing Solutions*

Hear more about digital dirt from Kristin Kane in a short video at www.mypearson marketinglab.com.

Company Web Sites

Companies constantly post open positions on their Web sites. And many companies do not use job boards or recruiters. Don't just rely on job boards to learn about open positions. Here are some tips about how to use company Web sites in your job search.

- **Visit Web sites for companies in your target industry.** In Activity 12.1, you will create a list of at least 25 target companies for which you would like to work. To create your list, you will use the research methods you learned in Chapter 4. You may want to review Chapter 4 as you are preparing your list. Here are a few reminders of resources you can use to identify your target companies:
  - Use the professional and trade publication Web sites as well as www.bizjournals.com, www.hoovers.com, www.yellowpages.com, and the business section of the local city newspaper or newspaper Web site to find the names of local companies in your industry or specialty.
  - Another good source for company names is the list of 100 Fastest Growing Companies. Because these companies are growing, they are usually hiring people. The Web site of the local major city newspaper or www.bizjournals.com will have a listing of local and/or regional fastest growing companies. National business publications such as *BusinessWeek* and *Fortune* publish national and international business lists.
  - Other lists published by local and national business publications could also be helpful, such as the Top Public Accounting Firms, Top Public Relations Agencies, Top Advertising Agencies, Top Interactive Marketing Agencies, Top Investment Banking Firms, Top Financial Services Firms, Best Companies to Work For, America's Most Admired Companies, Best Employers for New Grads, Top Companies for Women, Top Companies for Minorities, Top Companies for Leaders, Top Places to Start Your Career, Top Companies for Families, *Fortune* 500, Global 500.

    If you are looking for local business lists such as these, go to www .bizjournals.com or the Web site of your local city newspaper. If you are looking for national and international business lists, go to the Web sites of business publications such as www.wsj.com, www.businessweek .com, www.money.cnn.com/magazines/fortune/, as well as national trade publications such as *Advertising Age* at www.adage.com.

Find the Best Companies
Business lists are an excellent source to help identify target companies. The list of fastest growing companies in your city is an excellent place to start. Go to **www.bizjournals.com** to find business lists for your city.

Check It Out
Use the Recommended Web Sites in the **Brand You** Toolkit (at the back of the book) to complete Activity 12.1. It will give you some ideas about where you can find your target companies.

Your target company list should include professional services companies (such as advertising agencies if you want to go into advertising or accounting firms if you want to pursue a career in accounting, etc.) as well as companies that may a have a department in your target area. For example, if you want to go into finance, identify companies that have a finance department.

○ Business directories such as *Advertising Red Books*, *Directory of Corporate Affiliations*, and others can also help provide information about companies and agencies by geography and type. Many business directories are available online and at no charge in your campus library.

Following is a list that Amanda Burd compiled. Amanda is a marketing major at Saint Joseph's University who wants to pursue a job in advertising in the Philadelphia area. She completed Activity 12.1, My Target Web Site List, by using the research resources covered in Chapter 4 and highlighted here. She also used the Recommended Web Sites included in the **Brand You Toolkit** (at the back of the book). And she met with her professors, the librarian, and a counselor at the campus career center.

• For General Job Boards and Recruiting Web sites and Industry-Specific Job Boards and Recruiting Web sites, she researched the Web sites included in the Recommended Web Sites list in the **Brand You Toolkit**, went to her campus career center, and found out about some local job boards and industry-specific job boards.

• For Professional Organizations and Web Sites, Amanda is a student member of the American Marketing Association, so she added that to her list. She learned about the other professional organizations, including the Philly Ad Club, from her professor.
   She was pleased to find the Philly Ad Club Web site that includes a directory of hundreds of advertising agencies in the area in addition to a job board, news, and events. She added it to her list and is now planning on attending the next meeting.

• She asked her professor which business and trade publications were best, and she added all of them to her list. Her professor also recommended the *Philadelphia Business Journal*. She also went to the library to find some of the business lists mentioned above. The librarian showed her how to get the business lists that were compiled by the *Philadelphia Business Journal*. He also suggested she use the *Advertising Red Books* because it lists advertising agencies, company information, and key management names for each agency by city.

• She used the business lists from the *Philadelphia Business Journal*, a list of advertising agencies from the *Advertising Red Books*, and added some companies that were listed at the campus career center and some she had read about in the area to create her list of target company names and Web sites.

Figure 12.1 is the list Amanda complied for Activity 12.1. Her target company list actually included 26 companies; all are not shown here.

Figure 12.1 Amanda's Target Web Site List

General Job Boards and Recruiting Web Sites	Industry-specific Job Boards and Recruiting Web Sites	Professional Organizations and Web Sites	Trade Publications, Directories, and Web Sites	Target Company Names and Web Sites (Grouped by type)
Monster monster.com	**Marketing Jobs** marketingjobs.com	**American Association of Advertising Agencies** aaaa.org	*Advertising Age* adage.com	**Advertising Agencies Brownstein Group** brownstein.com
Yahoo! Hot Jobs hotjobs.yahoo.com	**Marketing Sherpa** marketingsherpa.com	**American Advertising Federation** aaf.org	*Brand Week* brandweek.com	**LevLane Advertising & PR** levlane.com
Career Builder careerbuilder.com collegegrad.com indeed.com	**Talent Zoo** talentzoo.com	**American Marketing Association** marketingpower.com	*PROMO* promomagazine.com	**1 Trick Pony** 1trickpony.com
The Vault vault.com	**The Creative Group** creativegroup.com	**Direct Marketing Association** dma.com	*Ad Week* adweek.com	**160over90** 160over90.com
Philly Jobs phillyjobs.com	**Aquent** aquent.com	**Search Engine Marketing Professional Organization** sempo.org	*Direct* directmag.com	**Packaged Goods and Food Companies Campbell Soup Company** campbells.com
South Jersey Jobs southjerseyjobs.com	**The Boss Group** thebossgroup.com	**Philadelphia Ad Club** phillyadclub.com	*Philadelphia Business Journal* bizjournals.com/philadelphia	**Tasty Baking Company** tastykake.com
Campus career Web site			*Advertising Red Books* redbooks.com	**Rita's Water Ice** ritaswaterice.com
				General Mills Generalmills.com
				Retail Companies Urban Outfitters urbanoutfitters.com
				Charming Shoppes charmingshoppes.com
				The Pep Boys pepboys.com
				Five Below fivebelow.com

My Target Web Site List

Instructions: Choose a specific industry in which you are interested, and then list the Web sites that you will use in each of the categories below. Complete a new chart for each industry you wish to pursue. Be sure to include local job boards and local professional organizations on your list. You may find it helpful to create your list in Word or Excel using the format below. Bookmark these Web sites on your computer so you use them frequently.

General Job Web Sites	Industry-Specific Job Web Sites	Professional Organizations and Web Sites	Trade Publications, Directories, and Web Sites	Target Company Names and Web Sites (Group by Type)

Here are some tips to help you maximize your results from applying for internships or jobs online:

- **Sign up for job alerts or job agents.** Whenever possible, use these tools to alert you to new jobs that are open.
- **Search Web sites regularly.** If a Web site does not offer job alerts, search the Web site at least three times every week for new jobs.
- **Search synonyms or similar words.** If you are interested in marketing, you can search for marketing, but also search for sales, promotion, advertising, interactive marketing, advertising agency, account executive, account coordinator, marketing specialist, or other marketing words that would be used to list marketing jobs.
- **Apply for jobs as soon as you find them.** Keep in mind that there are many other people who are applying for the same job.
- **Include your cover letter.** Always include a cover letter with your résumé when you apply for a job. A short e-mail note is not enough to set your brand apart.
- **Personalize your cover letter.** If a person's name is listed in the contact information, address your letter to "Dear Mr. Jones" or "Dear Ms. Jones." If the person's name is not listed, address your letter to "Dear Sir or Madam" or "Dear Employer."
- **Tailor your cover letter to the job.** Incorporate key aspects of your experience that reflect the job requirements. Avoid sending a generic letter; hiring managers only want to read cover letters that are relevant to them. For example, if you are applying for a pharmaceutical sales position, don't send your cover letter and résumé to an entertainment company. There's more information about how to do this in Chapter 13.

Real Questions, *Real Answers*

Q. Everyone says I should address letters to a person in a company. How can I find the names of the people in my target companies?

A. Once you identify your target companies, search the company Web site for names of key hiring managers. For example, if you are applying for a job in account management at an advertising agency, look for the names of the vice president of client services, account directors, account managers, and account executives. It's a good idea to include the human resources manager or recruiting manager. If you can't find the names and titles online, call the company and ask for the information, ask someone in your network if they know anyone at the company, or check your LinkedIn connections to see if anyone you know is connected to anyone in the company who can give you the information and make an introduction for you. Send as many targeted letters as possible to key people within each company; sending a letter to only one person in a company is probably not enough.

- **Save your résumé in multiple formats.** Microsoft Word is the standard format for all business communication. If you are sending your résumé to an individual e-mail address, it's expected that you will attach your résumé in **Word** format (PC or Mac). However, many job sites do not maintain the formatting of your résumé if it is submitted as a Word document. For job sites, it is best to submit your résumé in **PDF** or **plain text**. This will ensure that your résumé will be easy for the viewer to read.

- **Save your résumé as a PDF file.** You can convert a Microsoft Word document to PDF using some later versions of Microsoft Word, Acrobat 9 Standard or Acrobat 9 Pro, or visit www.acrobat.com and click on "Create PDF."

- **Save your résumé as a plain text document.** (In Word, click on File, Save As, then choose Plain Text in the Save As Type drop-down box.) Be sure to review your résumé in plain text before you save it, because you may need to make some modifications and delete some symbols that didn't translate. The plain text version can be submitted to those job sites that don't accept PDF.

- **If you are using Word 2007 or later version,** save the documents as Word 97–2003 documents to ensure that the recipient can open them. Don't forget to spell check your cover letter and résumé before you submit them online.

- **If you are using Pages** (Mac), save your document as a PDF file or convert it to Word before sending it to ensure that the recipient can open it.

- **Double check before you submit.** Take a minute before you submit to reread your cover letter and résumé to be sure the spelling and grammar are accurate, the greeting is correct, the date is correct, and any references to the company name are correct. This quick double-check can make the difference between your cover letter and résumé getting noticed or getting discarded.

Don't stop here! Web sites are only part of your integrated marketing communication plan. If you want results, read on.

Tricks of the Trade

"Don't reapply for the same job over and over again," according to Karen Carroll, Executive Recruiter, Blue Plate Minds. Your cover letter and résumé were already reviewed and rejected for the position. You are only wasting your time when you continue to reapply. It's a better idea to spend your time building your list of 25 target companies and finding the hiring manager at each company.

Direct Mail

One of the best ways to let prospective employers know about you and your value proposition is to send them a letter. Just like retailers who send you a catalog to showcase their new product lines, a cover letter and résumé can communicate your skills to the right person at a target company . . . even before a job is open or posted. Not all companies post open internships or full-time jobs online, so a letter is the perfect way to let a prospective employer know you are in the market. **And a hard-copy letter can make you stand out and break through the e-mail clutter.**

Keep in mind that direct mail usually yields a response of 1–2 percent, so it's best to send letters to as many target companies as possible. Send letters to all 25 of the companies on your target company list.

You should plan to send out at least 50 letters or more in each mailing (at least two to each company). You may want to do a few different mailings. For example, if you are targeting the public relations industry, you should have one mailing targeted to public relations and advertising agencies, one to companies with a public relations department, one to recruiting firms, and so on. Use the company groupings you created in Activity 12.1.

To ensure success from your mailing, follow these key guidelines:

- **Send by mail, not e-mail.** Always send a cover letter and résumé on paper via the U.S. mail. An unsolicited résumé (one that is sent to a prospective employer when a job is not posted) that is sent by e-mail is usually deleted.
- **Paper matters.** Use white or off-white résumé paper for both cover letter and résumé. Choose résumé paper (you can find it at your bookstore, office supply store, or office supply Web site).
- **Personalize your cover letter.** Address all envelopes and cover letters to a person in a department at a company (e.g., Ms. Kim Lu, Director of Finance, Home Depot). **Do not** send cover letters and résumés addressed only to a department or to a company because they will most likely end up in the trash (e.g., Finance Department at Home Depot).
- **Send cover letters and résumés to the right people.** Send a letter to the hiring managers such as the vice president, director, and manager of the department in which you would like to work as well as the vice president, director, and recruiting manager in human resources.

Timing Is Everything
Don't mail cover letters and résumés the week before a holiday. The people to whom you are mailing may be taking some time off.

What I Wish I Knew . . . *About Direct Mail*

Cait Walsh is a believer in direct mail! "It really works!" she said. Cait created her list of 25 target companies and the hiring manager at each company and then used the Mail Merge Manager in Word for Mac (also available in Word for PCs) to personalize and print her letters. Within days of mailing her letters, she had three interviews.

- **Send multiple cover letters and résumés to each company.** Send a cover letter and résumé to as many **appropriate** people as possible in each company. This will increase your chances for a response. You can send the same letter to each person; just be sure that each letter is individually addressed. (People do not compare letters, but they might pass them along to the appropriate person.)

Now that you have the big picture, you are ready to put together your mailings.

- **Create your mailing list.** The list of companies you created in Activity 12.1 is the basis of your mailing list of key people to whom you will send your cover letter and résumé.

Go to each company's Web site (or call the company) to find the name of the key decision makers to whom you will send your résumé. Common titles of key people are:

- Vice president of the department in which you would like to work
- Director of the department in which you would like to work
- Manager of the department in which you would like to work
- Account directors in professional services firms such as advertising agencies
- Vice president of human resources
- Director of human resources
- Recruiting manager
- Campus relations or internship manager (for internships)

Another good source for names and companies is local business and trade publications. Regularly read the articles that include the names and titles of people who have been promoted to key positions. Include them in your mailing list.

Be sure to spell all names correctly and use the formal name of the company in the address (e.g., Campbell Soup Company, not Campbell's). Don't forget to send your résumé to major recruiting firms that specialize in filling temporary and full-time entry-level positions such as Robert Half for finance and accounting jobs **(www.roberthalf.com)**, Aquent for marketing jobs **(www.aquent.com)**, Manpower **(www.manpower.com)**, and Kelly Services **(www.kellyservices.com)**.

See Figure 12.2 Sample Company Mailing List at the end of this chapter.

Creating Your Mailing Lists

Build your mailing list in an Excel spreadsheet or a table in Word using one column for each piece of information (one column for Mr. or Ms., one column for first name, one column for last name, etc.). See Figure 12.2 Sample Company Mailing List at the end of this chapter. Use a different spreadsheet or document for each mailing so that you can target your cover letter appropriately. Include phone numbers and e-mail addresses when you are conducting your research as that information will be helpful when you are doing follow-up.

- **Purchase your supplies.** Now that you know how many letters you will be sending, you should buy enough résumé paper (two sheets for each letter), envelopes, paper clips, and stamps. You can use #10 envelopes (standard size) that are perfectly acceptable. Or you can use 9″ × 12″ envelopes, which keep your résumé flat and make it easier for companies to scan.

- **Create a mail merge.** Because you will be sending approximately 50 letters (at least two to each of your target companies) in each mailing, you want to be able to print the letters and envelopes quickly and professionally. The Mail Merge tool in Microsoft Word allows you to personalize and print your letters and envelopes using the Excel spreadsheet or Word table you created earlier. You can even include the name of the company in the body of the letter.

Be sure to proof the letter and each name and address before you begin the Mail Merge.

- Open Microsoft Word; **if you are using Word 2003,** click on Tools, Letters and Mailings, Mail Merge, and follow the steps on the right of the screen to personalize and print your letters.

- **If you are using Word 2007,** click on Mailings, Start Mail Merge, then choose Step-by-Step Mail Merge Wizard. Follow the steps at the right of the screen to personalize and print your letters.

- **If you are using Word in Microsoft Office for Mac,** click on Tools, Mail Merge Manager, and follow the six steps in the pop-up wizard.

- After you print the letters, sign each one and paper clip your résumé to the letter.

- Use the mail merge process to print your personalized envelopes.

- Insert the appropriate letter into each envelope, seal, stamp, and mail.

Now that you have built your mailing list and set up your mail merge, you are ready to send another mailing at a later date if need be.

Practice Mail Merge

Instructions: Create your mailing list using Microsoft Word or Excel in Activity 12.2. Use the mailing list to create a mail merge in Microsoft Word. Follow the steps to create your mail merge to understand how the process works.

Career Fairs

Whenever you have an opportunity to meet a prospective employer in person, do it! Career fairs can be extremely productive. Follow these guidelines to ensure success:

- **Create an action plan.** Before the fair, review the list of employers that will be attending. Review open job listings to identify which employers you will target to meet. Make a list of the employers, contact name (if available), and location at the fair so you have a plan of action. Be open-minded and visit as many companies as possible. Career fairs are an excellent way to learn about companies with which you may not be familiar and jobs that you didn't realize were available. Use Activity 12.4 to prepare for each fair.

- **Bring copies of your "advertising."** Print more copies of your cover letter and résumé than you expect to give out. Print them on high-quality paper (use white or off-white résumé paper). Carry them in a folder or binder; bent résumés are never professional.

- **Always dress for success.** Wear business attire including shoes, hair, and makeup (if appropriate). Because you will be seeing different kinds of companies, this is not the time to be business casual. Stop in the rest room before you enter the job fair. It's a good time to do a last-minute check and use a breath mint just to be sure.

- **Make a personal contact.** Take the time to introduce yourself to each representative from the companies on your target list. This is an opportunity to introduce your brand, so be energetic, professional, and share your value proposition while you are presenting your résumé. You are the best advertising for yourself, so make each contact work.

- **Ask for a business card.** Follow up with a thank-you note (or e-mail) within 24 hours that refers to your meeting at the career fair. Also, add each person to your mailing list and set a reminder date to follow up in one week.

Networking

Networking is such an important part of your media mix that Chapter 14 is devoted to how and when to do effective networking.

Follow-up

When you implement an integrated marketing communication plan, you want to follow up quickly and consistently to maximize your return on your investment. Follow-up is one of the most difficult things to do but can be the most effective. When you follow up, you have the opportunity to make a positive impression. In addition, it gives you the chance to identify other people (or the correct people) to whom you should be directing your communication.

My Career Fair Action Plan

Instructions: Before each career fair, review the list of participating companies and complete this action plan.

Date of Career Fair _____

Time of Career Fair _____

Location of Career Fair _____

Target Company Name	Contact Person	How I Bring Value to This Company	Open Jobs	Location of Company Booth at Fair

Create Your Follow-up Plan

Using the Excel spreadsheet or Word table you created for your mailing list, add four additional columns:

- Date the cover letters and résumés were sent
- Date of follow-up
- Result of follow-up
- Date for second follow-up

This spreadsheet or table is an excellent tool to keep track of the dates you agreed to for follow-up. **See Figure 12.2 Sample Company Follow-up List at the end of this chapter.**

Here are some guidelines to make your follow-up appropriate and timely:

Follow up to:	When to Follow Up	How to Follow Up	Comments
Job posted on a job board or a Web site	1 week	Phone call to the contact listed in the posting	Many employers do not include a contact name; not all submissions to job postings can include a follow-up.
Direct mail	1 week	Phone call to the person to whom you sent the letter	It's best to call when you are able to talk to the person. Leave a voice-mail if necessary, but be sure to follow up again. It may not be possible to follow up on every letter sent; choose the top 10–20 for follow-up.
Career fair	1 day	Thank-you note or e-mail to the person you met at the fair	Set a date for follow-up in your thank-you note.
Networking	1 day	Thank-you note or e-mail to the person	Set a date for follow-up in your thank-you note.

ACTIVITY 12.5

Communications Time Line and Action Plan

*Instructions: Create your own Communications Time Line and Action Plan by filling in the dates in your work plan in the **Brand You** Toolkit (at the back of the book).*

Finding the right job is a big job. Sometimes it may seem that you aren't getting the response you want. Don't get discouraged! You are on the right track and you will find the internship or full-time job you want. Use all the "media" you have available and keep trying!

My Career Journal

Name five resources you will use to identify your target companies.

_____

_____

_____

_____

_____

Name five resources you will use to identify the names, titles, and addresses of people to whom you want to mail your cover letter and résumé at your target companies.

_____

_____

_____

_____

_____

List how you will use each of the seven "media" discussed in this chapter as part of your own integrated marketing communications plan.

_____

_____

_____

_____

_____

_____

_____

_____

Notes to **Myself**

13

Advertising Your Brand:
Crafting Your Résumé and Cover Letter

Do you have a compelling cover letter? Do you have a great résumé?

If you can't answer a resounding "yes" to both questions, it's likely you will have some challenges getting interviews.

Think about the reason you send out cover letters and résumés . . . to get an interview. So your cover letter and résumé are actually your "advertising" to help you get to the next step in the hiring process. Whether you are networking, applying for a job, or sending out your cover letter and résumé, your objective is always the same—to meet with someone personally.

It's not enough to simply have a cover letter and résumé; they need to stand out to get the attention of a recruiter or hiring manager. Remember, you're competing with hundreds, if not thousands of candidates for each open position. **If you only have a résumé, it's not enough. Many employers will not even look at a résumé without a cover letter**. Together, a cover letter and résumé tell a prospective employer who you are and why you are the right person for the job.

If you want to know how to make your brand stand apart from the pack, read this chapter carefully and follow the tips and examples. Then you can send out your cover letter and résumé with confidence . . . and practice your interviewing skills.

Brand You Checklist

✓ Explore the concept of NAB (Needs, Actions, Benefits) to help describe your brand.

✓ Learn how to write an effective résumé.

✓ Understand the role of your cover letter.

✓ Learn how to write a powerful cover letter.

real people, **Real Brands**

Jennifer
Wolf's Brand

The Philadelphia Business Journal *is the leading business publication and Web site for business in Philadelphia. Jennifer is responsible for planning and implementing all of the corporate events and awards for the newspaper.*
See Jennifer's video profile at www.mypearsonmarketinglab.com.

▼ **Q** & **A** with Jennifer Wolf, Event Manager at the *Philadelphia Business Journal.*

Jennifer's Profile

College: West Chester University

Major: Communications

Current profession: Event planning

First job: My first job was in nonprofit event planning

How I got my first job: Networking led me to my first job.

Brand key word: Enthusiasm

Description of my personal brand image: I am always striving to become an event expert. I'm willing to do whatever it takes to make an event come together.

My passion: To be a part of bringing a event together . . . working behind the scenes and taking care of every detail to orchestrate the perfect event.

Jennifer's Advice

Favorite advice about job searching: Set yourself apart. You need to prove why an employer should choose *you* for the job.

Favorite advice for students about building their brand: Get involved in school associations and clubs. Get experience in as many ways as you can; volunteer a lot on campus and off campus. A nonprofit organization is a perfect way to take initiative, make a contribution, gain experience, and build your brand and your network. Internships are a must.

Why internships are important: You get exposure, experience, and a chance to prove yourself. An internship is about learning. You might also learn what you don't want to do, which is just as important as learning what you want to do. Be open-minded and be willing to do anything.

What do you look for in an intern or entry-level candidate: A positive attitude. Show a prospective employer that you are ready to roll up your sleeves to get the job done right. Take initiative and go the extra mile.

What I look for in a résumé: Everyone has to start somewhere, so be honest about your experience, don't add fluff. Restaurant experience says a lot about how you can be customer-focused and multitask. Use specifics to describe your accomplishments in all of your positions and activities. I can see right through the fluff.

What makes me pass over a cover letter and résumé: Typos and grammar errors . . . they are not excusable. A cover letter or résumé with a typo or grammar error is a poor representation of your brand. Always use spell check and ask people to proofread your cover letter and résumé.

Favorite interviewing tip: Do your homework and know the basics about the company with whom you are interviewing. Come prepared to talk about how you can bring value to the company based on what you learned that the company is looking for.

The *worst* thing someone can do on an interview: Not dressing appropriately. Represent yourself as a professional by the way you dress for an interview, whether it's for an internship or a full-time job.

Real People, Real Advice ... About Résumés

"I have a résumé that I started when I was a freshman. I concentrated on getting a lot of things put on my résumé and a lot of times they weren't relevant to the job. . . . I could have done a better job of screening my activities to cater to the company I was applying to. . . . I could have highlighted some really important things."

—*Amanda Burd, student, Saint Joseph's University*

"You need to put tangible information on your résumé. . . . I have a current intern, I was most impressed by her résumé . . . she stated on her résumé that she sold $11,000 in advertising for a campus directory . . . that impressed me."

—*Jennifer Wolf, Event Manager, Philadelphia Business Journal*

Hear more tips about résumés in short videos featuring Amanda Burd and Jennifer Wolf at www.mypearsonmarketinglab.com.

The NAB Process

The secret to writing dynamic résumés and cover letters is using the NAB (Need, Action, Benefit) process. **Employers want proof that you have the skills you say you do.** This is critical to developing your own personal brand. **Employers believe that past performance predicts future performance.** So, if you can describe the skills and the results you have achieved, you will convince employers that you'll use these skills in the future. Once you've written the Action and Benefit statements, you have most of the information you need to construct a compelling résumé.

Student Profile—Amanda Burd

Amanda found a job description for the type of position she is seeking—a marketing assistant. She highlighted the skills, knowledge, and characteristics that the employer wanted. These are the employer's needs.

Marketing Assistant

We're Optibiz Corporation, a leading supplier of optics, photonics instruments and components, optomechanical components, positioning equipment, and vibration control. We are currently seeking a detail-oriented and highly motivated marketing assistant. Selected candidate will assist in the development and implementation of promotional marketing activities in our vibration control group. This will include: forecasting marketing trends of new/existing products; developing catalogs, brochures, and other collateral material; tracking and reporting advertising/collateral budget expenditures; implementing trade show efforts; and supporting product management processes. Requires a bachelor's degree in marketing or 3+ years applicable marketing experience. Knowledge of MS Excel is essential. We offer an excellent compensation and benefits package, a leading-edge work environment, and opportunities for professional growth. We invite qualified candidates to send or fax a résumé to. . . .

Appeal to Your Target

Most people gear their résumés toward getting other jobs just like their last ones. The secret to advancing your career is to focus on the needs of your *next* employer.

With the NAB process, you can demonstrate that you've actually used the skills the employer is seeking. You'll notice in the following examples that past jobs are not the only reference you can use. For instance, you can also describe skills you've acquired while completing class assignments, participating in campus activities, and completing internships.

Need. What does the employer need or want? Identify an employer's needs and the problems you can solve. Look at job descriptions, talk to employers, read trade journals, and visit Web sites.

Action. How have you demonstrated each skill? Write down a time when you used each skill or knowledge. Include who, what, where, and why.

Benefit. What was the result of your action? Describe the results you achieved—the benefit of your skills in the situation. Use numbers, dollars, and percentages whenever you can.

Next, Amanda completed a NAB worksheet. She listed the needs she had highlighted in the job description. Then she added some characteristics she knew from her research were important to hiring managers in marketing departments. After completing this activity, Amanda realized she had more experience related to marketing than she thought she had. She was much more confident about her chances to land the kind of job she wanted. You'll be happily surprised too.

Amanda's NAB Worksheet

Need: What does the employer need? (Skills, experience, knowledge)	Action: How have you demonstrated each skill or knowledge?	Benefit: What was the result?
Academic achievements	Recognized with multiple awards and scholarships	Ranked number 1 in SJU Marketing program, President's and Loyola Scholarship, Zonta International Women in Business Scholarship
Detail-oriented	Market research and analysis Developed reports and charts using Excel	Accurately compiled reports and managed direct mail databases; sent out monthly direct mail campaigns to 3,000 customers and prospects
Highly motivated	Worked while maintaining high grade point average	3.95 GPA
Forecast market trends	Marketing class—wrote paper forecasting market trends in publishing	Learned how to research and forecast trends
Powerful communication	Created presentations in PowerPoint	Created multimedia PowerPoint presentations to pitch new products to grocery store chains to increase product distribution
Leadership skills	Hawks Host Student Leader	Provided campus tours and answered questions for prospective students and their parents
Communication skills	Sales presentations	Learned to be comfortable informing and persuading people
Excel skills	Designed new format for reporting accounts receivable	Streamlined reporting and facilitated collections
Teamwork	Study group	Kept group on track by facilitating discussions—received an "A" on project and won the Business Policy team award

Writing a Dynamic Résumé

Writing a résumé can seem like a daunting task, but if you follow the steps outlined following, you'll find it manageable—not nearly as intimidating as filling a blue book or writing a research paper!

Get Organized

Review your NAB worksheet. Be sure you've included all relevant experiences such as jobs, internships, scholarships and honors, extracurricular activities, class projects, volunteer activities, and coursework. Gather addresses and dates for each experience.

ACTIVITY 13.1 ## Use NAB to Communicate Your Value

Instructions: Complete the following worksheet using a job description and other information about skills, knowledge, and characteristics that employers in your field seek in job candidates. Write these in the "Need" column. Use your experiences in school, work, internships, or volunteer activities to fill in the "Action" column. Describe the benefits of the results you achieved in the last column, using numbers or percentages whenever possible.

Need	Action	Benefit
What does the employer need? (Skills, experience, knowledge)	How have you demonstrated each skill or knowledge?	What was the result?

Never lie or exaggerate on your résumé. Employers can verify all the information you provide. They can confirm your education, previous employment, association memberships, and more. Stretching the truth will come back to haunt you. Most people are tempted to exaggerate because they lack confidence in their abilities or their experience. Remember that some employers prefer new college grads—your task is to find out which ones. Boost your chances by applying for jobs for which you are a good fit and by tailoring your message to their needs.

What I Wish I Knew . . . *About Résumés*

"You can leave the subjective descriptions off the résumé," according to an article titled *21 Things Hiring Managers Wish You Knew* on UpdatedNews .com. "Your résumé is for experience and accomplishments only," the article goes on to say. It's not appropriate to include subjective or fluffy profiles or descriptions, such as "good communicator" or "excellent with numbers and analysis." It's better to demonstrate your skills by focusing on accomplishments in your bullet points for each job description. Avoid just listing responsibilities; that doesn't set you apart and show a prospective employer what you have achieved in past positions.

Decide on Your Brand Stories

A great résumé starts with great stories. Think about your NAB (needs, actions, benefits), which you developed in Activity 13.1. Now, think about the following question:

What are experiences or accomplishments that make you unique and can bring value to an employer? You should be able to identify three powerful **brand stories** that you included in your NAB. These brand stories should be the foundation of your résumé, your cover letter, and ultimately your interviews. Think about your brand stories as three platforms on which you will talk about your experience and make it relevant. Some examples of brand stories are:

- Academic achievements
- Leadership experience
- Experience (in the industry in which you want to pursue a career)
- Entrepreneurship
- Community service
- Extracurricular activities
- Work ethic and commitment

Then, think about how you can best tell these brand stories on your résumé. While traditional résumés should be in chronological order, you can take some license when you are a student or recent graduate. In other words, you should change the order of your experience in order to tell your brand stories in a more powerful way. Use your headings to tell your brand stories. Make important things important by placing those headings that are the most relevant as high as possible on the page.

No matter how much you have done, you will need to keep your résumé to one page. You don't have to include everything you have done on your résumé. Include only the most relevant accomplishments and activities. **Remember, the objective of your résumé is just to get you an interview.** You can talk about your additional activities and accomplishments on the interview.

Build the Framework

Identifying Information

The top of your résumé should include your full name, both your campus address and your home address, phone number(s), and e-mail address. Your name should be the most prominent item on your résumé. Use bold face, 14- to 16-point type for your name.

Headings

Organize the content of your résumé by using headings. This makes it easier for readers to find the information for which they are looking. Following are headings for you to consider.

Objective. Every résumé should start with a clear objective. Don't make the hiring manager or recruiter have to work to figure out what you want to do. Karen Carroll, Executive Recruiter at Blue Plate Minds, says that she gets frustrated when she receives a résumé that doesn't include a clear objective, and she doesn't read it. Even if you don't know exactly what you want to do, create a clear objective that will help the reader understand the path you want to pursue. Don't worry about missing an opportunity by including only one specific objective. You will be opening up far more opportunities for interviews with a clear objective. The more specific you can be with your objective, the better. In fact, when you can, tailor your objective to the specific job and company at which you want to work. Here are some sample objectives that would be appropriate to include on a résumé.

Sample Objectives:
Seeking a position in food marketing
To obtain a sales position at WhatsNext.com
To obtain a teaching position in special education
Seeking a staff writer position at the *Los Angeles Times*

Education. For new graduates, education is often the most relevant qualification for the position. If this is true for you, it should be described right after your objective. List the school(s) you've attended and the degree you are earning. **If your GPA is 3.5 or higher, include it. If it is lower than 3.5, don't include it. Your GPA is not a requirement.** Don't list your high school unless you took some courses that are particularly relevant. As a general rule, high school should not be included on your résumé.

Honors and Scholarships. List honors, scholarships, or honor society membership. If you were named to the Dean's List, be sure to include this honor under this heading.

Résumé Essentials

- Name and contact information
- Objective
- Education
- Work experience and activities that make you unique and would bring value to a prospective employer
- Correct spelling and grammar

www.brandyou.com
Creating your own professional Web site can be a good way to supplement your résumé and demonstrate your skills and experience. Your Web site should include your résumé and examples of your work such as writing samples, internship projects, or volunteer events in which you had a role.

This is an important heading if you have been recognized in any way. It's important to note that this heading should be placed immediately below the heading for Education. That way the reader can see your awards and honors relative to your education. If you don't have any awards and honors, don't include this heading.

Work Experience.   Make this heading work for you by using a specific heading that says something about your experience. For example, if you've had an internship in marketing, this heading should be "Marketing Experience." If your experience is in sales, use "Sales Experience" as your heading. Avoid using generic headings such as "Work Experience," "Professional Experience," or "Work History."

Additional Headings.   Depending on your background, you may want to include additional headings, such as "Leadership Experience," "Athletic Achievements," "Entrepreneurial Experience," "Professional Associations," or other key brand stories. List any additional accomplishments in extracurricular activities ("Community Service") or ("Extracurricular Activities") or abilities such as fluency in another language. If a foreign language is relevant to the position you are seeking, you should use a heading title such as "Foreign Language Experience" or "International Language Skills" and move it higher on the page.

Skills: Include software and other skills. For example, *Proficient in Microsoft Word, Excel, PowerPoint, and Outlook*. It's important to include this heading because not every interviewer realizes that you learned and use these skills in school.

Describe Your Experience

The section titled "Marketing Experience" (or specific type of experience) should be the most important section of your résumé. Use the NAB process so that your résumé focuses on the needs of the employer. Most people gear their résumés toward getting other jobs just like their last ones. Now that you've earned your degree, you no doubt want to change careers—or at least your level of responsibility. That's why you want to emphasize your accomplishments that relate to what your *next* employer wants—not what your last one wanted.

Another advantage of using the NAB process is that it makes it easy to customize your résumé to specific employers. Think of your action and benefit statements as a database of information about your accomplishments. After researching an employer's needs (by referring to the job description, Web site, and insider information), you can change or rearrange your accomplishment statements so that the ones most important to this employer are at the top of each section.

- **List three to five accomplishments for each employment or internship experience.** If you have had an internship or other relevant work experience, be sure to include at least four to five bullet points about your accomplishments. Use fewer bullet points (and less space) for summer jobs. Make important things important by allocating the most space to the most important things such as internships and related work experience.

Video Résumés

A video résumé can be a novel approach to job searching, but do one only if you are extremely comfortable in front of the camera. Follow the same guidelines as a traditional résumé. And, be sure your résumé is also available as a Word document because less than 25 percent of companies currently use video résumés. Here are five tips for a successful video résumé:

- Keep it professional and businesslike.
- Keep it short (one to three minutes).
- Practice, practice, practice.
- Get feedback from mentors.
- Post to job sites such as **www.careerbuilder.com, www.jobster.com, www .linkedin.com,** and your professional Web site.

- Describe results, quantifying as often as possible. For example, "Developed copy for new company brochure, which was mailed to 1.5 million customers."
- Use bulleted statements starting with an **action verb**. See the list of verbs in Figure 13.1.
- Do not use phrases found in job descriptions such as, "Responsible for. . . ." Instead, describe what you did and the results you achieved using action verbs.
- Choose one tense, either past or present, and use it throughout your résumé.

Figure 13.1 Action Verb List

Action Verb List

Accomplish	Design	Install	Publicize
Achieve	Detail	Institute	Publish
Adapt	Determine	Instruct	Recommend
Administer	Develop	Integrate	Reconcile
Advertise	Devise	Interpret	Recruit
Advise	Direct	Interview	Rectify
Affect	Distribute	Invent	Redesign
Analyze	Draft	Investigate	Relate
Anticipate	Edit	Lead	Renew
Apply	Educate	Maintain	Report
Approach	Employ	Manage	Represent
Approve	Encourage	Manipulate	Research
Arrange	Enlarge	Market	Reshape
Assemble	Enlist	Mediate	Resolve
Assess	Establish	Merchandise	Review
Assign	Estimate	Moderate	Revise
Assist	Evaluate	Modify	Scan
Budget	Examine	Monitor	Schedule
Build	Exchange	Motivate	Screen
Calculate	Execute	Negotiate	Secure
Catalog	Expand	Obtain	Select
Chair	Expedite	Operate	Serve
Clarify	Facilitate	Organize	Staff
Coach	Familiarize	Originate	Standardize
Collaborate	Forecast	Participate	Stimulate
Compare	Formulate	Perceive	Strengthen
Conceive	Generate	Perform	Suggest
Conceptualize	Govern	Persuade	Summarize
Conduct	Guide	Plan	Supervise
Construct	Handle	Prepare	Survey
Consult	Hire	Present	Systematize
Contract	Identify	Preside	Teach
Contribute	Implement	Problem solve	Team build
Control	Improve	Process	Train
Coordinate	Increase	Produce	Update
Counsel	Index	Program	Utilize
Create	Influence	Project	Verify
Decide	Inform	Promote	Write
Define	Initiate	Prompt	
Delegate	Innovate	Propose	
Demonstrate	Inspect	Provide	

Format and Edit
Looks Count

- Choose a font that's easy to read, such as Times, Arial, Helvetica, or Palatino. Don't use different fonts within your résumé, although it is fine to use bold for headings or emphasis within the font you've selected. **Always use the same font for your résumé and cover letter.**

- Use a font size no smaller than 11 point.

- The easiest way to achieve formatting consistency is to **use a two-column table**. Use a narrow first column for your headings and dates; use a larger column for the descriptions of your accomplishments. When you're done, click the Format menu and delete the borders.

- Margins should be between 1/2″ and 1″. If the margins are too small, delete some information. It's better if your résumé has one less bullet point and is easy to skim. **If your résumé looks too cramped, people won't read it.**

- Use lots of white space so that your résumé is easy to read. **Your résumé should not exceed one page, unless you have over five years of full-time industry experience**.

- Highlight job titles, employers, and other résumé categories such as education with bold type. Avoid using all capital letters, underlining, or italics. Be consistent—use the same style for each corresponding heading (e.g., Objective, Employment).

- **Be absolutely certain there are no typos or misspellings.** Ask someone (such as a professor, your parents, or a working professional) to proof your résumé for you.

- Don't use a template—your résumé, like you, should be unique. Also, templates don't always translate in saved documents.

- Before you save your résumé, be sure it will print on only one page.

- Print your résumé on white or neutral-colored résumé (24-pound bond) paper. **Do not use colored paper.**

See a sample résumés in Figure 13.2 and 13.3.

Tricks of the Trade

It's important to save your résumé in several different file formats to ensure that the recipient sees the documents in the format you intended. When you submit your cover letter and résumé to a job board, the formatting will not be maintained if you save your files as a Word document.

- Save your cover letter and résumé as a PDF file. This will ensure that the formatting is preserved. If your software does not include this option, go to www.acrobat.com to convert your files at no charge.

- Some job boards will not allow a PDF to be submitted. In this case, save your cover letter and résumé as text files. In Word (PC or Mac), choose File, Save As, then use the drop down menu and choose Text File (.txt) or Rich Text File (.rtf). Be sure to review your documents as some of the items may have shifted. If this is the case, simply make the adjustments and save again the same way.

Tips for a Scannable Résumé

With the latest in technology, organizations, particularly in the government sector, are turning to the electronic process of scanning. It will search for degrees, titles, organizations, and other information specific to a particular opening.

- Include key words—nouns that are listed in the job description. Match the words exactly. Computers can't evaluate; they can only match.
- Use standard typefaces and fonts between 11 and 14 points in size.
- Avoid italics, underlines, and shadows.
- Shoot for simplicity.
- Avoid vertical and horizontal lines, graphics, and boxes.

Figure 13.2 Sample Résumé for Carlos Miranda

Carlos Miranda
120 Stapley Street
San Francisco, California 94105
(415) 352-6834; cmiranda@hotmail.com

Objective

To obtain Marketing Assistant position involving market research and analysis

Education

Golden Gate University, San Francisco, CA
Bachelor of Science in Business Administration, Marketing, expected 2011 ◄

> Carlos emphasizes his education and course work related to his career objective.

Honors and Activities

National Honor Society Speech Club Treasurer
Peer Tutor in Accounting Principles, 2009–2011
Program Chair, Marketing Club
• Developed monthly plans to increase sales, resulting in increased ◄ profits
• Calculated daily sales, and wrote accurate sales reports

> In his descriptions, Carlos tells what he did and the results he achieved.

Marketing and Sales Experience

American Heart Association, San Francisco, CA, Intern   Fall, 2010 ◄
• Created fund-raiser publicity, raising $1,800
• Coordinated targeted marketing plan, resulting in new corporate sponsors
• Assisted in research and prepared data and figures for reports to Board of Directors

> Carlos groups his experience together and gives it a relevant heading.

Crate and Barrel, San Francisco, CA, Accounting Clerk   2001–2003 ◄
• Maintained accounts receivable, reducing delinquent accounts by 20%
• Improved tracking of accounts receivable by creating reports using Excel software
• Implemented new accounting procedure, increasing accounting process efficiency

> Carlos provides specifics so that the reader can easily see the value of his contributions.

Computer Skills

Microsoft Word, Excel, PowerPoint, Outlook

Figure 13.3 Sample Internship Résumé for Christine Marren

Christine Marren
813 E. Wetmore Place
Tucson, AZ 85710
(520) 345-7888; CMarren23@msn.com

Objective	Seeking internship in market research
Education	**University of Arizona,** Tucson, Arizona Bachelor of Science, Marketing major, expected June, 2012
Scholarship	Selected as member of Blue Key National Honorary Society Work full-time while maintaining a 3.8 GPA
Market Research Experience	**The Householder Group**, Tucson, AZ Account Services Intern　　　　　　　　　　　　Summer 2010 • Researched client demographics for this retail seafood consultancy • Updated Web site including content and photography for 200 new per month, increasing site visitors by 45% • Created daily Web site report for senior management using Coremetrics Web analytics tool • Managed over 500 paid search keywords, which accounted for over 30% of Web site sales, decreased cost per click by 4% • Assisted in writing marketing brochures and other collateral used at trade shows
Customer Service Experience	**Anthropologie**, Tucson, AZ Salesperson　　　　　　　　　　　　Sept. 2009–Present • Awarded Associate of the Month for six different months • Provide personal selling consultations to help customers make wardrobe choices **Ten Restaurant**, Tucson, AZ Server　　　　　　　　　　　　Sept. 2008–June 2009 • Took orders and served customers • Used Aloha computer system
Community Service	• As a volunteer, wrote a fund-raising brochure for Breast Cancer Foundation of Arizona; campus event raised $1,800 for the charity • Canvassed neighborhoods to promote reelection of County Commissioner candidate
Skills	Proficient in Microsoft and Mac applications including Word, Excel, PowerPoint, Keynote, Pages, Adobe Acrobat, HTML

Chris includes her expected graduation date and degree.

Chris lists other internship first to highlight her most relevant experience.

Amanda Burd's Résumé— Before and After

Before

Amanda Burd, student at Saint Joseph's University, has a very impressive background. She created her résumé to showcase her skills. The résumé that she created *before* her Brand You experience is shown in Figure 13.4 on the following page. While this résumé is very good, there is some room for improvement.

After

Amanda started by completing her NAB (needs, actions, benefits) and answering the question, "What are three things that make you unique and would bring value to a prospective employer?" Amanda refocused her brand around the following three brand stories:

- **Academic Achievements**—Her scholarships, honors, and inclusion on the Dean's List demonstrate that she is smart; her international study is an excellent supplement to her education.
- **Marketing Experience**—Her three internships in marketing underscore her accomplishments in the industry.
- **Leadership Skills**—Her campus activities and involvement show that she is willing and able to take on leadership roles.

Using this as her foundation, Amanda reviewed her résumé again and reorganized and refined it. Here are some of the key changes she made:

- **Reformatting**—She used a simple two-column format. For the body of her résumé, she inserted a table with two columns, moved the vertical line to the left of the table, and then when she completed the information, she removed the lines of the table. This makes her résumé format clean, easy to read, and easy to update. Also, she changed the font and used upper- and lowercase font instead of all uppercase.
- **Reorganization and Headings**—She reorganized the information so that her three brand stories were easy to see at a glance. Her education is complete including her degree, international study, and scholarships and honors all in a prominent place on the page. Notice that she included her grade point average because it is so high, but she also supplemented it by including the Dean's List honor. She also organized her internships into a strong category of Marketing Experience. Then she created the heading for Leadership Experience and included her campus activities that demonstrated this point.
- **Job Descriptions**—She added more description to her internship descriptions with more focus on accomplishment and results. She made her most current internship the most important by using the most space to describe it. By contrast, she made her first internship less important

by using only two bullet points. This use of space helps make important things important for the reader.

Review Amanda's résumé before her *Brand You* experience in Figure 13.4, and then review her résumé after her Brand You experience in Figure 13.5 and see the difference. Also review the other examples of résumés on the next pages and in the *Brand You* **Toolkit.**

Writing a Powerful Cover Letter

Your résumé is not complete without your cover letter. It can be your most important advertising. Although a potential employer is interested in your résumé, your cover letter positions your brand and gets your résumé read. Many résumés are never even seen because of bad cover letters. **In fact, some hiring managers and recruiters won't look at a résumé without a cover letter.**

Real People, Real Advice ... About Cover Letters

"I'm still kind of confused about how a cover letter works and what you should really do with it. . . ."

—*Amanda Burd, student, Saint Joseph's University*

"A cover letter is very important . . . it is your only one opportunity to express yourself fully."

—*Jennifer Wolf, Event Manager, Philadelphia Business Journal*

Learn more about a cover letter and why you need one in short videos featuring Amanda Burd and Jennifer Wolf at www.mypearsonmarketinglab.com.

Real Questions, *Real Answers*

Q. Why do I need a cover letter?

A. Your cover letter is not only an opportunity to set yourself apart, but it is a necessity when you are looking for a job. Your cover letter should be a summary of why you are sending your résumé (the hiring manager or recruiter may be working on filling several positions), what makes you unique, and why you would bring value to the company. Your cover letter should be short, concise, and professional. It should always be addressed to a person, not a department or company. And there should be no typos, misspelled names, or grammar errors.

Figure 13.4 Amanda Burd's Résumé Before *Brand You*

Amanda Burd
abb406@zoommail.com
777-888-5555

Permanent Address: School Address:
1234 Main Street   200 Ash Street
Home, PA 19801   Philadelphia, PA 19131

Education:
Saint Joseph's University   Philadelphia, PA
Bachelor of Science Business Administration   May, 2010
Major: Marketing
    Major GPA: 3.98/Overall GPA: 3.95

Honors and Awards:
Ranked 1st in SJU Marketing Program   Business Policy Case Competition Winner
President's Scholarship & Loyola Scholarship   National Society of Collegiate Scholars
Beta Gama Sigma Scholarship   William McGowan Scholarship
Zonta International Women In Business   Philly Ad News Magazine "Rising Star"
Scholarship   Award

Marketing Experience:
General Food and Beverage   Dresher, PA
  Business Management Intern   June 2009–August 2009
    • Worked in conjunction with the Wakefern (ShopRite) and Wegman's team on various cost
     analysis projects
    • Analyzed Nielsen data and produced sales presentations to increase distribution of
     General Foods and Beverage's products
    • Pitched two new items to ShopRite grocery buyers
H2L2 Architects/Planners LLC.   Philadelphia, PA
  Marketing Intern   October 2008–May 2009
    • Conducted market research and data management
    • Assisted with all in-house marketing activities and facilitated all direct mail promotions
    • Aided in a strategic marketing rebrand initiative
SJU Summer Scholars Program   Philadelphia, PA
  Market Research Assistant   May 2008–August 2008
    • Partnered with a marketing department faculty member to construct a "green" business
     prototype that relies on collaboration between employees and consumers
    • Co-authored editorial to appear in the "Handbook of Contemporary Marketing in China:
     Theories and Practices"
The National Aviary   Pittsburgh, PA
  Marketing Intern   May 2007–Aug 2007
    • Generated, executed, and analyzed a study of visitor demographics
    • Formulated and implemented fresh grassroots marketing tactics

Additional Experience:
Hawk Host Student Leader   Philadelphia, PA
                                                                    Feb 2006–Present

    • Effectively communicated personal experiences and campus information to prospective
     students and their families

Meeting and Lunch with Warren Buffett   Omaha, Nebraska
                                                                        March 2009

    • Discussed Mr. Buffett's successful investment strategies, business practices, and life philosophy

Marketing Study Tour   Belgium, Germany, Switzerland
                                                                        March 2009

    • Interacted with business leaders and government officials to gain a better understanding of
     European business practices
    • Toured business sites and other areas of cultural significance

Figure 13.5 Amanda Burd's Résumé After *Brand You*

Amanda Burd
abb406@zoommail.com
777-888-5555

Permanent Address:
1234 Main Street
Home, PA 19801

School Address:
200 Ash Street
Philadelphia, PA 19131

Objective

To obtain a marketing assistant position in a consumer products company

Education

Saint Joseph's University, Philadelphia, PA
Bachelor of Science, Business Administration, May, 2010
Major: Marketing, GPA—3.95, Ranked #1 in Marketing Program

International Study

Marketing Study Tour, Saint Joseph's University, March 2009
• Interacted with business leaders and government officials
  in Switzerland, Belgium, and Germany

**Scholarship
and Honors**

• Dean's List—2007–2010
• President's Scholarship
• Loyola Scholarship
• Beta Gamma Sigma National Honor Society Scholarship
• Zonta International Women in Business Scholarship
• Meeting and lunch with Warren Buffett

**Marketing
Experience**

General Food and Beverage, Dresher, PA   June–Aug. 2009
Business Management Intern
• Researched competitive and market conditions in the grocery trade as
  part of the ShopRite and Wegman's team
• Analyzed Nielsen data including market share, brand perception, and
  purchase patterns in the cracker segment
• Identified customer preferences for packaging options and presented
  findings and recommendations to internal marketing team
• Used research data and recommendations to produce sales presentations
  to increase distribution of General Food and Beverage's products
• Pitched two new items to ShopRite grocery buyers

H2L2 Architects/Planners LLC, Philadelphia, PA   Oct. 2008–May 2009
Marketing Intern
• Conducted market research and data management to acquire new
  customers for the 100-person architectural firm
• Assisted with marketing activities including facilitation of all monthly
  direct mail campaigns to over 3,000 customers and prospects
• Tracked results of direct mail and identified 6 qualified prospects of
  which 2 became customers of the firm within 3 months
• Aided in a strategic marketing rebranding initiative by conducting
  and analyzing customer research

The National Aviary, Pittsburgh, PA   May–Aug. 2007
Marketing Intern
• Generated, executed, and analyzed a study of visitor demographics
• Formulated and implemented grassroots marketing tactics

**Leadership
Experience**

SJU Summer Scholars, Saint Joseph's University   May–Aug. 2008
Hawk Host Student Leader, Saint Joseph's University   Feb. 2006–Present

Skills

Proficient in Microsoft Word, Excel, Access, PowerPoint

Figure 13.6 Amanda Burd's Cover Letter Before *Brand You*

Amanda Burd
1234 Main Street
Home, PA 19801
abb406@zoommail.com
(777) 888-5555

October 13, 2010

General Food and Beverage is comprised of champions. Excellence is exhibited through not only stand-out products but stellar people. Most recently, my introduction to General Food and Beverage at the Saint Joseph's University career fair, follow-up information session, and preliminary interviews have given me a taste of the vitality and opportunity present at General Food and Beverage. As a junior marketing major, the prospect of spending my summer as an intern with General Food and Beverage is exciting. Contributing to the dynamic culture all the while gaining insight and understanding of the company would be inimitable. Furthermore, interning opens doors for full-time work with General Food and Beverage and the chance to work alongside the best and brightest in the industry.

Driven, results-oriented people are the force behind the success of General Food and Beverage. The experiences I have already undertaken illustrate my goal-oriented and ambitious attitude. My former intern experience at The National Aviary gave me practice solving real business problems and analyzing data. Likewise, conducting my own research over the summer with the Saint Joseph's marketing department led me to know the satisfaction that comes from producing paramount work. Partnering with a faculty member, we developed a business prototype that successfully integrates environmental initiatives within an organization. Our work will be published in several upcoming sources. Even in the classroom, SJU has challenged me to take on real-world problems and produce results. In one honors class, teams of students conducted and analyzed alumni data for the Executive MBA office at the university. Other volunteer projects and extracurricular activities have also shown me the merits of being well rounded in all areas of one's life. SJU has selected me to be a campus ambassador. This leadership role has given me the opportunity to interact with alumni, faculty, and prospective students and their families on a weekly basis. General Food and Beverage is looking for optimistic, intelligent, and level-headed achievers. I want to be part of the General Food and Beverage team.

Please feel free to contact my references listed below:

Dr. Brent Smith: bsmith@sju.edu—Co-author and Research Mentor, Professor of Marketing
Terese Waldron: twaldron@sju.edu—SJU Executive MBA Director
Dr. Rick Sherman: rsherman@sju.edu—SJU Professor of Honors Accounting

Thank you for your time and consideration.

Sincerely,

Amanda Burd

Amanda Burd

Cover Letter Formats

There are two styles of cover letters—narrative style or the narrative style with bullet points. Both use the same basic elements described following.

The narrative style is a traditional business letter and is written in full sentences throughout. This style gives you an opportunity to showcase your writing skills.

Amanda Burd used the narrative style before she started the *Brand You* process, as shown in Figure 13.6. Amanda reworked her cover letter using

Figure 13.7 Amanda Burd's Cover Letter After *Brand You*

Amanda Burd
1234 Main Street
Home, PA, 19081

October 13, 2010

Mr. Jason Caldwell
General Food and Beverage, Inc.
One Corporate Circle, Suite 300
Dresher, PA 19808

Dear Mr. Caldwell:

It's clear that General Food and Beverage is comprised of champions.

My introduction to General Food and Beverage at the Saint Joseph's University Career Fair, follow-up information session, and preliminary interviews have given me a taste of the excellence, vitality, and opportunity present at the company. As a junior Marketing major, the prospect of spending my summer as a Marketing Intern at General Food and Beverage is exciting.

I feel that my experience, work ethic, and intellectual curiosity can be an asset to General Food and Beverage. Some highlights of my background include:

- **Academic Achievements**—I am currently ranked number one in the Marketing Program at Saint Joseph's University with an overall GPA of 3.95. I have been named to the Dean's List for every semester I have attended the university. In addition, I have earned several scholarships including the President's Scholarship, Loyola Scholarship, and Beta Gamma Sigma National Honor Society Scholarship.

- **Marketing Experience**—I understand the attention to detail and focus on the customer that is necessary to be successful in marketing. I have had two previous Marketing internships in which I managed databases of 3,000 customers, facilitated monthly direct mail campaigns with 100% accuracy, and participated in a strategic rebranding of the architectural firm.

- **Leadership Experience**—As part of the Saint Joseph's University Summer Scholars Program, I partnered with a Marketing Department faculty member to construct a "green" business prototype. I co-authored an editorial to appear in the "Handbook of Contemporary Marketing in China: Theories and Practices." In addition, I participated in marketing the university as a Hawk Host Student Leader, which helped increase student admissions.

I believe I can bring my passion for marketing and willingness to work hard to General Food and Beverage. I would like the opportunity to show you samples of my work. I will contact you next Wednesday to set up an appointment that is convenient for you. In the meantime, I can be reached at abb406@zoommail.com or 777-888-5555.

Sincerely

Amanda Burd

Amanda Burd

Attachment

the bullet point style after she read this chapter. You can see how much more powerful her revised cover letter is in Figure 13.7.

Amanda's cover letter is well written and clearly states why she is the best person for the job. However, there are some areas that should be modified before she sends this cover letter.

- The letter should be addressed to a person and should include an inside address.
- There should be a personal salutation (Dear Mr. Caldwell) at the beginning of the letter.
- It is not necessary or appropriate to include references in a cover letter (see section later in this chapter about references). References should be provided only when requested by the prospective employer.
- The letter is difficult to skim quickly; the narrative format requires the reader to take the time to read the entire letter to understand what Amanda has to offer.
- The uppercase font is difficult to read.

Figure 13.7 shows Amanda's cover letter rewritten in the bullet point format after her *Brand You* experience. Here are the highlights of the changes she made.

- Notice how easy it is to skim the letter and see Amanda's brand stories of academic achievements, marketing experience and leadership experience.
- The letter is short and to the point.
- The letter includes all of the elements of a formal business letter as shown in Figure 13.8.

You can also review Amanda Burd's cover letter and résumé side-by-side in Figure 13.9 to see how the cover letter introduces the résumé. In addition, there are other cover letter samples in this chapter. Christine Marren's cover letter (Figure 13.11) is an example of narrative style.

The narrative style with bullet points incorporates bullet points in the second paragraph to highlight the key benefits of your brand. Carlos Miranda's cover letter (Figure 13.10) is an example of this style. **The advantage of the narrative style with bullet points is that it makes it easier for the reader to visually scan rather than read the entire letter.** When an employer scans a good cover letter, he or she usually reads it completely, and then reads the résumé. And the narrative style with bullet points can be easier to write.

Paragraph One—The Introduction

The introduction provides your chance to grab readers and entice them to read on. Most cover letters are very boring reading. Find something interesting to say, create visibility and impact, and your letter will leap out from the stack recruiters are reviewing. **Talk about the position you are seeking, how you learned about the position, and whatever it is that interests you most about the position.**

Carlos Miranda wrote the cover letter in Figure 13.10 to reply to a specific ad online. Note how he researched the company on the Internet to find a good way to open his letter and gain the reader's attention. A colleague referred Christine Marren to Mr. Lang, so she gets the reader's attention by mentioning the mutual contact in the first paragraph (see Figure 13.11).

See More

There are more sample cover letters and résumés in the **Brand You** Toolkit (at the back of the book).

Don't Forget Your Keywords

It's important that you use keywords in your résumé as well as your cover letter so employers can scan (by computer and visually) to see exactly what your brand represents.

Figure 13.8 Anatomy of a Cover Letter

Jonathan Vital (1)
541 North Elm Street
Dayton, OH 12345

(2)
April 18, 2011

Mr. Michael Woods
Account Director
(3) Ludlow Interactive Advertising
4040 Century Boulevard; Suite 1501
Boston, MA 03456

(4) Dear Mr. Woods:

(5) Congratulations on landing the Dominos Pizza account. I'm sure it's an exciting time at the agency. If you are looking for a motivated individual with a passion for the Internet on your team, I am that person.

(6) I am currently a junior at Brookstone College pursuing a major in Marketing with a focus in Interactive Marketing. I'd like to bring my energy and Internet savvy to Ludlow Interactive Advertising for a summer internship position on one of your client service teams. Some highlights of my background are as follows:

(7)

- **Marketing Trade Group Involvement** – I have gained exposure to the interactive advertising industry as a member of the local chapter of the American Marketing Association and a student member of the Boston Advertising Club.

- **Leadership Experience** – As the Student Chairperson of the Event Committee for the Saint Katherine's Youth Group, I have organized over 8 fund-raising events. As a result of the increased fund-raising, our group was able to provide financial assistance and personal support to over 300 local families in need.

- **Passion for the Internet** – I thrive on the fact that the Internet is continuously evolving and providing new and untapped opportunities for brands. I want to play a role in building brands online. As an experienced Internet and technology user, I have the experience and insight to understand how current interactive marketing works and ideas as to how it might work even better.

(8) With Dominos as a new client, you need only the best people to support the brand. I am focused and willing to work hard in order to learn the business. I would like the opportunity to show you some examples of my work. I can be reached at 615-333-5555 or via e-mail at jvitale@brookstonecollege.edu. I will touch base the week of April 25 to see what day will be most convenient for you. I look forward to discussing your new challenges.

(9) Sincerely,

Jonathan Vitale

(10) Jonathan Vitale

(11) Attachment

1. **Your name and return address**. Should be bold face and in a type size at least one size larger than the body of the letter. *Leave at least one line between your return address and the date.*
2. **Date**. Use month, date, year; spell out month. *Leave one line between the date and the inside address.*
3. **Inside Address**. The name, title, company and address (including suite number if applicable) of the person to whom you are sending the letter. Always use Mr. or Ms. before the first name. Use the person's formal first name and middle initial, if available. *Leave one line between the inside address and the greeting.*
4. **Greeting**. Always use Mr. or Ms. with the last name if you do not know the person on a first name basis. The greeting should be followed by a comma or a colon (Dear Ms. Williams,). If a name is not included in a job posting, the greeting should be, Dear Sir or Madam, or Dear Employer. *Leave one line between the greeting and the first paragraph.*
5. **First paragraph or lead-in line**. This is where you create interest or make a statement about the company. This paragraph may also include your introduction. *Leave one line between first paragraph and second paragraph.*
6. **Second paragraph**. This is where you establish how you can bring value to the company. This should also include your introduction and the position in which you have interest if you didn't include this in the first paragraph/lead-in line.
7. **Bullet points**. Here is where you make your NAB come alive and make it easy for the reader to see what you have to offer to the company at a glance. Use bold face to highlight the key lead-in words. *Leave one line between bullet points.*
8. **Closing paragraph**. This is your call to action; offer to show samples of your work if you have them. Also state when you will follow-up. Give your contact information for easy follow-up. *Leave one line between the last paragraph of the letter and the closing.*
9. **Closing**. "Sincerely" is the standard professional closing. The closing always includes a comma. *Leave four lines between the closing and your name.*
10. **Signature**. Your name. You sign the letter in the space between "Sincerely," and your name. *Leave one line after your name.*
11. **Attachment designation**. Type the word "Attachment" to signify that there is an attachment to the letter (this is comparable to the paperclip that appears on e-mail messages that have an attachment).

TIP: If you are sending a cover letter and résumé via direct mail, paperclip your résumé to your cover letter to prevent them from being separated.

Figure 13.9 Amanda Burd's Cover Letter and Résumé After *Brand You*

Amanda Burd
1234 Main Street
Home, PA, 19081

October 13, 2010

Mr. Jason Caldwell
General Food and Beverage, Inc.
One Corporate Circle, Suite 300
Dresher, PA 19808

Dear Mr. Caldwell:

It's clear that General Food and Beverage is comprised of champions.

My introduction to General Food and Beverage at the Saint Joseph's University Career Fair, follow-up information session, and preliminary interviews have given me a taste of the excellence, vitality, and opportunity present at the company. As a junior Marketing major, the prospect of spending my summer as a Marketing Intern at General Food and Beverage is exciting.

I feel that my experience, work ethic, and intellectual curiosity can be an asset to General Food and Beverage. Some highlights of my background include:

- **Academic Achievements**—I am currently ranked number one in the Marketing Program at Saint Joseph's University with an overall GPA of 3.95. I have been named to the Dean's List for every semester I have attended the university. In addition, I have earned several scholarships including the President's Scholarship, Loyola Scholarship, and Beta Gamma Sigma National Honor Society Scholarship.

- **Marketing Experience**—I understand the attention to detail and focus on the customer that is necessary to be successful in marketing. I have had two previous Marketing internships in which I managed databases of 3,000 customers, facilitated monthly direct mail campaigns with 100% accuracy, and participated in a strategic rebranding of the architectural firm.

- **Leadership Experience**—As part of the Saint Joseph's University Summer Scholars Program, I partnered with a Marketing Department faculty member to construct a "green" business prototype. I co-authored an editorial to appear in the "Handbook of Contemporary Marketing in China: Theories and Practices." In addition, I participated in marketing the university as a Hawk Host Student Leader, which helped increase student admissions.

I believe I can bring my passion for marketing and willingness to work hard to General Food and Beverage. I would like the opportunity to show you samples of my work. I will contact you next Wednesday to set up an appointment that is convenient for you. In the meantime, I can be reached at abb406@zoommail.com or 777-888-5555.

Sincerely

Amanda Burd

Amanda Burd

Attachment

Amanda Burd

abb406@zoommail.com

777-888-5555

Permanent Address:
1234 Main Street
Home, PA 19801

School Address:
200 Ash Street
Philadelphia, PA 19131

Objective	To obtain a marketing assistant position in a consumer products company
Education	**Saint Joseph's University,** Philadelphia, PA Bachelor of Science, Business Administration, May, 2010 Major: Marketing, GPA—3.95, Ranked #1 in Marketing Program
International Study	**Marketing Study Tour,** Saint Joseph's University, March 2009 • Interacted with business leaders and government officials in Switzerland, Belgium, and Germany
Scholarship and Honors	• Dean's List—2007–2010 • President's Scholarship • Loyola Scholarship • Beta Gamma Sigma National Honor Society Scholarship • Zonta International Women in Business Scholarship • Meeting and lunch with Warren Buffett

Marketing Experience

General Food and Beverage, Dresher, PA   June–Aug. 2009
Business Management Intern
• Researched competitive and market conditions in the grocery trade as
  part of the ShopRite and Wegman's team
• Analyzed Nielsen data including market share, brand perception, and
  purchase patterns in the cracker segment
• Identified customer preferences for packaging options and presented
  findings and recommendations to internal marketing team
• Used research data and recommendations to produce sales presentations
  to increase distribution of General Food and Beverage's products
• Pitched two new items to ShopRite grocery buyers

H2L2 Architects/Planners LLC, Philadelphia, PA   Oct. 2008–May 2009
Marketing Intern
• Conducted market research and data management to acquire new
  customers for the 100-person architectural firm
• Assisted with marketing activities including facilitation of all monthly
  direct mail campaigns to over 3,000 customers and prospects
• Tracked results of direct mail and identified 6 qualified prospects of
  which 2 became customers of the firm within 3 months
• Aided in a strategic marketing rebranding initiative by conducting
  and analyzing customer research

The National Aviary, Pittsburgh, PA   May–Aug. 2007
Marketing Intern
• Generated, executed, and analyzed a study of visitor demographics
• Formulated and implemented grassroots marketing tactics

Leadership Experience

SJU Summer Scholars, Saint Joseph's University   May–Aug. 2008
Hawk Host Student Leader, Saint Joseph's University   Feb. 2006–Present

Skills   Proficient in Microsoft Word, Excel, Access, PowerPoint

Carlos Miranda
120 Stapley Street
San Francisco, CA 94105

May 15, 2008

Ms. Diane Thomson
Director of Marketing
Optiflex Corporation
4333 West 56th Street
San Francisco, CA 94000

Dear Ms. Thomson,

The introduction of the FXY-09 must be creating exciting opportunities within the Marketing Department. After exploring the Optiflex Web site, it is apparent that Optiflex is marketing specifically to consumers for the first time. You will require someone to develop marketing strategies that achieve your goals and are delivered on time and on budget. I would like to be a part of this effort.

Recently, I earned my Bachelor of Science degree in Business Administration with an emphasis in Marketing from Golden Gate University. My degree along with my work experience in marketing, sales and accounting makes me uniquely qualified for a position in the Marketing Department. Some highlights of my achievements are the following:

- **Marketing Experience**. As an intern at the American Heart Association, I worked with a team to create the advertising materials for a successful direct marketing campaign that raised $1,800. I conducted the research on the local market and recommended the targets for the campaign.

- **Sales Experience**. I understand what it takes to make sales happen at the store level. In my role as Assistant Store Manager at Gap, I conducted research and analysis to identify new customers and designed new marketing strategies that increased store traffic by 25 percent.

- **Leadership Skills**. I have demonstrated responsibility, accountability, and leadership in my roles as Speech Club Treasurer and Program Chair of the Marketing Club during my academic career.

I'd like the opportunity to show you samples of my work and discuss in more detail how my experience and skills are a good fit for the Optiflex Corporation. I will call you during the week of May 19 to set up a convenient time to meet. I can be reached at (415)352-6834 or cmiranda@hotmail.com. Thank you for your consideration. I look forward to speaking with you.

Sincerely

Carlos Miranda

Carlos Miranda

Attachment

Paragraph Two—The Body of the Letter

Use the body of the letter to emphasize your experience and its relevancy to the specific position. Describe examples to show that you have the qualifications the employer is seeking. Cite accomplishments as they relate to the desired characteristics. List particular skills and academic achievements that demonstrate you are a good match for the job. Use your NAB activity to determine the two to four key points you want to make.

Figure 13.11 Christine Marren's Cover Letter—Narrative Style

Christine Marren
813 E. Wetmore Place
Tucson, AZ 85710

August 10, 2010

Mr. Adam Lang
MRS Research, Inc.
One Corporate Drive, Suite 600
Baltimore, MD 04132

Dear Mr. Lang,

Dana Kowwa suggested that I contact you regarding an entry-level research position with your firm. I worked with Dana on my senior marketing research project. He was the Project Manager at the client, TeleServe. He felt there could be a good match between my skills and your firm.

I recently graduated from Arizona State University with a Bachelor of Science degree in Marketing. I have had experience working in interactive marketing research as an intern at The Householder Group. I have used the Coremetrics Web analytics tool to track consumer behavior on the company Web site. In addition, I have managed over 500 paid search keywords using Google Ad Words, which accounted for over 30% of the Web site's traffic. Under my leadership the cost per click was reduced by 4%.

I grew up on the East Coast and would be very interested in relocating to the Baltimore area. I will call you next week to set up an appointment to discuss my qualifications in further detail. I am planning on being in the Baltimore area during the second week of September. Thank you for your time and consideration.

Sincerely,

Christine Marren

Christine Marren

Attachment

Note the difference in style between Christine's cover letter (Figure 13.11), which uses the narrative style, and Carlos's cover letter, which uses the narrative style with bullet points (Figure 13.10).

In his cover letter, Carlos discusses his degree and experience as it relates to the marketing position he wants. He describes how his internship gave him the opportunity to put his education to work and achieve real results.

Paragraph Three—The Closing

End your cover letter with an active strategy to get the interview. Offer to show samples of your work and tell the reader that you will call to set up a convenient time to meet and discuss your qualifications further. Thank the reader for his or her time and consideration. Remember to follow up with a phone call.

Review and Proof Your Cover Letter and Résumé

Believe it or not, a typo or grammar error can be the reason you don't get called for an interview. Professionals have no tolerance when it comes to cover letters and résumés. Proofread and spell check your cover letter and résumé. Then ask a professional such as a counselor at your Career Services office to proof your cover letter and résumé.

Real People, Real Advice ... About Proofing Your Cover Letter and Résumé

"I would say what makes me pass over it right off the bat ... is poor grammar and spelling errors ... it's really a poor representation of who you are. Something as simple as that (a typo or grammar error) really does work against you."

—*Jennifer Wolf, Event Manager, Philadelphia Business Journal*

See the entire video featuring Jennifer Wolf to hear what it takes for your résumé to break through at www.mypearsonmarketinglab.com.

Cover Letter Style Requirements

While there is some flexibility in choosing your cover letter format, there are some elements that are required. See Figure 13.8—Anatomy of a Cover Letter. And be sure to use the same font for your cover letter and résumé.

My Career Journal

After completing NAB, what are your three brand stories that will be the focus of your résumé and cover letter?

_____

_____

_____

List 10 action verbs you could use on a résumé from your last job, internship, or volunteer experience.

_____

_____

_____

_____

_____

_____

Write the three bullet points for each of your brand stories for your cover letter.

_____

_____

_____

_____

_____

_____

_____

_____

Notes to **Myself**

14

Personal Selling:
How Networking Can Help You Achieve Your Goals

Networking can be one of the most effective ways to get an internship or job. In fact, it's said that 80 percent of jobs are filled as a result of networking—people who know people and recommend people to other people. **Networking is one of the most important things you can do to get an internship or job.** But networking can be one of the most daunting activities for anyone to do, especially for students and young people.

Brand You Checklist

✓ Learn how to use networking to help you find an internship or job.

✓ Recognize how to use professional social networking to connect with people and build your professional network.

✓ Learn about informational interviews and how to get them.

Real People, Real Advice ... About Personal Branding

"The idea of networking can be kind of intimidating."

—*Amanda Burd, student, Saint Joseph's University*

"The more people you know, the more people who can help you, and the more people they may know that can help you. That's what networking is all about."

—*Stephen Facenda, President, ViaMark Advertising*

Watch short videos featuring Amanda Burd and Stephen Facenda discussing networking tips at www.mypearsonmarketinglab.com.

Networking—How It Works

Think about it . . . if someone tells you about a great new restaurant, you'll probably make it a point to go there. Or if a friend recommends a Web site, a new brand of jeans, or even a song on iTunes, you'll give it extra consideration. The same thing happens in the professional world when it's time to hire for internships or full-time jobs. That's why networking is so important.

With as many as 80 percent of jobs being filled through networking, you might be wondering why there are so many internship and job postings online. You might assume that's how most jobs are filled. **The fact is, most hiring managers hate to post open positions.** They have to sift through the hundreds of résumés they receive from job postings with no real information about candidates except what each candidate submits. It's far more efficient (and effective) for the hiring manager to talk to people he or she knows and trusts and ask them who they know who might be a good fit for the position. Even though the hiring manager might not know the person who is being recommended, he or she trusts people in his or her network to refer good people to him or her. The secret to effective networking is to connect and keep in touch with enough people so that you are the person being recommended even before a job is posted. It's been said that by the time the job is posted, it's too late to apply. The best prospects come from networking.

Although you might find the prospect of networking scary, it's a simple method of connecting to people that you already know how to do. You've probably developed a network at school—people you can call on when you've missed a class or need help understanding an assignment. You've probably also learned that networking is about more than just meeting people; it's about building relationships. For example, you will be more likely to ask someone you know to borrow his or her notes or to work in your team for a team project than to ask a complete stranger.

If you think about your personal network, you've probably already learned the three keys to successful networking:

1. You have to **work at keeping in touch** with people in your network.
2. You should always **help people in your network**, especially when you don't want anything in return.
3. When you develop strong relationships with people in your network, you can **expand your network** with people who are in your network's network (think about how you have met friends of your friends).

The same principles that apply to your personal network also apply to your professional network. The bottom line is that networking works because you develop an ongoing relationship with people and you give willingly, even when it's not convenient. When you consistently do this, your network of people expands because people tell other people about you. **There's nothing more powerful than someone referring you for an internship or a job.**

Networking can be a great way to learn about industries, find out about companies, and meet people in positions you may never have known about. It's important to start networking as early in your professional career as possible. The more you network, the easier it becomes. But networking takes time and effort.

It's important to understand what networking *is* and *is not*. Networking is a way to share information and help people. Networking is *not* a way to ask for a job. **Remember that networking is based on building and maintaining relationships.** When you provide value to others (such as volunteering, providing information, sharing an article, or even sending a thank-you note), others will respond by helping you connect to the people who can help you.

real people, **Real** Brands

Stephen
Facenda's Brand

ViaMark Advertising is a full-service advertising company that creates award-winning advertising campaigns for local and regional businesses.
See Stephen's video profile at www.mypearsonmarketinglab.com.

▼ **Q** and **A** with Stephen Facenda, President of ViaMark Advertising.

Stephen's Profile

College: Drexel University

Major: Marketing

Current profession: Sales

First job: My first job was as an account executive at a radio station.

How I got my first job: Networking was invaluable to help me get my first job.

Brand key word: Relater. I think it's important to be able to relate to all kinds of people.

Description of my personal brand image: I would say knowledge, honesty, passion, and fun.

Value I bring to my clients: What I bring my clients is my knowledge, experience, and ability to listen.

Stephen's Advice

Favorite advice: You have two ears and one mouth, so you should listen twice as much as you talk.

Favorite advice about job searching: Don't be shy. Tell people what you are looking for; people want to help you.

How to choose your path: Tap into your current network—your parents, their friends, neighbors, older brothers and sisters, alumni—and ask questions to learn what you think you might want to do.

What impresses me about a young person: When someone has command and knowledge without cockiness. Show me that you know what's going on by reading business publications, books, and being fluent about current events. Don't pretend that you know all the answers.

What *not* to do on an interview: Don't complain. Be honest, but don't bad-mouth anyone, including a previous boss, employer, or co-worker. Take responsibility for your actions and don't blame bad experiences on anyone else, even if they are not your fault.

Where to Start Networking

The first step in developing a professional network is to start with the people you already know. You might think you don't know anyone to build your professional network, but you'll be surprised. Start by making a list of people in your network starting with **family and friends, then list friends of the family as well as friends' family members.** Before you know it, you will have a longer networking list than you thought. If you think that networking with family and friends doesn't make sense, you might be overlooking a great opportunity. Abby Siegel-Greenberg, senior account executive at *Philadelphia Business Journal*, says, "With social media networks now, LinkedIn, Facebook, and things like that, there might be people that your parents know that you had no idea—that Aunt so-and-so or people who have been coming to barbecues at your house for years—are in this industry."

Expand your list to include people you meet every day—guest speakers in your classes, people you meet at campus events and professional meetings, professors, and advisors. And don't overlook other people who are in your personal network such as your hair stylist, mechanic, or personal trainer. They may know someone who might be able to help you get the internship or job you want. Activity 14.1 will help you create your networking list.

Developing Relationships in College

College is the perfect time to begin developing professional contacts and relationships. Your campus is full of people who can provide essential information about the world of work, as well as connections when you begin your job search. Here are six excellent ways to start your professional networking while you are in college.

Your Peers

Nearly everyone you meet in college will one day be working, and some of them will be working in companies of interest to you—as potential suppliers, customers, or employers. You can build positive relationships with peers by sharing notes, studying for exams, and participating in joint class projects. Use these experiences to learn how to work with others, assert your viewpoint, and collaborate to achieve results. **Stay in touch with classmates after graduation**—you have already built a network that can lead you to others in your field.

Program Advisors

The more your advisor knows about your work goals, the more he or she can help you select the courses most beneficial to you. Advisors are in touch with employers in your field of study, so they can provide you with contacts to help you learn more about work opportunities. Advisors may also be aware of internships, co-op experiences, and employers looking for job candidates.

Career Center Counselors

Most colleges have career centers where you can access information about career fields, internships, job-search techniques, and on-campus interviews. A career center counselor can help you find work related to your field while you're in school. Many career centers maintain useful Web sites linked to the campus home page. Although career center Web sites are useful, they cannot provide the personal relationship and insights that a counselor can.

Professors

Many students think to contact their instructors only when they're having trouble with an assignment. Professors, however, can also be invaluable in helping you prepare for your future career. **If you share your career direction with them, they can help you identify resources that will help you achieve your goals.** Instructors serve on community boards, consult with businesses, and read numerous publications about workplace trends. Many times, professors know about available internships and jobs. If all of your professors know what you're looking for, they can probably connect you to people who are hiring.

Clubs

Your campus has many clubs for students to learn more about careers in particular fields. **Clubs and professional organizations also provide a setting where you can develop relationships with peers who will be working in your profession.**

Alumni

People who have gone to your college or university have an emotional connection to the school and **want to help those who have come after them**. Visit your campus alumni office to find out the best way to contact alumni who work in the area you wish to work. If you belong to a sorority or fraternity or any other campus organization, contact the alumni from these groups. It will be very likely that they will want to help you.

Alums Care
Tap into your schools' alumni organization on campus and on **www.LinkedIn.com**. Alumni have an emotional connection to the school and want to help you succeed. Reach out and network with as many as possible.

ACTIVITY 14.1

Identify Your Network

Instructions: Using the categories below, write the names of at least 25 people who are members of your network. Don't worry about addresses and phone numbers now; you can look those up later. Stretch your mind to list as many people as possible, including teachers, advisors, friends of your parents, bank tellers, auto mechanics, and so on.

Group	People to Include in Your Networking List
Family/friends—family members, neighbors, friends	
Acquaintances/neighborhood contacts—club members, church groups, community groups	
School—advisors, instructors, classmates	
Professional colleagues—former bosses, current and former co-workers, association members, customers, suppliers	
Service providers—doctors, lawyers, hair stylists, mechanics, trainers	
Volunteer work/internships—community groups, contacts from internships	

Ways to Expand Your Network

The key to starting a new networking relationship: communicate a mutual interest and a valid reason for connecting with the person. Even busy executives will take your call if your appeal is legitimate. For example, Jim Lawrence, vice president for Darden Restaurants, speaks at seminars at Cornell University. He says a student in the seminar can seek his advice by following up afterward. He states, "If they have a good reason for meeting with me, I'll find the time. I've given tours and advice to students who have contacted me in this way. After all, they are potential customers, stockholders, or employees, so it's in Darden's interests for me to be helpful."

Tricks of the Trade

When you are networking, be memorable. **It's a good idea to have business cards made with your name and contact information.** When you are in networking situations, give your business cards to people whom you meet. Ask everyone you meet for his or her business card and provide yours in return. Then, follow up with a personal thank-you note to each person whom you met. It's a perfect way to be memorable . . . and make it easy for someone to contact you.

No matter how many people you know, you may need additional ways to connect with people who have the inside scoop on your industry sector or profession. The following ideas will help:

- **Join a professional association.** Many associations have student chapters on campus or offer reduced rates for student members. All of them welcome students or new graduates aspiring to work in their profession. To find a professional organization in the area in which you may be interested, visit http://www.quintcareers.com/professional_organizations .html. And visit your campus library and review the Gale *Encyclopedia of Associations* to see what organizations are active.

- **Talk to speakers in class, at conferences, and at professional meetings.** Take the time to introduce yourself to all guest speakers after class and get their business cards so you can send them thank-you notes. If you are attending a conference, call ahead and ask conference speakers if they have time to meet with you after their presentations. Many conferences need volunteers to help with logistics at the event. They will usually waive the conference fee in exchange for help. You'll still have time to attend presentations and meet attendees.

- **E-mail or call authors of articles in trade journals or magazines.** Authors spend time writing to gain visibility and recognition. They appreciate hearing from people who have read their material, and they may have good ideas about other people you could talk to about your job search.

- **Inform your favorite bloggers about your search.** Blog hosts are often leaders in their industry, so they have many contacts. Although they may not post your inquiry, they may be willing to share information with you if you ask. To appeal to their generous side, start your query with a statement about why you enjoy reading their blog.

- **Reach out to your Facebook or other social network and ask for people you can contact for help with your search.** Keep expanding your network so you can ask questions about professions, industries, and companies and get good information. Note: First, be sure your social networking pages are appropriate for business contacts. The pictures of the spring break trip are probably *not* what you want your prospective employer to see.

ACTIVITY 14.2 Ways to Expand Your Network

*Instructions: List below the ways you will **expand** your network. Include names of people or groups you can contact.*

Source	People to Include in Your Networking List
Professional organizations—list on-campus and off-campus organizations that may be beneficial for you to join	
Guest speakers—in class, at conferences and meetings	
Authors of articles, blogs—people who write about things that you are interested in	
Facebook and other social networks—let everyone you know (and everyone they know) what type of job you are looking for	

How LinkedIn Can Help You Build Your Network

You're probably familiar with social networks like Facebook and MySpace to connect with your friends. **But did you know that professional social networks like www.LinkedIn.com can help you connect to professionals in the area in which you would like to work?** Professional social networks work well with in-person networking for a powerful combination for connecting to the right people.

www.LinkedIn.com is the largest professional social network with eighty five more than 50 million people. Chances are, the people with whom you need to connect to get the internship or job you want are on LinkedIn.com. Now, you just need to connect with them.

There are six key tips to leveraging www.LinkedIn.com.

1. **Create a profile.** Include all of your relevant positions including internships, work experience, volunteer experience, and involvement in campus, athletic, and community service organizations and activities.
2. **Ask people to join your network.** Start with your college friends. Then invite professors, supervisors, internship mentors, advisors, and athletic leaders.

"I'm not on LinkedIn. I'm still a little bit unfamiliar with how to best use that to my advantage."

—*Amanda Burd, student, Saint Joseph's University*

"LinkedIn is a laser-focused way to build your network."

—*Stephen Facenda, President, ViaMark Advertising*

Watch short videos featuring Stephen Facenda discussing the power of www .LinkedIn.com at www.mypearsonmarketinglab.com.

3. **Use your network's network.** Identify people who are in the networks of those to whom you are connected and ask your connection for an introduction. That way you can connect with someone who is in the area or company at which you would like to work. Build a relationship and even ask if you can meet the person so you can learn more about how he got into the business.

4. **Search for people or companies.** Use the search box at the upper right corner to help you find people you may know that would be good to connect with. Also, search for companies at which you may want to work and find out whom you are connected to at the company. Ask your connection for an introduction to the person so you can make contact with someone who works where you want to work.

5. **Ask for recommendations.** People look for people who have been recommended by someone in authority. Ask your supervisor from your summer or campus job or internship, athletic coach, or volunteer manager to write a recommendation about your work ethic, skills, and character.

6. **Join groups.** Use the search box (drop down to search for groups) and find groups in your areas of interest. For example, if you are interested in PR, put PR into the search box and you will get several groups including PRSA, PRSA in your city, and other public relations organizations. You should join some that are of interest to you. Once you join, get involved in discussions. Respond to and start discussions. And use the search box on the left to identify the group members to see if there might be someone to whom you are connected or might connect including your school alumni group, your sorority or fraternity, and professional groups.

Watch video demonstrations about how to use www.LinkedIn.com at www .mypearsonmarketinglab.com.

ACTIVITY 14.3 Using LinkedIn.com to Build Your Network

Log on to www.LinkedIn.com and complete the following activities. Refer to the videos at www .mypearsonmarketinglab.com for detailed instructions about how to use each of the features on LinkedIn.com.

- Create your profile.
- Ask at least 10 people you know to join your professional network on LinkedIn. (Tip: Be sure to send a personal note with your request to add each person to your network.)
- Join at least five groups. (Tip: Use the search box in the upper left corner and drop down the menu to search for "Groups." Use keywords for your school's alumni group and other groups in the areas in which you are interested, such as accounting, finance, marketing, corporate law, etc.)
- Ask at least 10 people that are in your network's network or are members of groups to join your professional network.
- Ask at least two people for a recommendation, such as a professor, a mentor, or a supervisor.

Real Questions, *Real Answers*

Q. Do employers really check Facebook and other social networks before they hire?

A. When you think about your Facebook page, you probably think about the conversations, pictures and videos you share with your friends. According to a recent survey conducted by CareerBuilder, prospective employers check Facebook and other social networks before they hire. In fact, 45 percent of employers search candidates on social networks, and 35 percent say they found content that has caused them not to hire a candidate.

Here are some social networking tips from Rosemary Haefner, Vice President of Human Resources at CareerBuilder:

DO: Clean up your digital dirt NOW . . . before you begin your job search.

DO: Remove all inappropriate conversations, pictures, and images.

DO: Participate in professional discussions and other leadership roles online.

DO: Keep your conversations positive.

DON'T: Complain about an employer, co-worker, or boss.

DON'T: Mention that you are looking or have another job while you are currently employed.

The Ultimate Networking—Informational Interviews

You learned about informational interviews in Chapter 4, but now that you are at this stage in your personal branding process, it's worth revisiting this topic. You should use informational interviews at all times throughout your job search (and throughout your career). **An informational interview is exactly that—an opportunity to meet with someone and learn about how she started her career and get advice as to what you can do to be successful.** When you meet someone who does what you want to do, ask him for an informational interview. An informational interview is the best way to learn more about an industry, job, or company in which you may be interested in working. When you use your networking skills, you increase your chances of meeting people in different areas and from different companies. These contacts are excellent resources to help you learn about the industry and how to get into the industry. Generally, people want to help young people find their path (everyone was in your shoes at one time).

Keep in mind that when you are networking and conducting informational interviews, you are also building long-term relationships. Be honest about your intentions. In other words, it's not appropriate to go on an informational interview and ask for a job. Your objective is to learn about the industry. While an informational interview might ultimately lead to a job, don't ask about it in the interview. Stay focused on learning as much as you can and connecting with and impressing as many people as possible.

Real People, Real Advice … About Informational Interviews

"An informational interview is when you go in and you just talk to someone about their job . . . and connect with someone in an informational and informal way."

—Amanda Burd, student, Saint Joseph's University

"People inherently want to help you, so don't be shy about that . . . find out what people do and ask lots of questions."

—Stephen Facenda, President, ViaMark Advertising

See video comments from Amanda Burd and Stephen Facenda about informational interviews at www.mypearsonmarketinglab.com.

What I Wish I Knew . . . *About Networking*

Jessica Goodman, a 22-year-old college graduate, shares these five tips about networking for college students in her blog, Brazen Careerist:

1. **Stay connected with your professors.** They are professionals and know people that you may want to know. Keep in touch.

2. **Get experience.** Get an internship or volunteer. Either way, you need to put yourself out there and learn the area you want to pursue. It's a great way to meet and impress people.

3. **Start networking prior to graduation.** Don't wait until you need to start networking to start the process. Get involved with professional organizations and meet people so you can provide value before you ask for a favor (or a job).

4. **Go outside your comfort zone.** You don't know what you don't know, so get out there and experience as much as you can.

5. **Be professional.** Remember that no matter where you are (in person or online), you are making an impression. Be yourself, but always be appropriate. That means taking down those spring break pictures from your Facebook page.

My Career Journal

Networking (in person and online) is critical to career success. Identify three ways you can network in person in the next 30 days.

_____

_____

_____

_____

_____

_____

_____

_____

Networking starts with the people you know. Using your networking list you created in Activity 14.2, add at least one more networking source to your list. (Hint: Think about professors, mentors, and other people whom you know.)

_____

_____

_____

_____

_____

_____

_____

_____

Get more familiar with how to leverage the features on www.LinkedIn.com. Find at least 10 people who work at companies that are on your target 25 company list. How might you approach each one for networking, and possibly an informational interview?

_____

_____

_____

_____

_____

_____

Notes to **Myself**

Delivering Your Value Proposition

Step 5

(Chapters 15–16)

Going on interviews and evaluating job offers might seem a long way off right now, but be prepared. It will happen sooner than you think.

When it's time for a face-to-face meeting with your prospective employer, you want to be as prepared as possible in every way. You've done a lot of work to get the interview; now you want to turn it into a job offer. Learn the ins and outs of interviewing so you can get the internship or full-time job you want.

It's exciting to receive a job offer. But before you accept it, do you know everything you need to know about the company, the job, and the compensation? What if you are interviewing with two companies and receive an offer from one but really want the offer from the other one? What if you receive two job offers? How do you determine which one is really better?

Read Chapters 15 and 16 now. And reread them again before each interview. Every time you read them, you will feel more confident, ask better questions, learn more about negotiating a job offer, and even enjoy the process.

Welcome to the Real World! ➤

15
Delivering Value:
How to Make Every Interview Successful

Brand You Checklist

✓ Learn how to prepare for job interviews.

✓ Understand how to research a company prior to the interview.

✓ Consider the kinds of questions to expect on an interview.

✓ Learn the appropriate way to dress for an interview.

Be Prepared

Bring a few extra copies of your résumé printed on résumé. paper in a folder or portfolio. Even though the interviewer already has your résumé, it might not be handy at the time of the interview. Or you might be asked to meet with someone who was not originally on the interview schedule.

You can never be too prepared for a job interview.

A job interview is actually a sales call. If you're successful, you'll sell yourself and build relationships that could last a lifetime. If you're not successful, you'll be trying to do it all over again with a different company.

A seasoned salesperson doesn't call on a potential customer without preparation. Salespeople find out as much as they can about their client's history, buying habits, and product needs. They thoroughly plan their presentation, focusing on the benefits that will appeal most to this particular customer. With preparation, a sales professional enters the customer meeting with confidence. In fact, the steps of an interview are just like the steps of a sales call.

This chapter includes advice and videos from several of the professionals featured throughout the book to give you different perspectives on the interviewing process. The theme is common from each professional-prepare, prepare, prepare.

Prospecting and Qualifying

Even for experienced professionals, job hunting is an emotional roller-coaster ride. Some days, you'll soar with anticipation and hope. Other days, you'll find your confidence slipping after a rejection. Everyone needs resiliency during a job search. You'll find it much easier to keep up your momentum if you have several prospects in the works. Your list of 25 target companies will keep you on track—you'll already know whom to pursue next. **Inexperienced job hunters often make the mistake of singling out one employer at a time.** Instead, you want to do what experienced salespeople do. You will achieve success sooner if you develop a comprehensive job-search campaign, working on a mix of activities at any one time. Even while you're interviewing with one employer, stay connected to your network and send out résumés to other firms in your target market.

Preapproach

Success! You've researched companies, written your résumé, implemented your communication plan, networked, and now your hard work has paid off—you've been invited for an interview. Once you've made it to this stage, you know the employer is interested in you. Now it's time to close the deal.

Get a Complete Job Description

The way to stand out from the competition is to gather background information about the company and specific position so you can plan your interview. You want to know everything you can about the company and the job. Most people don't think to call the company, but you can call the human resources department and request a full job description. This is important because many job postings sometimes show only the highlights of the requirements—a full job description gives the details. When you call, the person answering your request may also be willing to give you "insider" information that you can use in the interview. Ask about new company initiatives, new management, or new products—anything you can discuss in the interview to show that you've done your homework and have learned about the culture you hope to join.

Employers *expect* candidates to research the company and be prepared during an interview. A surefire way to be eliminated from consideration is to wing it on the interview instead of doing real research about the company.

Real People, Real Advice ... About Researching
a Company Before an Interview

"I always start with the company's Web site.... There are definitely some things you can do to prepare yourself."

—*Amanda Burd, student, Saint Joseph's University*

"You definitely need to know the basics (about the company) to get your foot in the door.... You have to be aware of how the organization runs itself and understand the product ... Show that there is interest in learning more."

—*Jennifer Wolf, Event Manager, Philadelphia Business Journal*

See short videos featuring Amanda Burd along with Jennifer Wolf and other professionals discussing interviewing at www.mypearsonmarketinglab.com. See Jennifer Wolf's profile in Chapter 13.

Research the Company Online

Every interviewer expects a candidate to visit the company Web site. Be sure to review all the pages, especially those in the "About Us" section. The company Web site can give you valuable insights about the company, its products and services, its customers, and its culture.

You can also find key information about most companies by doing an Internet search or going to **www.hoovers.com**. Your campus library may have a subscription. Here are some of the basic facts employers expect you to know:

- How many locations and employees does the company have?
- What are the key products or services offered by the company?
- Are their customers other businesses or consumers?
- How long has the company been in business? Have they merged or been acquired recently?
- How does the company's market share compare to that of competitors?
- Does the company have any new products or services? Is the company expanding globally?
- Have the CEO or others received awards or published a book or article recently?

All of the information you gather about the company and the position will help you determine how you should position your brand, what stories you should tell that will be relevant, and what questions to ask.

Prepare Your Interview Questions

Inevitably, you'll be asked if *you* have any questions. Even though you may have questions about salary and benefits, **don't** ask about them at this time. (Review Chapter 11 about the compensation conversation.) Show your interest in the job by preparing great questions to ask in the interview. These questions show that you've thought about the position and the company.

Real People, Real Advice ... About Researching the Interviewer

"If you're going on a job interview, look the person up before you go in. Find out something about that person, maybe two or three things. What was their first job? What do they do at their current job? Where did they go to school? It now becomes a friendly conversation . . . it loosens up the room . . ."

—*Ike Richman, Vice President of Public Relations, Comcast-Spectacor*

Hear Ike Richman's advice for interviewing at www.mypearsonmarketinglab.com. See Ike Richman's profile in Chapter 9.

Tricks of the Trade
Phone Interviews

Phone interviews can be especially challenging because you don't have the benefit of eye contact and non-verbal communication. However, phone interviews are the screening method to determine which candidates will be invited for an in-person interview. So it's critical to be prepared for a phone interview. Here are a few important tips for successful phone interviews from Kristin Kane.

- **Never take a phone interview on the fly.** Always plan for it. If an interviewer calls you without an appointment, it's acceptable to say that you are busy and set a time when the interviewer can call you back.
- **Always do a phone interview in a quiet room.** It's important to focus on your conversation and listen to the interviewer's questions.
- **Whenever possible, use a land line for a phone interview.** This will avoid a possible dropped call or other interruption due to poor cell service.

See a short video of Kristin Kane providing several helpful tips for successful phone interviews at www.mypearsonmarketinglab.com. See Kristin Kane's profile in Chapter 12.

Think about your questions into major groups. That will make them easier to remember (although you should always feel comfortable referring to your notes). And you will be able to ask questions as they relate to the topic you are discussing.

Company

- What is one word you would use to describe the company culture?
- What do you think the company will look like in three years.

Position

- What would the ideal person for this position be like?
- What is the single most important skill the person in this position must possess?
- What is one word you would use to describe your management style?
- What are some challenges facing the department in the next 90 days? What role will the person in this position play in tackling those challenges?
- What are the next steps in the hiring process?

After the interviewer responds to your questions, follow up by restating your strengths. For example, suppose the interviewer tells you the ideal person would be committed to achieving goals and learning new skills. Follow up by telling about a specific time when you achieved a goal or discuss how much you've enjoyed learning as a college student.

The Best Interview Preparation
Practice!
Practice!
Practice!

Advice Straight from Recruiters

- "Can I work with this person? Do they fit in with our corporate culture? These are the two questions that are in my mind when I interview. I use scenarios to see how the person responds to actual events. I select candidates who show enthusiasm, strong interpersonal skills, and good judgment when answering questions."—Manager for a large non-profit organization

- "I look for a person's ability to solve logical problems. I want real-world experience (school experience isn't enough). The person must be good at verbal and written communications and be able to work independently because I'm a hands-off manager."—Anonymous manager

- "First, seriously assess yourself—strengths, weaknesses, and preferences. Second, research prospective employers. Third, don't put on an act you can't sustain day in and day out if hired."—Manager at a major chemical corporation

- "Learn how to dress, speak, WRITE!"—R. Gately, President, Gately Consulting

- "Be sincere, ask questions when you are confused, don't play hardball, and read a book on interview tips. Don't talk about drinking or sex habits, and keep clean the night before an interview. I have had people come in late and hung over. They think because I'm young that I would laugh. They were wrong."—HR representative of a *Fortune* 500 electronics company

Real People, Real Advice ... About Questions to Ask on an Interview

"In doing your homework for the interview, you should have questions . . . your questions should show that you are invested and that you did your preparation to get this far . . . "

—*Kristin Kane, Director of Social Media and Recruiting,*
Kane Partners Staffing Solutions

Hear tips from Kristin Kane about asking questions during a job interview at www .mypearsonmarketinglab.com. See Kristin Kane's profile in Chapter 12.

Research the Interviewer Making a personal connection is so important during every interview. There are several ways to learn about your interviewer even before the interview. Use the Internet, especially LinkedIn.com to gain some insight about your interviewer's personal and professional background.

Prepare Your Key Selling Points

An interview is a sales call. You want to be prepared with the key selling points for your brand.

During the interview, your objective is to be sure the interviewer knows what you have to offer while answering his or her questions.

Read the section titled "NAB the Interview with Memorable Stories." Learn how to use NAB (Need, Action, Benefit) to make your brand come alive in interviews.

What I Wish I Knew . . . *About Interviewing*

Zack Benson was a confident, bright senior who had a passion for technology and a flair for sales. So when he got the call for an interview with a major media company for a sales position, he was thrilled. He was always good on his feet and knew that if he could just get in front of the sales manager, he would surely impress him. But Zack learned the hard way that he needed to do far more research about the company and be much more prepared to tell his brand stories in a short but compelling way. "I thought I was prepared for the interview. I had no idea about the tough questions I was going to be asked," he said after the interview. "I wasn't as prepared as I should have been."

Zack's tips for interview preparation include being ready with five or six stories about your experience that reflect with what the company is looking to accomplish. Practice them out loud so you avoid rambling. And he is a firm believer in not only looking at the company Web site, but also reading everything you can about the company and using the company's products. Zack's motto for interviews now is, "You can't be too prepared."

The key is to keep your NAB stories short, conversational, and focused. **Keep rehearsing them until they come naturally to you.**

Get Directions

Get directions to where you are going, including which building and floor. Be sure you are familiar with the travel time, especially during rush hours. Find out about parking or public transportation. Allow extra time for transportation.

Approach

The first few minutes of the interview are critical! **Approach your interviewer with a smile, a firm handshake, and eye contact.** Start off by finding ways to break the ice and establish rapport. You might mention something you've learned about the company (perhaps their new product is just now hitting the market). Or you can bring up something personal, like interesting items on the interviewer's desk. You'll feel more comfortable if you can get the interviewer to talk about him- or herself for a few minutes before jumping into the questions.

We make quick judgments about people we meet for the first time; interviewers are no exception. **That's why it's important to dress professionally, make eye contact, and wear a big smile.**

Sales Presentation

An astonishing thing often happens when searching for work—people who are normally articulate start to falter and stammer the minute they hear those famous four words: "Tell me about yourself." It even happens to experienced people!

Perhaps it would be easier if you could just go in and give a sales presentation, laying out the benefits of your abilities. But that's not the way an interview works. **You do want to focus on your benefits; however, you must do that in response to questions.** Interviewing takes more preparation than a regular sales presentation because you have to be able to think on your feet. You have to figure out how to relate the points you want to make to the questions you're asked. **Be ready to answer the "Tell me about yourself," question with your value proposition or elevator pitch you prepared in Chapter 9.** It's the perfect way to start an interview because it leads you down the path of discussing your strengths, experience, and what you can bring to the company.

Handling Objections

You won't hear objections during a job interview. Managers and recruiters are trained to remain neutral, and they rarely give feedback about how you're doing. They may follow up a question by probing for more information. That may be a cue that they're very interested in you. Or it could just mean that your answers are not specific enough. If you're going on lots of

Smile!
Nothing is better for building rapport.

Last-Minute Check
Arrive early and ask the receptionist if you can use the restroom. Take a quick look to be sure your hair is in place, your clothes are straightened, and use a breath mint. Bring along a business publication such as the *Wall Street Journal* in case you have to wait.

interviews and not getting job offers, you might try to get feedback from an interviewer. It is rare that they will be candid, however—interviewers are wary of discrimination lawsuits. A better way to get feedback is to ask a professional in your network to practice with you. **Some college career centers offer workshops on interviewing skills and videotape mock interviews.** This is a very good way to see how you're doing and get feedback to improve.

The Close

Close

Summarize your strengths and ask for the job!

Every sales situation involves a close—the point at which the salesperson asks the customer to commit to a purchase. **Most job seekers fail to close the interview.** An example of an appropriate close would be, "After the research I did before coming in, I was interested in working for your company. Now that I have a better understanding of the job and the advantages of working for your company, I'm even more excited about it. I would really like the opportunity to contribute to your success." **No matter what your impression is at this point, it is important to let the interviewer know you want the job.** The interview is not the time to make a decision about whether you'll accept the position. You can always say no if it is offered to you. But it may not be offered at all if you don't ask for it.

Follow-up

Say Thank You

Always send a thank-you note within 24 hours of an interview. An e-mail note is acceptable, but a handwritten note makes you stand out. See sample thank-you notes in the *Brand You* Toolkit.

No matter how well your interview went, it's important to follow up in order to seal the deal. **The first thing to do is to write a thank-you note within 24 hours.** A handwritten note is best, but an e-mail has become acceptable. Follow up your thank-you e-mail with a handwritten thank-you note. Your note should include the following:

- thank the interviewer for his or her time and information;
- refer to something specific in the interview—a mutual contact, some connection with the interviewer, or a topic you discussed;
- briefly describe the key reasons you feel you are a good match for the position;
- reiterate your interest in the job; and
- be sincere.

Real People, Real Advice ... About Thank-You Notes

"You quickly want to e-mail that person after the interview. . . . I definitely think that e-mail followed up by a handwritten note is important because then it shows how serious you are."

—*Jennifer Wolf, Event Manager, Philadelphia Business Journal*

Hear about the dos and don'ts of thank-you notes in a short video with Jennifer Wolf at www.mypearsonmarketinglab.com. See Jennifer Wolf's profile in Chapter 13.

Call in about a week if you haven't heard from the employer. Just ask the status of his or her decision. Often pressing business matters interrupt the hiring process. Your phone call will send a signal regarding your interest and motivation. You don't want to become a pest; on the other hand, it's okay to check in once a week to ask about the progress. It's always better to know where you stand than to wonder what is happening.

Real Questions, *Real Answers*

Q. Is it better to send a thank-you note after an interview by e-mail or should it be handwritten?

A. *Always* send a thank-you note after an interview and thank the interviewer for his or her time. It's a good idea to send both—an e-mail thank-you note within 24 hours of your interview and a handwritten thank-you note written at the same time and mailed immediately. If you're wondering about why you should send two thank-you notes, consider this . . . the e-mail thank-you note gives immediacy, while the handwritten note shows thoughtfulness. **Interviewers agree that a thank-you note (e-mail or handwritten) sets a candidate apart.** It's a good idea to send a thank-you note to everyone with whom you interviewed as well as anyone who set up the interview, such as the recruiter. Even if you didn't get the job (or didn't want the job), it's appropriate to send a thank-you note.

Need some inspiration for how to write an appropriate thank-you note? Review the Sample Thank-You Notes in the *Brand You* **Toolkit** in the back of the book.

NAB the Interview with Memorable Stories

Interviewers want to know about your accomplishments and the results you achieved. Many applicants give answers that are too general. They list personal skills and characteristics. After listening to five applicants in a row say they're dependable, hardworking, flexible, and team players, the interviewer's eyes begin to glaze over—everyone sounds the same. These adjectives are not action words. They don't sound convincing and don't show your potential benefit to the company.

How can you stand out from the other applicants? How can you convince the interviewer you can solve his or her problems? By using storytelling narratives to illustrate what you can do.

The interviewer will remember personal, real-life stories. **Your stories provide the context in which you used skills and show that you are a person who takes action to achieve results.** A positive side effect of telling stories is that you take yourself back to a time when you were with people you like and were accomplishing something important. The retelling will relax you and at least temporarily take your mind away from the stress of the interview.

A word of caution is needed here. Stories create interest for the listener. However, your stories should be factual, not fiction and should be , used to illustrate that you have accomplished things relevant to the employer's needs.

Become a Storyteller
Use NAB (Need, Action, Benefit) to stand out from the competition.

To create your memorable stories, complete a NAB (Need, Action, Benefit) worksheet like the one you wrote to develop your résumé. Dedicated candidates who want several offers from which to choose have found that NAB is the secret to acing an interview. They complete NAB worksheets prior to each interview. From their cache of experiences, they select stories that relate to the specific needs of each employer.

Here's how to use the NAB worksheet to prepare for an interview. In the Needs column, write the knowledge, skills, and abilities mentioned in the job description. For each entry in your Action column, create a story that explains the situation thoroughly. Be sure to clearly describe what you did and emphasize the results you achieved. Whenever possible, quantify the results (for example, "We increased profits by 10 percent"). You might want

ACTIVITY 15.1   Identifying Organizational Culture

Instructions: Knowing the culture of an organization can help you prepare for your interview. The information will help you decide what to say and which stories to tell. Select an actual company in your chosen field and create a list of resources you can use to identify the organization's culture. List what you found from each resource.

	Company	Organizational Culture
Resource 1		
Resource 2		
Resource 3		
Resource 4		
Resource 5		

to write the story first. Then practice telling the story until you can say it clearly. The final step is to look at the **Frequently Asked Interview Questions** described later in this chapter. Decide which of your stories would be a good answer for each question.

Sample Stories

How would you handle working at a trade show?

"I think I would be good at representing your products at trade shows—I like talking to people and giving them information. When I was a member of a campus club, we went door-to-door asking people to vote for local candidates. As a group, we decided which neighborhoods were the most critical. I helped write the script we used and kept everyone's motivation up on the days we canvassed. We met our goals in less time than we expected. I enjoyed talking to people about our candidates' views on the issues—I think I convinced a number of people to vote for them. I'm sure these are the same skills you would need to talk to potential customers at a trade show." Notice that this person doesn't have experience with trade shows, but tells an interesting story about a time when he used similar skills. A much stronger response than admitting he doesn't have experience!

Tell me about a time when you worked on a team.

"One of my favorite classes was a class on market trends and research. The professor assigned us to teams. Our assignment was to write and present a market research project. Our group chose distance learning for college students. In the beginning, we had so many ideas about how we could do this that we couldn't focus very well. I volunteered to lead our discussions so we could decide on a plan of action and get busy on the project. People in the group seemed relieved that someone took charge. I made sure everyone had input into our decisions, but I didn't allow the group to waste time, either. We had one member who wasn't contributing much at first. I talked to him privately and together we identified a part of the project that he was interested in doing. In the end, he developed all the visuals that really added to our presentation. We developed some innovative ways to research our topic, and we gathered comprehensive information. There was a lot of interest from the class when we made our presentation—and we got an A on our project!"

This story has lots of detail about a group project. She assumed a leadership role and helped another student succeed. A compelling story—the fact that it's a school project instead of a work team doesn't matter.

Keep Your Preparation Simple

Internet sites have lengthy articles filled with numerous interviewing techniques. Although it's mostly good advice, it can be overwhelming, and

Tell Your Story
Give specific descriptions of past experiences—don't talk in generalities.

Keep It Simple
Develop six great NAB (Need, Action, Benefit) stories and practice them until they're perfect. Then think about the kinds of questions for which you can use them.

impossible to remember everything during the stress of an interview. **So keep it simple. Develop six great stories based on your NAB worksheet.** Bring each story to life by filling in the details and making it interesting. Practice your stories until you can say them without hesitation. In the interview, look for ways to transition from a question into your story. With these six great responses, you'll demonstrate commitment and enthusiasm.

Stories are compelling because they are remembered. When the interviewer is evaluating all the candidates, he or she will remember your stories and be able to put your face with the interview.

How to Handle Behavioral Interviews

Many managers use an interviewing approach called *behavioral interviewing*. It is based on the premise that past behavior most likely predicts future behavior. Thus, if you've demonstrated the skill or knowledge in the past, you will do it at this company, too. Interviewers are looking for positive behaviors—real-time examples of things you've done—not generalities, traits, or personality characteristics.

Behavioral interviewing questions start with, "Tell me about a time when . . ." or "Give me an example of . . ." Interviewers then continue to probe and ask questions about this particular experience until they have a clear, realistic picture of the event. **You'll be a star if you respond with one of your prepared answers, using one of your NAB (Need, Action, Benefit) experiences to paint a picture of your accomplishments.** Always describe the results you achieved and their benefit. Choose situations with positive outcomes. If you're asked to describe a stressful experience, talk about the event in a positive, upbeat manner.

Interview Checklist
See the complete Interview Checklist in the ***Brand You* Toolkit** at the back of the book.

Take time to organize your thoughts before answering a question. You don't want to ramble or appear off track. **It's okay to say, "Let me think about that for a minute." It's also okay to ask a question if you don't understand something.** You may be asked to describe the situation in greater detail, as the interviewer looks for examples of specific behaviors. If you've studied the job description, you'll know the behaviors they're looking for, and you'll be able to include them in your response.

With this style of interviewing, the recruiter strives to create a comfortable environment, encouraging the applicant to describe and tell more. Beware of becoming too comfortable and saying things you will regret later. **Even though recruiters may seem very friendly, they are still evaluating your responses.** Always give a favorable impression. There are stories of people who described how they told off their last boss or went over the heads of their teachers to get their grades improved. One applicant told the interviewer he was getting married in a few months and would be moving to another city. Be natural, but be careful what you say on every interview.

"My favorite interview question is asking a candidate what type of supervision they like or require. . . . I'm looking for someone that's really independent . . . and takes their own initiative to get the job done."

—Jennifer Wolf, Event Manager, Philadelphia Business Journal

Watch videos featuring Jennifer Wolf and other professionals discussing their favorite interview questions at www.mypearsonmarketinglab.com. See Jennifer Wolf's profile in Chapter 13.

Frequently Asked Interview Questions—and How to Answer Them

Although it's impossible to predict the questions you'll be asked, practice answering these typical questions. The secret to a great interview is to be prepared to discuss your skills and how you can benefit the company. Your NAB stories will do this for you. **Remember to practice your answers out loud—things that sound good in your head don't always come out right.**

The Best Interview Preparation
Rehearse!
Rehearse!
Rehearse!

Interview Question	How to Answer
Tell me about yourself.	Interviewers often ask this broad question to build rapport and begin the interview. Launch your value proposition. Focus your answer on your skills and interest in the field, giving a brief chronological overview. Avoid discussing personal or family information.
Tell me about a time when you achieved more than was expected.	The interviewer wants to know about your personal commitment to a task. How motivated are you? Are you results-oriented? Do you inspire others? How have you shown initiative in the past? Use examples from your education or work experience. The recruiter is most interested in the behaviors you exhibited to achieve a particular goal.
Describe a time when you had a conflict with someone.	You can't avoid this question by saying you've never been involved in a conflict. Everyone has conflicts. The interviewer wants to know how you handle and resolve them. What happened and how did you react? Are you the kind of person who blows up and adds fuel to the fire, tries different ways to keep peace, or avoids conflict and walks away? Your answer should describe a time when you successfully resolved conflict in a reasonable and appropriate way. Choose a small conflict at work or school, and focus on what you did to resolve the problem.

When asked this question, the most recent or troubling conflict you've experienced might pop into your head. Don't describe these situations or any issues that you feel emotional about, and avoid talking about parents, roommates, or spouses. You want to appear rational and even-tempered. Stay away from blaming or berating anyone. Instead, discuss an issue like differences in work styles, and describe how you resolved the problem. Don't pick a situation you walked away from, such as dropping a class or quitting a job. |

Continue on the next page . . .

Interview Question	How to Answer
Give me an example of a time when you had to work under pressure.	The recruiter wants to know how you handle stress and deadlines. What do you consider stressful? Can you meet deadlines? Do you thrive under pressure or buckle under deadlines? Describe a situation with pressure that has to do with deadlines rather than personalities of co-workers. Talk about strategies you successfully used to stay calm.
Tell me about a time when you dealt with an angry customer.	The interviewer wants to know how you react to angry people. Do you use different strategies to calm irate people? Do you do everything you can to make sure customers walk away happy? Do you strictly enforce company policies or often bend them to keep customers coming back? Talk about an exchange that ended positively—a time when you successfully calmed an angry customer and resolved the situation. Don't use examples in which you referred an angry customer to others.
Describe a situation when you analyzed a problem and arrived at a solution.	The recruiter wants to evaluate your decision-making skills. Did you use a systematic approach or intuition? Were you impulsive, or did you delay and overanalyze the problem? Choose a situation that you systematically analyzed, and describe how you handled it.
What are your strengths?	The interviewer looks to see if your strengths match the skills needed in the position. Use this opportunity to talk about your strengths that are related to the job. Give examples of times when you demonstrated them. Describe skills by using one or two of your NAB experiences.
What are your weaknesses?	This question is used to assess your self-confidence. Pick a real weakness (but not your worst one!) and then describe how you overcame it. For example, "I sometimes volunteer to take on too many tasks because I see they need to be done. When this happens, I may ask my supervisor to help me prioritize them." Don't talk about problems with past bosses, co-workers, or roommates.
Why do you want to work for this company?	This question seeks to find out what you know about the company. It gives you the opportunity to show you have done your research. Don't just say, "It's a great company that's growing." Instead, look the interviewer in the eye and say, "I really want to work for your company because . . . ." Talk about what you can do to solve a problem or add value to the team. One recruiter told us, "We asked an applicant why she wanted to work for our company. Her reply, 'It must be a good company to work for' wasn't enough and I didn't hire her. I think anyone should be able to express why they want the job they are applying for."
Why should I hire you?	Tell specifically how you can be an asset to this organization, and let the interviewer know that you want to work there (even if you're not sure yet). You would be surprised how many applicants never ask directly for the job.
What did you like best about your last job?	Focus on similarities between that job and this one. Share another NAB experience.
What did you like least about your last job?	The interviewer is hoping you will reveal conflicts—don't do it. Beware of complaining! A basic principle of job-hunting is to never say anything negative about a former employer. So you could answer: "I enjoyed my work at XYZ Company, but I guess one thing I didn't like was . . . ." Pick something that is not critical in the job for which you are applying. End your response on a positive note by talking about your readiness for new challenges.

Continue on the next page . . .

Interview Question	How to Answer
Where do you see yourself in five years?	The recruiter wants to know if you set goals and plan to keep learning. Talk about skills you can reasonably learn in this position and responsibilities you could meet as a result. Don't talk about promotions within the company or long-term employment—that may not be in the cards. Don't mention returning to school full-time or any plans that might indicate a short commitment to the employer.
What was your favorite class in college?	Describe a class related to the type of work for which you are interviewing. Tell about relevant class activities, assignments, and group projects you enjoyed.

Dress for Success

What's the best way to dress for an interview? Unless you are interviewing for a job to be a rock star, keep it professional.

Dressing for success can be challenging in today's casual work environment. Some industries are more formal than others, and every company is different. You never know what the environment is until you get there. You can ask the person who is arranging the interview about what to wear. However, even if that person says the dress code is casual or business casual, be prepared to dress for success.

You might be tempted to dress for the environment, but you might not know what that means. When in doubt, dress professionally. No matter what the profession, you can't go wrong dressing professionally or conservatively; you can make a mistake dressing too casually or too trendy. You can always dress down after you get the job. Even if you are interviewing in a more casual industry such as advertising, position yourself as the professional you are.

Here are a few guidelines for dressing for success:

Women: Professional Dress

- Wear a professional dress or suit (skirt or pants with blazer) in a conservative color (black, beige, brown, or navy are always appropriate). If you wear a colored jacket, your blouse and accessories should be coordinated for a total business-like look.
- Do not wear a sundress or dress with thin straps or low necklines.
- The hemline of a skirt should be at or slightly above the knee.
- The neckline of your blouse should be conservative; a camisole is not appropriate.
- Your suit or dress should fit you well. If it's too tight or too loose, invest in a new one. You'll use it when you are working. If the suit or dress needs to be tailored, have it done. Fit makes you look and feel more confident.

Think Twice about Your First Impression

"When a candidate asks me what to wear, I tell him or her that you only have one chance to make a good first impression. You decide."— Ike Richman, Vice President of Public Relations, Comcast-Spectacor.

real people, **Real Brands**

Carla

Showell-Lee's Brand

A seasoned television personality and fashion expert, Carla provides insight to job seekers of all ages about how to dress for success.
See Carla's video profile at www.mypearsonmarketinglab.com.

▼ **Q** and **A** with Carla Showell-Lee, television personality and host of "Attire for Hire" workshops.

Carla's Profile

College: Temple University

Major: Broadcast Journalism

Current profession: Television personality

First job: Temple University campus radio station

How I got my first job: I volunteered at the campus radio station after I graduated.

Brand key word: Reliable.

Description of my personal brand image: Reliable is the best description of my brand image. I'm very conscientious. If you tell me to do something, you know I'm going to show up and I'm going to be there.

My passion: My passion is writing. I love telling someone's story ... putting the story and visuals together like puzzle pieces to creatively tell an authentic story.

What I love about my job: It gives me a sense of being creative.

Carla's Advice

Favorite advice about job searching: Find out what really makes you tick, what makes you get goose bumps, what makes you juicy. You need find the craft that makes you tick, then do the research to find out if it's what you really want to do.

Favorite advice about job searching: Do a "dress rehearsal" before each interview. Actually get dressed in the suit, shoes, and accessories that you will wear on the interview. It gives you a chance to be sure everything is cleaned, pressed, and fits properly.

Advice about electronic devices on an interview: Turn off you electronic device before you go into the building. It's never appropriate to hear your electronic device during an interview. It's not appropriate to be on your electronic device while you're waiting for the interview, either.

What I wish I knew about job searching: It's all about building rapport. I wish I knew how powerful sending a handwritten thank-you note can be. Thank-you notes really make you stand out and people remember you when you write a thank-you note.

Real People, Real Advice ... About How to Dress for an Interview

"It's always an unspoken that you're suppose to wear business formal to a job interview."

—*Amanda Burd, student, Saint Joseph's University*

"First impression is so key and I've had students come in for an interview not dressed appropriately. Right off the bat, that really speaks volumes about who you are."

—*Jennifer Wolf, Event Manager, Philadelphia Business Journal*

Watch short videos featuring Amanda Burd and Jennifer Wolf discussing dressing for success at www.mypearsonmarketinglab.com. See Jennifer Wolf's profile in Chapter 13.

- Wear conservative shoes or basic pumps in a neutral color. Leave the stilettos, platform shoes, and flip flops at home. Definitely avoid strappy or casual sandals.
- Hair and makeup should look natural; no heavy eye shadow or bright lipstick.
- Wear appropriate accessories; no big bracelets, chandelier earrings, or large rings.
- No tattoos or body piercings should be visible other than pierced ears.
- Carry a professional handbag or briefcase; no backpacks, please.

Real People, Real Advice ... About Interview Dressing for Women

"I think you should find the suit, the style of dress, that makes you "pop" every time you walk in the door. It's your power suit ... "

—*Carla Showell-Lee, Television Personality and Host of "Attire for Hire" Workshops*

Hear all of Carla Showell-Lee's tips for women about how to dress for an interview at www.mypearsonmarketinglab.com.

Women: Business Casual

- Same as above; you can be a bit more flexible with your color choices, but don't go overboard.

Men: Professional Dress

- Wear a suit in a conservative color (navy, gray, or black are best); white or light colored solid shirt and coordinating tie.
- Your suit should fit you well. If you don't have a good suit, invest in one and have it tailored to fit. You will use it when you start working. A well-fitting suit makes you look and feel more confident.
- Your shirt should fit you well and be pressed. A wrinkled shirt makes a bad impression.
- Wear polished conservative shoes in a color to complement your suit with appropriate color of hosiery.
- Don't wear any jewelry except a watch and ring.
- Tattoos or body piercings should not be visible.
- Carry a professional portfolio or briefcase; no backpacks, please.

Men: Business Casual

- Wear a blazer (navy is the standard color for a blazer) and a shirt in white or a pale color with a coordinating tie.
- See notes above about fit and a pressed shirt.
- Wear appropriate shoes; nothing that resembles an athletic shoe, a sandal, or a flip flop.
- Wear appropriate color of socks.
- Don't wear jewelry except a watch and ring.
- Tattoos or body piercings should not be visible.
- Carry a professional portfolio or briefcase; no backpacks, please.

Be ready for every interview by reviewing the Interview Checklist in the *Brand You* Toolkit.

Show Your Skills with a Portfolio

One of the most powerful things you can do on an interview is to show samples of your work. No matter what type of job or what company you are interviewing with, bring samples of class projects, internship or volunteer projects,

Show Them What You Can Do

Put samples of your work in a binder or portfolio and bring it on every interview. Include class projects, internship projects, and volunteer efforts. You can stand out when you show an interviewer what you have done rather than just telling her.

Real People, Real Advice ... About Work Samples

"I've never actually brought samples of my work to an interview.... I should probably have a portfolio.... I guess I never really thought about it."

—*Amanda Burd, student, Saint Joseph's University*

"Definitely, the more the better. I think it's great if you bring samples of your work. It shows that you're motivated and this is what you've done, it's showing your own experience. It definitely shows extra effort ... that you are going the extra mile to bring samples of your work."

—*Jennifer Wolf, Event Manager, Philadelphia Business Journal*

"I think it's important to bring samples of your work ... You're branding yourself when you're showing your work. It shows that you are aggressive, assertive, and that you care enough to think about bringing the samples with you."

—*Ike Richman, Vice President of Public Relations, Comcast-Spectacor*

Watch videos featuring Amanda Burd, Jennifer Wolf, Ike Richman and other professionals discussing portfolios and work samples for interviews at www.mypearson marketing lab.com. See Jennifer Wolf's profile in Chapter 13 and Ike Richman's profile in Chapter 9.

or other activities that demonstrate your skills. While a portfolio is required for creative jobs such as Web site designer or copywriter, it can be a powerful tool in any profession to help set you apart from the other candidates.

Your portfolio should be a collection of the best samples of your work. Here are a few pointers for your portfolio of work samples:

- Choose four to six samples that demonstrate your skills. Copies of PowerPoint presentations, papers, brochures, flyers, blogs, social networking pages, posters, pictures of events, writing samples, press releases or any other project are appropriate.
- Include clean copies that are not shopworn. Do not include copies that have been graded or include writing or comments.
- Put your work samples into a binder or other portfolio including plastic sleeves.
- Be creative. If you're looking for a job in public relations, write the press release that announces you in the job and include it in your portfolio.

Read more about professional Web sites and portfolios in the *Brand You Toolkit* at the back of the book.

My Career Journal

Go back to Chapter 9 and review your Value Proposition. How could you rephrase or change this statement to relate your features and benefits to the company you chose in Activity 15.1?

_____

_____

_____

_____

_____

Write a NAB (Need, Action, Benefit) statement to answer the following FAQs:

What are your strengths?

_____

_____

_____

_____

_____

What are your weaknesses?

_____

_____

_____

_____

_____

Give an example of a time when you worked under pressure. (Be sure to pick a time when you were successful!)

_____

_____

_____

_____

_____

Write down three questions you will ask on a job interview.

_____

_____

_____

_____

_____

Notes to **Myself**

16

Evaluating and Finalizing Your Offer:
Get What You Want

This is it! This is where it all comes together. You have gone on interviews, impressed your prospective employer, and now you are about to get a job offer. This step in your work search is just as important as each of the others. Even though it seems like you have arrived, don't relax just yet. Take the time to carefully read this chapter. Then, reread this chapter and complete the activities as soon as you receive a job offer. It's an exciting time, but don't get caught up in the excitement and miss something important. You don't want to be disappointed when you start your job.

Brand You Checklist

✓ Learn how to determine if an offer is a good offer.

✓ Understand how to negotiate a better offer.

✓ Determine what to do if you get one offer before another offer.

✓ Establish what you need to do to accept the offer.

✓ Realize why you need an offer letter for an internship or a full-time job.

Real People, Real Advice ... Getting an Offer

"I'm really excited. After graduation I'll be working with a large food manufacturing company recognized as one of the best companies to work for in the country ... I actually got the job from completing an internship with the company ... Little did I know I was doing something really, really important by getting that internship."

—*Amanda Burd, student, Saint Joseph's University*

Hear about Amanda Burd's job offer at www.mypearsonmarketinglab .com.

Salary Discussions

For most people, salary is an important factor in evaluating a job offer. It shouldn't be your only consideration, especially if career satisfaction, flexibility, and lifestyle options are important to you. No matter where salary fits in your list of incentives, you'll get the best possible compensation package if you understand how to discuss salary and how to negotiate it.

There are two basic principles that every job seeker should know:

1. Don't go to an interview without knowing what you're worth.
2. Delay discussion of salary as long as possible.

Although employers have a salary range for their open positions, you should calculate your market value. Study typical salaries for the job you're considering. Then analyze how you'll contribute to the profitability of the company. This analysis should be based on the value of your education, experience, and the responsibility of the position. Reread Chapter 11 – Pricing the Product to review resources you can use to establish your value.

Real People, Real Advice ... About Answering the Salary Question

"It's important to have a number in your head that you're willing to live with . . ."

—*Karen Carroll, Executive Recruiter, Blue Plate Minds*

Hear Karen Carroll's tips for negotiating a job offer at www.my pearsonmarketinglab.com.

Why should you delay salary discussions? Think about other sales situations. When a salesperson wants the consumer to buy a high-end product, he or she presents all the features and benefits. The salesperson waits until he or she knows the consumer is sold on the product before he or she brings up cost. The best time to discuss salary is when both of you have a strong interest in one another.

Sometimes it's not possible to completely delay salary discussions. You may be asked to disclose your salary expectations in response to a job posting or in your first screening interview. Remember that you usually can't negotiate up from the lowest figure you name. Here's how you can handle these situations:

• In your cover letter, you can ignore the request. Or you can say, "I expect to earn market value for the responsibilities of the position." However, be aware that your résumé may be ignored if you don't provide a figure when asked (human resources managers like people who follow directions). **Never include salary expectations in your letter unless asked.**

• During the interview, one way to respond to a question about your salary expectations is to reply with a question of your own. You can ask, "What would a person with my background, skills, and qualifications typically earn at your company?" Or, you can simply state, "I'm looking for a competitive entry-level compensation package, but I'm most interested in joining the company with the right fit for me."

• Sometimes the interviewer won't answer that question and will probe again for your requirements. Be as nonspecific as possible. "I know I can contribute value to your organization, but I'd like to wait until we're both sure I'm the right person for the job." Another possible response is to say, "I'm comfortable with the salary range you are offering. I'd like to discuss the specifics when I know more about the responsibilities of the job." If pressed to name an actual figure, respond with a broad range. Be sure you would accept the lowest figure in your range—that could be the one you are offered in the end.

If salary comes up at the end of the interview, thank the interviewer for making the offer. An appropriate response would be, **"Thank you for offering me the position. After learning more about your company and the responsibilities of the job, I'm excited about the opportunity to work for the XYZ Company. I'm sure I can make an impact and I'm ready to consider your best offer."** At this point, the employer may name a salary or provide a range. It's always appropriate to think about a job offer for a few days. It is perfectly acceptable to respond by saying something like, "I'm very excited about receiving this offer and about the opportunity to work at XYX Company. This is a big decision. I'd like to give you an answer by Thursday." This will give you some time to think about the offer and determine if there are any elements of the offer that you want to negotiate.

Usually the offer won't come during the interview. Instead, the hiring manager or recruiter will call you and make the offer later. Have paper and pen handy so you can take notes (it's okay to ask the person to hold while you get a pencil and paper). When the offer is made, don't be afraid to ask questions to find out everything you need to know to evaluate the offer. That might include some of the following questions. But don't feel as if you have to ask all of these questions at the time you get the offer.

- What is the entire compensation package, including benefits?
- What exactly does the benefits package include?
- What are the opportunities for your personal development and promotion?
- When will your salary be reviewed? What do you need to do to earn at a higher level?
- What salary increases can you expect in three to five years?
- Is the offer subject to any conditions, such as a background check, verification of work history, drug testing, or security clearance?

Regardless of whether you are offered the job in the interview or on the phone, don't accept immediately. Tell the person offering the job, **"Thank you for offering me a position with your company. I'd like a little time to consider your offer. Can we talk again later this week?"** New college grads have a tendency to be so grateful for employment, that they don't take time to evaluate the offer. This is an important decision for both you and the employer. Now that they've offered you the job, they want an enthusiastic employee, not someone who accepted only because he or she couldn't say no. Employers don't expect you to answer immediately—they won't withdraw the offer if you ask for a few days to consider it. So take time to evaluate whether this is the right job for you. Also, it's a good time to gather your questions so you know exactly what information you need to know before you accept the offer.

What I Wish I Knew . . . *About Accepting a Job Offer*

"Don't jump at the first offer," says a recent graduate who found out the hard way. He accepted the first offer because he was afraid he wouldn't find anything else. Within three months, he knew he had made a mistake and was looking for another job. "Ask questions and take some time to review the offer, the company and the position," he advises. "Don't feel pressured, if it's not the right job for you, keep looking. You'll know when you find the right fit."

Evaluating the Offer

No Secrets

Don't be afraid to ask about details of a job offer. It's a good idea to ask for a copy of the company benefits package to be sure you understand every benefit that is offered . . . or not offered. And, it's very acceptable (and usually encouraged) to call back the company while you are considering your offer to get additional information about the offer. Use the evaluation sheet in Activity 16.1 as a guide as to what questions to ask.

It's hard to turn down an offer for a job, especially if your search has taken a long time, but you want to be confident that you'll be happy in your new position. No matter how excited you are, it pays to sit back and assess the match between you and the work. Think back to the activities you completed at the beginning of this book. Is this the industry where you want to be right now? Is this the specialty in which you want to start paying your dues? How will you feel in a year when you see this job on your updated résumé?

The best way to see how the offer adds up is to complete Activities 16.1 and 16.2.

One mistake new grads often make is to fail to take into account the benefits that are offered. If you're like many people starting your career, you might think you're invincible and you'll never get sick. But health and life insurance are important and expensive. Health plans and other benefits actually represent a hefty chunk in the equation—they often equal as much as 30 percent of your pay. **Even if you can't negotiate salary, companies will often increase benefits if you ask for them.**

Employee benefits vary from company to company. Many offer a cafeteria plan of benefits, allowing employees to choose what they like best from a variety of options. Benefits are constantly changing as companies scramble to remain competitive. Here are some of the most common benefits about which you should ask:

- **Vacation, sick leave, personal holidays, and time off.** Many companies now lump together vacation, personal holidays, sick leave, and time off, calling it *paid time off*, and you can use it as you wish. (Personal holidays are paid days off that you can take when you want. Holidays are paid holidays that fall on major federal holidays such as Fourth of July,

Thanksgiving, Christmas, etc.) You may be able to negotiate another week of vacation in lieu of higher salary. Be sure to ask when you are eligible to use the vacation, sick leave, time off, and personal holidays.

- **Health insurance.** Most companies provide medical insurance for full-time employees. Companies may pay a percentage of health insurance costs for employees and their families, and the employee pays the rest. Coverage can vary dramatically. Insurance options include medical savings accounts, HMOs, PPOs, dental, and vision.

- **Life insurance.** Term or whole life insurance may be offered. Usually the policy terminates when employment ends.

- **401(k) or pension plan.** A 401(k) plan allows you to build a tax-deferred retirement nest egg. Some employers match your contribution or a portion of it. Employer matching is a valuable benefit as it is additional income that is deposited in your 401(k) account. If a pension plan is offered, the employer puts money into a fund for your retirement.

- **Stock options (ESOPs).** This option allows the employee to buy a certain amount of company stock at a discounted price. Employees may buy the stock, pocketing the difference between the option price and the market price.

- **Signing bonus.** Bonuses have been a popular way to entice employees to join the company. They are commonly offered during good economic times or to high-demand employees. Based on the current economic conditions, signing bonuses are not very common. Typically, the bonus is paid to the employee upon successful completion of the probationary period or after one year.

- **Child care/elder care assistance.** Some companies offer on-site day care for children of employees. Other companies offer pretax savings accounts to meet child care or elder care expenses; the company may or may not contribute money to the account.

- **Tuition reimbursement.** This is an important benefit if you plan to pursue a graduate degree. Rules for reimbursement vary, so find out the company's policy.

- **Relocation expenses.** If you are relocating to another city to take the job, many companies offer a relocation allowance. The amount varies by company, location, and position.

Relocation Information

Before you accept a job that requires relocation, be sure you understand exactly which relocation costs will be paid by the company. Go to **www.rileyguide.com/relocate.html** to find out what you can expect.

Tricks of the Trade

Take the time to consider a job offer before you accept it. Even if you know it's the right job and right offer for you, it's worth taking a few days to think about it and consider the elements of the offer. Companies expect candidates, even those for entry-level jobs, to think about an offer for a few days. This is the perfect time to review all of the elements of compensation, ask any questions you may have, and determine if there is anything you want to negotiate. Once you accept the offer, you are no longer in a position to negotiate.

ACTIVITY 16.1 Compensation Comparison Worksheet

Instructions: When you receive a job offer (or offers), fill in the information next to each compensation element to objectively evaluate the offer (or offers). Use this worksheet to evaluate one offer or to compare multiple offers.

Compensation Element	Job Offer from _____ (Company Name)	Job Offer from _____ (Company Name)	Job Offer from _____ (Company Name)
Position			
• Title	_____	_____	_____
• Key Responsibilities	_____	_____	_____
Salary			
• Base salary *(annual salary)*	_____	_____	_____
• Commission *(dollar amount or percentage of annual salary and conditions of payment)*	_____	_____	_____
• Bonus *(dollar amount or percentage of annual salary and conditions of payment)*	_____	_____	_____
• Signing Bonus *(dollar amount or percentage of annual salary and conditions of payment)*	_____	_____	_____
• Stock Options *(number of options, option price, and vesting)*	_____	_____	_____
Benefits—Vacation			
• Vacation Days *(number of days and when earned)*	_____	_____	_____
• Personal Holidays *(number of days)*	_____	_____	_____
• Holidays *(number of days)*	_____	_____	_____
• Sick Days *(number of days)*	_____	_____	_____
• Other *(number of days)*	_____	_____	_____
Benefits—Insurance			
• When available after start date	_____	_____	_____
• Medical *(cost per pay period)*	_____	_____	_____
• Dental *(cost per pay period)*	_____	_____	_____
• Optical *(cost per pay period)*	_____	_____	_____
• Life *(cost per pay period)*	_____	_____	_____
• Long-term Disability *(cost per pay period)*	_____	_____	_____
• Short-term Disability *(cost per pay period)*	_____	_____	_____

Continues on the next page . . .

Compensation Element	Job Offer from _____ (Company Name)	Job Offer from _____ (Company Name)	Job Offer from _____ (Company Name)
Benefits—Other Income/Savings			
• 401(k) Plan (*yes or no; # of waiting days to participate*)	_____	_____	_____
• 401(k) Matching (*percentage of contribution*)	_____	_____	_____
• Other	_____	_____	_____
Benefits—Other			
• Tuition Reimbursement	_____	_____	_____
• Day Care	_____	_____	_____
• Elder Care	_____	_____	_____
• On-site Amenities	_____	_____	_____
• Car Allowance (*dollar amount paid monthly*)	_____	_____	_____
• Relocation	_____	_____	_____
• Other	_____	_____	_____

But Is It the Right Offer for YOU?

Once you have established the monetary value of your offer or offers, it's just as important to evaluate whether this is the offer that's right. Don't take an offer just because it's the only offer you have. You have to go to work every day so you want to be sure that you accept the offer that's right for YOU.

Real People, Real Advice ... About Evaluating an Offer

". . . (You have to ask yourself) what else is important to me? . . . Have this on paper . . . Are benefits important to me? Is vacation? Is personal time off, holidays, flex hours, is it just gaining the experience, is it working for *that* company? . . . The more you know about what's important to you and what you're willing to negotiate on and what you're not, (makes you more prepared) when you're going into negotiations."

—*Karen Carroll, Executive Recruiter, Blue Plate Minds*

Listen to Karen Carroll discuss how to evaluate a job offer in a short video at www .mypearsonmarketinglab.com.

Take a few minutes after you determine the value of your job offer and consider the pros and cons of the offer or offers. It's not always the salary that should be the deciding factor in accepting a job offer. Some other elements in addition to compensation are

- Distance and time of the commute to work
- Option to work remotely
- Work environment
- People with whom and for whom you will work
- Culture of the company
- Dress code (casual vs. formal)
- Employee turnover
- Opportunity for personal development and career advancement
- Job function (is it or will it lead you to what you want to do)
- Social responsibility of the company
- Community involvement of the company
- Reputation of the company
- Stability of the company
- Travel requirements/opportunity
- Relocation requirements/opportunity

Use Activity 16.2 to consider all the elements that are important to you. Keep in mind that any one pro or con can make a job a great fit . . . or a not-so-great fit. Only **you** can determine that based on what's important to you.

ACTIVITY 16.2   Pros and Cons of Your Job Offer

Instructions: When you get a job offer or offers, complete the following worksheet. Think about all of the elements that are important to you and put them in the appropriate column. You can use this to evaluate one job offer or multiple job offers.

Job	Pros	Cons
Job Offer #1		

Continue on the next page . . .

Job	Pros	Cons
Job Offer #2		

Negotiating An Offer

Now that the job has been offered and you've decided you want it, you're ready to negotiate. Keep in mind that you should complete Activities 16.1 and 16.2 after you receive a job offer or offers but before you accept an offer. **You should not officially accept the offer until you have negotiated the offer that you will accept.** If you accept the position before you negotiate, you lose your negotiating power.

Real People, Real Advice ... About Negotiating a Job Offer

"I didn't know if I was supposed to talk about the conditions of the job offer or just accept it. As an entry-level employee, I didn't know (if I could negotiate).

—*Amanda Burd, student, Saint Joseph's University*

"(Compensation) is absolutely negotiable . . . for entry level, you tend to have a little less pull because you're looking for experience and that's the most important thing . . . but if everyone's not happy, it's not going to be a relationship that works."

—*Karen Carroll, Executive Recruiter, Blue Plate Minds*

Watch a short video clip featuring Karen Carroll discussing how to negotiate a job offer at www.mypearsonmarketinglab.com.

About half of all job seekers accept the first offer that's put on the table, but some employers expect candidates to counteroffer. Remember that the employer won't withdraw the offer just because you counter it. So go ahead and ask for what you want—you have nothing to lose and perhaps a lot to gain. Prepare a counteroffer, including salary and benefits. Complete Activity 16.3 Pre-Negotiation Worksheet before you begin negotiating. This will help you identify those items that are most important to you during the negotiation. You probably won't be able to negotiate on every aspect of the offer, so pick the one or two things that are most important to you. Your **pre-negotiation goals** are those things that you consider to be "deal breakers"; if you don't get those, you won't accept the offer. Your **counteroffer** is what you will ask for in each area. Your counteroffer should be for a little more than your pre-negotiation goals in order to allow some room for negotiation.

Also be prepared to review your strengths—the ways you will add value to the firm—as justification for the terms you are seeking. It is also helpful to discuss current market values for this type of position to support your request.

Keep a positive outlook during the negotiation. **Settle the issue of salary first and then move into a discussion of benefits.** Sometimes with entry-level positions there isn't much room for negotiation of salary, but a signing bonus, an extra week of vacation time, or an early salary review are all items that may sweeten the deal for you.

Some things for which you might consider negotiating:

- Additional vacation time
- Availability of medical insurance at start date (some companies have a 30–90 day waiting period)

Negotiate to Win
Identify one or two key items (such as increased salary, additional vacation days, etc.) that you want and keep your negotiations focused on those. You will be more likely to get want you want if have a targeted approach.

Real Questions, *Real Answers*

Q. What if I am getting ready to accept an offer, but I have a vacation planned that is already paid for. Should I mention that during the negotiation?

A. It's always good to be upfront with your new employer about plans that were made prior to your employment. That conversation should be separate from an offer negotiation. In other words, that is a one-time event that you should establish with your employer in regard to compensation (e.g., will you take the days off without pay or will they go toward your vacation accrual?). Cover this after you have negotiated your job offer. You don't want to use this one-time episode as a negotiating point because it's not. Basically, you are asking to take some days off without pay to cover the plans that were already finalized. If you discuss this while you are discussing any other elements of your offer negotiation, you will be disappointed that you won't get more for your negotiation.

Pre-Negotiation Worksheet

Instructions: Complete this worksheet after you receive your offer, but before you negotiate the offer. Use the detailed listing in Activity 16.1 to identify areas you would like to increase. The Current Offer is what you have been offered. The Pre-Negotiation Goal is the minimum you must have in order to accept the offer. The Counteroffer is what you will go back to the company and ask for, which should be slightly more than your Pre-Negotiation Goal.

Compensation Element	Current Offer	Pre-Negotiation Goal	Counteroffer
Salary			
Vacation			
Insurance			
Other Income/Savings			
Relocation Benefits			
Other Benefits			

- Waiving of one or two months of health care insurance premiums
- Signing bonus
- Performance bonus
- Stock options

Coordinating Timing of Multiple Offers

Because you are probably interviewing with multiple companies at the same time, it's likely you can expect offers from more than one company. However, not every interviewing process moves at the same pace, so you probably won't get multiple offers at exactly the same time. If this is the case, when you get your first offer (and tell the company you want some time to consider it), it's best to call the other company (or companies) and ask your contact person about the timing for the next steps in the interview process. An example of how you might handle this is

"I wanted to touch base and see if you can give me some insight as to when you will be making your decision (*let person respond*). I'm very interested in the position and working for your company. I am considering another offer right now and I want to be sure I make my decision with as much information as possible."

It's always best to call the second company so you can get some feedback about timing and if you are still being considered as a candidate. You may not be able to move the process any faster, but you can signal your situation and get some insight before you make your final decision.

Using One Offer to Negotiate Another Offer

What if you have an offer from the first company and want to use it to negotiate an offer from the second company? As mentioned earlier, it's good to negotiate. But keep in mind that you are negotiating with a future employer, not buying a house. **You want the negotiation to be professional and positive.**

Keep your negotiation focused on exactly what you want from the negotiation and underscoring your value. It's acceptable to mention that you have another offer at a higher salary (or more extensive benefits or more vacation time, etc). **But don't disclose the company name, or exact compensation package.** Chances are the company will not match an offer just for the sake of matching an offer unless there is a severe shortage of entry-level candidates (remember, you don't have any experience yet). Companies pay what they consider the job to be worth. Your objective is to establish your value to get the additional salary, vacation or other benefits that you want.

Negotiating Your Start Date

You may want to take some time off before you start work; your new employer may want you to start right away. **Discuss your start date after you negotiate your salary and benefits.** Your start date is a short-term consideration; your compensation package is a long-term consideration. It's important not to trade off compensation for a later start date.

Discuss your intentions with your new employer and come to an agreement as to what date will work best. It's acceptable to start at least two to four weeks after you accept the job. In some industries, such as accounting, you may accept a job offer up to a year in advance. An internship may have a longer or shorter lead time depending on the industry, company, and time of year.

Accepting the Offer

Once you have agreed to a final offer, you should verbally recap all the elements of the offer. Then you should ask for an offer letter. Every internship and full-time job offer should formally be extended with an offer letter. If the company will not provide an offer letter, don't take the job.

"... I accepted by job offer by signing an offer letter that was mailed to me."

—*Amanda Burd, student, Saint Joseph's University*

Hear Amanda Burd talk about how she received her job offer at www.mypearson marketinglab.com.

An offer letter is a letter of agreement of the terms of the offer. It usually contains the following as appropriate:

- Title of the position which you are being offered
- Person to whom you will report (optional)
- Location of office (optional)
- Starting salary (either hourly or annual)
- Bonus, commission, signing bonus, car allowance or any additional compensation
- Number of stock options, option price, and vesting schedule
- Vacation days (may reference company benefits package)
- Other benefits (may reference company benefits package)
- Start date
- Any offer contingencies such as passing a company-paid drug screening, background or security check, and/or references

Examples of offer letters are shown here and in Figures 16.1 and 16.2.

You should have an offer letter within one to two days of accepting the offer. It is acceptable if the offer letter is sent via e-mail as long as it is on the company letterhead.

When you get your offer letter, review it carefully to be sure it includes all of the elements to which you agreed. If it doesn't, call the author of the letter immediately to get clarification and resolution on the issue. Some companies require you to sign the offer letter and return it to the company. It's best to make a copy of the signed offer letter before you return it. **Keep your offer letter along with all other information from the company in a reference file.**

Congratulations! It's time to enjoy your career. Here's to brand YOU.

A Personal Touch
After you accept an offer, it's a good idea to send a hand-written thank-you note to everyone with whom you interviewed. It's a nice touch to thank each person for his or her support and tell him or her how excited you are about joining the company. Each person will appreciate your note and you will start off your new job on the right foot.

Offer Letter
An offer letter is standard for internships and full-time positions. Be sure you get an offer letter within one to two days of accepting the offer verbally. **If you are already working, don't give notice at your current job until you receive your offer letter for your new job.**

Figure 16.1 Offer Letter for Full-time Job

Rich, Talbot and Wells Advertising
1 North Wacker Drive, Suite 3100
Chicago, IL 60600

June 11, 2010

Mr. John Morton
4851 Hudson Avenue
Chicago, IL 60606

Dear John,

We are pleased to extend this offer of employment to you as Account Coordinator reporting to Sarah Welch, Account Director. Your compensation package will include the following:

- Annual salary of $45,000 with performance and salary review on an annual basis.

- Annual performance bonus of 5% of your base salary based upon meeting agreed performance objectives. Your bonus will be prorated for 2010.

- Two weeks of vacation according to the company vacation policy.

- Participation in the 401(k) program upon eligibility outlined in the enclosed *Employee Benefits Package.*

- Participation in the company health plan after 90 days of employment.

- Participation in all other company benefits outlined in the enclosed *Employee Benefits Package.*

Your start date will be July 1, 2010. We are looking forward to you joining our team. If I can be of any further assistance, please don't hesitate to call me.

Sincerely,

Anne Sullivan

Anne Sullivan
Director of Human Resources

Enclosure

Figure 16.2 Offer Letter for Internship

AJA, Inc. 4545 City Avenue
Philadelphia, PA 19104

May 1, 2010

Ms. Christine Spenser
1102 Main Street
Philadelphia, PA 19191

Dear Christine,

I am pleased to confirm your acceptance of employment as Accounting Intern reporting to Leslie West, Accounting Manager. As agreed, your start date is May 19, 2010. Please report to the Accounting Department located on the 5th floor at 4545 City Avenue at 8:45 a.m.

You will be entitled to all benefits outlined in the attached copy of *A Guide for New Employees*. Your hourly wage will be $16.00.

Our offer of employment is contingent upon your ability to verify that you are lawfully allowed to work in the United States as well as our receipt of satisfactory reference and background checks.

Please accept my personal welcome and well wishes for success in your new position. Welcome to AJA, Inc.

Sincerely,

Pat Ryan

Pat Ryan
Manager of Recruiting

Attachment

My Career Journal

Name three compensation elements that are most important to you.

_____

_____

_____

Name three elements of a job that are important to you but are not part of compensation, such as culture, location, work environment, social responsibility of the company, etc.

_____

_____

_____

Thinking about your future job, what is the most important element to you about your job? About the company for which you will work? About the culture of the company?

_____

_____

_____

Notes to Myself

Notes to **Myself**

Toolkit

Table of Contents

Getting Started—Creating Your Action Plan and Timeline

Every successful marketing campaign starts with a plan. Now it's time to create your work plan. Your work plan will be your road map. And it will be a tool to help you pace your career planning and work search so that you don't feel as if you are rushing to get an internship or full-time job at the last minute.

The Best Time to Conduct Your Job Search

When is the best time to start your career planning and work search? It's never too early. **The 5 Steps to Real Success** is a process that is iterative. That means that you can go through the steps many times. Or you may want to revisit one or two of the steps as you progress through your academic career. The earlier you do your career planning, the better prepared you will be when you want to apply for an internship or a full-time job.

When are companies hiring? It depends. In some areas, such as accounting and finance, internships and full-time jobs are usually filled in the fall with starting dates in the spring. Generally, this is also true for large companies that have structured internships or training programs. However, advertising agencies, PR agencies, event planning companies, and other professional services providers are usually hiring all year because their staffing needs depend on their acquisition of new clients.

Keep in mind that there is even more competition for internships and full-time jobs at the end of the school year. You want to get your cover letter and résumé out early to avoid getting lost in the crowd.

General Time Line and Action Plan

The best way to get something done is to put your plan on paper. Now that you have identified some areas that you are interested in pursuing, it's time to create your work plan.

Following is a general time line for **The 5 Steps to Real Success**. This time line is designed to complete the steps in a time frame as short as a semester or as long as six months. In the blank Action Plan and Time Line on the next page, you will be able to create your own Action Plan and Time Line and adjust the time frames so they work for your schedule.

General Time Line—The 5 Steps to Real Success

Step	Approximate Time to Complete	Notes
Step 1—Choosing Your Path • Read Chapters 1–3. • Complete activities in Chapters 1–3.	3 weeks	It's best to complete this step as soon as possible so you can begin thinking and gathering information to choose your path. You may want to revisit these chapters later in your academic career and reevaluate or refine your path.
Step 2—Researching the Market • Read Chapters 4–7. • Complete activities in Chapters 4–7.	4–6 weeks	Do extensive research on the market, your target industries, and target companies. You will use this research in Step 4—Communicating Your Value Proposition.
Step 3—Creating Your Value Proposition • Read Chapters 8–11. • Complete activities in Chapters 8–11.	4–6 weeks	This is where you actually start crafting Brand You. The activities will help you create the framework for your résumé and cover letter.
Step 4—Communicating Your Value Proposition • Read Chapters 12–14. • Complete activities in Chapters 12–14. • Create your résumé. • Write at least one cover letter directed to your target audience. • Send out your cover letter and résumé using as many media as possible.	3–6 weeks	This is the step where Brand You comes alive for your "customers"—prospective employers. You will want to use every method to get your cover letter and résumé to as many people as possible in your target audience. "Advertise" as much as possible and let prospective employers know about you.
Step 5—Delivering Your Value Proposition • Read Chapters 15–16. • Complete activities in Chapters 15–16. • Reread Chapter 15 prior to each interview.	2–8 weeks	This is your opportunity to impress your prospective employer and learn if the company and position is what you want. Don't just grab the first job that's offered. If you get out enough cover letters and résumés, you will have plenty of job offers. Be sure you evaluate your offers completely and ask the right questions.

Creating Your Personal Action Plan and Time Line

It's time for you to create your own work plan, including your action plan and time line. You may adjust it based on changes in your schedule, but it's best to create your work plan and revise it as needed.

Organization is key for your work search. Keep your work plan easily accessible so you can stay on track. You may want to set up task reminders so you don't lose track of the steps you want to complete by your due dates.

*Instructions: Fill in your Estimated Start Dates and Estimated Completion Dates for each of **The 5 Steps to Real Success** based on your schedule. Stay organized and review this work plan weekly. Update your Actual Start Dates and Actual Completion Dates so you can stay on your schedule.*

My Work Plan and Time Line

Date of Work Plan _____

Action Plan	Estimated Start Date	Estimated Completion Date	Actual Start Date	Actual Completion Date	Notes
Step 1—Choosing Your Path					
• Read Chapters 1–3.	_____	_____	_____	_____	_____
• Complete activities in Chapters 1–3.	_____	_____	_____	_____	_____
Step 2—Researching the Market					
• Read Chapters 4–7.	_____	_____	_____	_____	_____
• Complete activities in Chapters 4–7.	_____	_____	_____	_____	_____
Step 3—Creating Your Value Proposition					
• Read Chapters 8–11.	_____	_____	_____	_____	_____
• Complete activities in Chapters 8–11.	_____	_____	_____	_____	_____
• Create your résumé.	_____	_____	_____	_____	_____
• Write at least three versions of your cover letter directed at different target audiences.	_____	_____	_____	_____	_____

Continued on the next page...

My Work Plan and Time Line

Date of Work Plan _____

Action Plan	Estimated Start Date	Estimated Completion Date	Actual Start Date	Actual Completion Date	Notes
Step 4—Communicating Your Value Proposition					
• Read Chapters 12–14.	_____	_____	_____	_____	
• Complete activities in Chapters 12–14.	_____	_____	_____	_____	
• **Online.** Complete a list of target Web sites including job boards, professional organizations, and at least 25 companies.	_____	_____	_____	_____	
• **Online.** Set up e-mail alerts on job boards, professional organizations, and target company Web sites.	_____	_____	_____	_____	
• **Online.** Review existing personal social networking pages to ensure all content is appropriate.	_____	_____	_____	_____	
• **Online.** Join professional social networking Web sites.	_____	_____	_____	_____	
• **Online.** Create professional Web site including résumé and work samples.	_____	_____	_____	_____	
• **Direct Mail.** Conduct research on target companies to identify names, titles, and addresses of people in companies to whom you want to send your cover letter and résumé. Create your mailing lists in Microsoft Word or Excel.					
• **Direct Mail.** Purchase mailing supplies.	_____	_____	_____	_____	

Continued on the next page...

My Work Plan and Time Line

Date of Work Plan _____

Action Plan	Estimated Start Date	Estimated Completion Date	Actual Start Date	Actual Completion Date	Notes
• **Direct Mail.** Complete mail merge and mail letters.	_____	_____	_____	_____	_____
• **Career Fairs.** Research dates and locations of upcoming Career Fairs.	_____	_____			
• **Career Fairs.** Complete a Career Fair Action Plan (Activity 12.4) for each fair.	_____	_____	_____	_____	_____
• **Follow-up.** Add follow-up columns to mailing lists. Set dates for follow-up.	_____	_____	_____	_____	_____
• **Follow-up.** Monitor follow-up dates daily and call, write, or e-mail as appropriate.	_____	_____	_____	_____	_____
Step 5—Delivering Your Value Proposition					
• Read Chapters 15 and 16.	_____	_____	_____	_____	_____
• Complete activities in Chapters 15 and 16 (as appropriate).	_____	_____	_____	_____	_____
• Reread Chapters 15 and 16 prior to each interview.	_____	_____	_____	_____	_____
• Enjoy your new job!	_____	_____	_____	_____	_____

Recommended Web Sites

Review these Web sites and descriptions. Visit those that you think will help you target your job search. Use this list as a reference when you complete Activity 12.1. Don't forget to include Web sites for local professional organizations (such as the local advertising club) and local job boards.

Web Site Type	URL	Description
Career Planning	www.rileyguide.com	Comprehensive career site with links for researching careers and jobs in all disciplines and international jobs
Career Planning	www.bls.gov/OCO	*Occupational Outlook Handbook* from the U.S. Department of Labor
Career Planning	www.salary.com	Salaries for varies jobs; compares salaries in various cities; includes links to www.careerbuilder.com
Career Planning, Job Board, and More	Usually listed on your school's Web site	Your campus career center, library, and alumni organization are excellent resources
Career Planning and Job Board	www.experience.com	Articles, tips, blogs with career planning insights including section for internships; includes job board
Career Planning and Job Board	www.collegegrad.com	Career information geared to college students; includes job board
Career Planning and Job Board	www.wetfeet.com	Career planning information and job board; includes job board
Career Planning and Job Board	www.career-advice.monster.com/	Career planning and job search articles; also includes one of the largest job boards on the Internet, www.monster.com
Career Planning and Job Board	www.job-hunt.org	Career planning information, links to other Web sites, and job board
Career Planning and Job Board	www.careerbuilder.com	Career planning articles and one of the largest job boards on the Internet
Career Planning and Job Board	www.jobweb.com	Web site of the National Association of Colleges and Employers; career planning articles and tips; links to college career center Web sites
Career Planning and Job Board	www.black-collegian.com	Career information, news, and job board with a focus on African Americans
Career Planning and Job Board	www.hispanicbusiness.com	Information about Hispanic businesses with link to www.hirediversity.com job board
Career Planning and Job Board	www.vault.com	Information and articles on career planning, salaries, and more, including internships; includes job board
Job Board	www.aftercollege.com	Job board focused on internships and entry-level jobs

Continued on the next page...

Web Site Type	URL	Description
Job Board	www.craigslist.com	One of the largest job boards on the Internet
Job Board	www.hotjobs.yahoo.com	Large job board; also includes articles on conducting a job search
Job Board	www.nationjob.com	Large job board for jobs of all kinds
Job Board	www.monstertrak.com	Large job board with focus on internships and entry-level jobs
Job Search Engine	www.indeed.com	An aggregator of job listings; search by keyword and location
Job Search Engine	www.internshipprograms.com	Search engine for internships
Job Search Engine	www.internweb.com	Search engine for internships
Professional Networking	www.linkedin.com	Largest professional social network on the Internet; search for jobs using the "Jobs" link at the top of the page
Professional Networking	www.ryze.com	Professional social network
Professional Networking	www.jobster.com	Professional social network
Professional Networking	www.ziggs.com	Professional social network
Professional Association Job Board	www.associationjobboards.com	Links to Web sites of professional associations and job boards
Accounting and Finance	www.afponline.org	Web site for Association for Financial Professionals; includes job board
Accounting and Finance	www.fpanet.org	Web site for the Financial Planning Association; includes job board
Accounting and Finance	www.accountingjobstoday.com	Job board specializing in accounting jobs
Accounting and Finance	www.garp.com	Web site for Global Association of Risk Professionals; includes job board
Accounting and Finance	www.aicpa.org	Web site of the American Institute of Certified Public Accountants; includes job board
Accounting and Finance	www.theiia.org	Web site for the Institute of Internal Auditors; includes job board
Accounting and Finance	www.jobsinthemoney.com	Job board specializing in accounting and finance jobs
Accounting and Finance	www.accounting.com	Job board specializing in accounting jobs
Accounting and Finance	www.bankjobs.com	Job board specializing in accounting and finance jobs
Advertising	www.aaaa.org	Web site of the American Association of Advertising Agencies; includes job board
Advertising	www.aaf.org	Web site of the American Advertising Federation; includes a job board
Advertising	www.redbooks.com	Directory of advertising agencies and key management members

Continued on the next page...

Web Site Type	URL	Description
Advertising	www.adage.com/talentworks	Career advice and job board of *Advertising Age* magazine
Entrepreneur	www.inc.com	Web site of *Inc.* magazine; information, articles, and resources for entrepreneurs
Entrepreneur	www.entrepreneur.com	Web site of *Entrepreneur* magazine with business ideas, opportunities, tools, and services for entrepreneurs
Entrepreneur	www.score.org	Web site for SCORE, Counselors to America's Small Businesses and partner with Small Business Association (SBA); free business counseling available
Event Planning	www.bizbash.com	Event planning organization; excellent free magazine
Freelance/Independent Contractor	www.ifreelance.com	Job board for freelancer service providers and open projects
Freelance/Independent Contractor	www.sologig.com	Consulting, contract, temporary, or freelance opportunities
International	www.intljobs.org	Job board for international jobs
International	www.ihipo.com	Social network based in Singapore; includes job board
International	www.monster.com/geo/siteselection	International portion of Monster.com; search jobs by country
Internet Marketing	www.sempo.org	Web site of Search Engine Marketing Professional Organization; includes job board
Internet Marketing	www.marketingsherpa.com	Online marketing articles and job board
Internet Marketing	www.shop.org	Web site of the National Retail Federation; includes job board
Internet Marketing	www.webanalytics-association.org	Web site of the Web Analytics Association; includes job board
Internet Marketing	www.iab.net	Web site of the Internet Advertising Bureau focused on the continued growth of interactive advertising
Management	www.amanet.org	Web site of the American Management Association; includes job board
Management	www.shrm.org	Web site of Society for Human Resource Management; includes job board
Marketing	www.the-dma.org	Web site of the Direct Marketing Association; includes a job board
Marketing	www.fmi.org	Web site of the Food Marketing Institute
Marketing	www.stylecareers.com	Job board for fashion, apparel, and retail jobs
Marketing	www.marketingjobs.com	Job board for jobs in marketing
Marketing	www.marketinghire.com	Job board for jobs in marketing
Marketing	www.talentzoo.com	Job board for jobs in marketing, advertising, and PR

Continued on the next page...

Web Site Type	URL	Description
Marketing Research	www.mra-net.org	Web site of the Marketing Research Association
Public Relations	www.prsa.org	Web site of the Public Relations Society of America; includes job board
Public Relations	www.prssa.org	Public Relations Student Society of America; includes job board
Public Relations and Communications	www.iabc.com	Web site of the International Association of Business Communicators; includes job board
Sales and Marketing	www.smei.org	Web site of Sales and Marketing Executives International; includes job board

Your Digital Brand: Do's and Don'ts of Online Job Searching and Social Networking

Whether you are submitting your cover letter and résumé online, via e-mail, or posting your professional profile or video résumé to a professional social network Web site, there are mistakes that could cost you the opportunity for an interview. It's a good idea to know the proper online etiquette for the professional world. Your brand is available to prospective employers 24/7.

Here Are the Practices You Should DO:

- **DO:** Spell check and proof every communication you send or post. That includes cover letter, résumé, professional profile, and every e-mail you send. One typo or grammatical error can eliminate you from consideration for an interview. Ask someone (a professor, a parent, or someone in the business world) to proof your résumé and cover letter before you post them or send them out.

- **DO:** Submit your cover letter and résumé in PDF format when applying for jobs through an online job board because it will maintain the formatting. Go to **www.acrobat.com**, click on Create PDF, and follow the prompts. Review the PDF documents to be sure page breaks are correct.

- **DO:** Also save a copy of your cover letter and résumé in Microsoft Word (PC or Mac) because most companies require this format. If you are using Word 2007, save the documents as Word 97–2003 documents so all recipients can open them. If you are using Pages, save your documents as PDF files to ensure that those who are using a PC can open them. Also save a copy of your cover letter and résumé as a plain text file using Microsoft Word (File, Save As, choose Plain Text in the drop-down menu). Be sure to fix any line breaks or odd characters before you save it. If a job board does not accept a PDF, submit your résumé as a plain text document. This will make it easier for employers to read.

- **DO:** Review the privacy policy of job boards and Web sites before you post your résumé. Based on the privacy policy, you may want to consider applying for specific jobs rather than posting your résumé to minimize your exposure for identity theft and getting unwanted e-mail solicitations.

- **DO:** Identify keywords to search for jobs on job boards and other Web site job listings. The right keywords increase your chances of seeing relevant jobs.

- **DO:** Incorporate your keywords into your cover letter and résumé so that when companies put your information into their databases, you increase your chances of your résumé being included in the search results. Need help identifying keywords? Stop by the library and get some ideas from the librarian or stop by the campus career center and ask for ideas.

- **DO:** Include the job code from the Web posting in the subject line of the e-mail when applying for a job. Be sure to also mention the job title for which you are applying in your cover letter.

- **DO:** Join professional social networks such as **www.linkedin.com** and create a profile, start a professional network, and ask for introductions to other people in your target industry, and search for jobs.

- **DO:** Create a professional Web site including your résumé and samples of your work. Include writing samples, projects, papers and presentations from your internships, volunteer work or major classes, and other business-related content. Be sure this is all your work and does not violate any copyright or privacy issues. This Web site serves as your online branding statement. You should limit the amount of personal information (such as address and phone number) to minimize the risk of identity theft.

- **DO:** Search your name on all major search engines such as Google, Yahoo!, Bing, and Ask. The search results are those that your prospective employers will see. Be sure all pages are consistent with your brand message.

- **DO:** Set up a Google News alert, **www.google.com/alert** for all target companies and any companies with whom you may be interviewing. You will get an e-mail about any breaking news as it happens so you will be informed about company news for an interview.

- **DO:** Send thank-you notes within 24 hours to everyone with whom you interview. An e-mail thank-you is very acceptable; a handwritten note is especially effective.

Here Are the Practices That Are DON'Ts:

- **DON'T**: Include pictures, videos, blogs, or other entries on your social networking pages or other Web sites that are not appropriate for a prospective employer to see. You are marketing your personal brand 24/7, so edit your pages accordingly. (That means removing the spring break video from YouTube!)

- **DON'T**: Use abbreviations or text messaging language in business communications, even if you know the person with whom you are communicating. Keep your communications professional.

- **DON'T**: Send your cover letter and résumé unsolicited to your target companies via e-mail. Because the addressee doesn't know you, your résumé will most likely be deleted or treated as spam. Also, don't use services to e-mail blast your résumé to companies or recruiters. Direct mail is a more effective way to contact people in companies that are on your target list. And, your paper cover letter and résumé will stand out in the sea of daily e-mails.

- **DON'T**: Save documents such as your résumé and cover letter with file names other than your name and type of document. For example, a file name for a résumé such as "official version" is not appropriate to submit to a job posting. Make it easy for a prospective employer and reflect professionalism by saving your résumé and cover letter documents with file names such as "Michael Boyers résumé" and "Michael Boyers cover letter."

- **DON'T**: Use a personal e-mail address that isn't professional for business communications. If your current personal e-mail address is something like **partygirl@gmail.com**, set up a new e-mail account with Gmail, Hotmail, or other Internet service provider. Use the new e-mail address or your college or university e-mail address on your résumé. Also, if you have graduated, it's a good idea to use your personal e-mail address rather than your school e-mail address (it demonstrates that you have made the transition to the real world).

- **DON'T**: Use a video résumé just because it is a novel use of technology. A video résumé should be used only to supplement a traditional résumé and cover letter. Only use one if you are extremely comfortable in front of the camera and you can produce the video professionally. Also, keep in mind that some companies won't use video résumés due to potential discrimination issues (e.g., hiring someone based on appearance rather than skills).

- **DON'T:** Leave electronic devices turned on during an interview. Turn off your cell phone or PDA (don't just put it on vibrate) and put it out of sight before you go into the building for the interview. Leave your iPhone, iPod, iPad, Kindle, PSP, or any other electronic devices at home. Demonstrate that the interview is the most important thing to you by not having any disruptions.

- **DON'T:** Forget that the online world meets the real world. Use courtesy, professionalism, and a personal touch in every communication.

Networking Made Easy— 10 Tips You Should Know

Networking can be daunting for college students as well as seasoned professionals. Here are 10 tips that can make networking less overwhelming and more productive.

Networking Tip #1—Make a networking list. It might sound simple, but a list can really help you get focused. Include all of your friends, your family, your family's friends, your friend's family, your mechanic, hair stylist, personal trainer, people with whom you volunteer, friends at school, friends at home, everyone with whom you come in contact. The list will help you to contact everyone you know, not just those that are top of mind.

Networking Tip #2—Join a professional organization. The best way to get to know people in the industry in which you want to get a job is to join a professional organization such as Sales and Marketing Executives International, American Accounting Association, 4As, AIGA, or others that are relevant to the industry. There are on-campus organizations as well as local professional organizations that can increase your network significantly. Don't wait until you're a senior . . . it's never too early to join. **The secret to making your membership in a professional organization work is to get involved.** When you join a committee or take on a leadership role in the organization, it goes a long way on your résumé. Employers look for activities in which you got involved, made a contribution, and generated results. When you join a professional organization and get involved in it, you will find that professionals will be your best advocates and will actually help you get the job you want.

Networking Tip #3—Get business cards. The exchange of business cards at a professional networking event or a casual chance meeting is critical so that someone can contact you and you can follow-up. Don't wait until you get a job to get business cards. You can have your own business cards made inexpensively online or at any office supply retailer. Having a business card signals that you are a professional. In addition, it makes it easier for you to ask for someone's business card when you offer yours in exchange. Choose a simple, conservative business card design that provides your name, your specialty (if you have one), and your contact information. Avoid flashy colors and complicated designs and keep it simple. You'll impress professionals in any field with the fact that you took the time and effort to have a business card made.

Networking Tip #4—Be ready with your elevator pitch. You never know when you're going to meet someone who might be able to help you get the internship or job you want. Whether you're attending a networking event or meeting someone unexpectedly, it's important to be prepared with your elevator pitch (your value proposition). Rehearse your elevator pitch out loud several times so that it becomes natural to say in any situation.

Networking Tip #5—Ask for informational interviews. The best way to learn about a profession is to talk to people who are in it. Informational interviews can be as simple as having coffee with someone to learn about how he or she got into the profession and what he or she recommends you do to get into it. Find people who do what you want to do and then ask them for informational interviews. You'll learn a lot and start great relationships.

Networking Tip #6—Keep in touch regularly. Networking isn't about collecting business cards, it's about developing relationships. Most people connect at networking events or other gatherings, but then don't follow-up. If you want networking to work for you, establish relationships and keep in touch regularly. You should contact people in your network on average every 30 days. A good way to keep in touch is to send a note including a relevant article or video. Even if the person doesn't respond, keep in touch. It's the best way to stand out and build a lasting relationship.

Networking Tip #7 —Create a LinkedIn.com profile. Professional social networking starts with a comprehensive profile that highlights your strengths and accomplishments. You have the opportunity to have your profile viewed by thousands of professionals, so use it to your advantage. Start with a professional photo of yourself. **Don't use a picture taken at a social event or with your friends.** While that is appropriate for Facebook, your picture on LinkedIn.com should reflect your professional brand; a simple headshot (a picture of you from the shoulders up) is perfect. **Complete the Summary, Specialties, and Experience portions of your profile.** Connect in-person networking with social networking by asking people to join your LinkedIn.com network including your friends and everyone on your networking list. Also, connect with people you meet such as at networking events, meetings, or guest speakers in your classes. **Make it easy for others to view your LinkedIn.com profile by adding your LinkedIn.com URL to the signature of your e-mails.**

Networking Tip #8—Leverage your network's network on LinkedIn.com The power of LinkedIn.com is the fact that you have access to the network of everyone in your network. Review the networks of your connections to see if anyone works at a company that is on your target company list. You can search for connections by using the drop-down search box and choosing "Companies"; enter the name of a company and you will see who in your network or your network's network works at that company. You can connect directly with that person and ask for an introduction to the hiring manager.

Networking Tip #9—Ask for recommendations on LinkedIn.com LinkedIn.com includes a section for recommendations. Ask your professors, supervisors, leaders, and other people who can speak on your behalf to write a recommendation on LinkedIn.com. (After you create your profile, go to the "Profile" button at the top of the page and click on "Recommendations," and then click on the link for "Request Recommendations.")

Networking Tip #10 —Help others whenever possible. Networking is about giving, especially when you don't need something in return. When you establish the fact that you are willing to go out of your way to help people, people will return the favor when you need help. You might think that you can't help any professionals right now, but you would be surprised. Consider volunteering, introducing people, and even helping with social networking skills. Everyone needs something, and you just might have the skills or access to help someone else. Going the extra mile makes networking work.

Internships 101: What You Should Know About Internships

Why an Internship?

One word says it all—experience.

If you have an internship on your résumé, you have an advantage over students who don't have internships. An internship allows you to stand out, be different, offer value, get experience, impress a prospective employer, add to your personal network, and get the job you want. Don't underestimate the power of an internship on your résumé.

Where Is the Best Place to Look for an Internship?

Follow **The 5 Steps to Real Success** in *Brand You*. The process is the same for internships and full-time jobs. Chapter 4—Career Information and Research and Recommended Web Sites in the *Brand You* Toolkit are excellent sources to help you conduct research and identify internship opportunities.

When Is the Best Time to Look for an Internship?

Timing depends on the industry and company. Fall is the best time to apply for spring and summer internships at companies that have structured internship programs. Many company Web sites list cutoff dates for internship applications. For some industries, including many advertising agencies, public relations agencies, interactive marketing agencies, and other professional services providers, internships are usually created based on need, and timing depends on when new clients come onboard. These companies hire all year round. Read the business journals and trade publications to see who recently won a new account. Chances are they will be looking to ramp up fast.

The bottom line is it's never too early and it's never a bad time to start investigating and applying for internships.

Paid versus Unpaid Internship—Which Is Better?

You might think the obvious answer is that a paid internship is better than an unpaid internship. But that's not always the case. What's important is to get experience in the industry you think you want to pursue. In some industries, an internship is a requirement in order to be considered for a full-time job. If you can find a paid internship that will give you the experience you want, take it. But don't be short-sighted when you search for an internship. If you can afford to give up the income, choose your internship based on what experience you will get. You'll find it will pay you back when you look for a full-time job.

Test Drive Your Career Choice

An internship is great experience and it can lead to a full-time job in the same company or industry. But an internship is also a great way to find out what you DON'T want to do. You may not like your internship. You may want to change your career path as a result of an internship. That's great news because you can focus your efforts on another industry or specialty that you might like better. And, you still get the benefit of having experience on your résumé. So go ahead, test drive your career choice with an internship.

An Internship Is What You Make It

Just because you get an internship doesn't mean you've arrived. An internship can include a lot of repetitive and sometimes boring tasks. And, it also can include stimulating and thought-provoking assignments including exposure to senior management and clients, challenging projects, inclusion in major meetings, and more.

When you land an internship, get involved. Sometimes managers are too busy to spend the time to train interns. If that's the case, train yourself. Ask questions of co-workers, read as much information as you can, learn the company systems, get involved in anything that's going on in your department, volunteer to work on projects even if they are boring, work overtime when needed, walk through the office with your head high and introduce yourself to anyone you pass; make people remember you. Think of your internship as a 10-week job interview. Just like an interview, an internship is what you make it.

Sample Cover Letters and Résumés

Sample Cover Letter for Jessica Freeman

Jessica Freeman
8724 Ninth Avenue
Oak Park, IL 60301

April 17, 2010

Ms. Janice Phillips
Director of Marketing
Advance Insurance Group
421 Corporate Drive; Suite 300
Chicago, IL 60606

Dear Ms. Phillips:

Can Advance Insurance benefit from an innovative and hard-working Marketing Specialist?

I am currently a senior at City State University and will be graduating in May with a Bachelor of Science degree in Marketing. I believe my educational achievements coupled with my intellectual curiosity and personal energy can bring a fresh perspective to your Marketing Department. Some highlights about my background are as follows:

- **Marketing Experience** – As a Marketing Intern at The Sage Group, I was a member of the client team that repositioned Noah's Dairy Products. The initiative included developing a new positioning statement, media strategy, and creative strategy. I am also fluent with Internet search tools including Google Ad Words, Blue Hornet e-mail tool, and Omniture Web analytics tool.

- **Academic Excellence** – I have been named to the Dean's List for the past 2 years. In addition, I am a recipient of the 2010 Loyola Scholarship Award, which recognizes outstanding academic performance and community service.

- **Community Service** – I am the Marketing Coordinator of Coats for Kids, a nonprofit organization that provides coats to elementary schools. This year, we donated a record $25,000 worth of new coats to over 500 children in the Chicago metropolitan area.

I would like the opportunity to show you some samples of my work, which include marketing strategy, market research, sales promotion, and advertising. I'll call you the week of April 26 so we can set up a meeting time that is convenient for you. You can reach me at 312-555-1212 or jfreeman123@gmail.com. I look forward to discussing this marketing opportunity.

Sincerely,

Jessica Freeman

Jessica Freeman

Attachment

Sample Résumé for Jessica Freeman

Jessica Freeman

8724 Ninth Avenue
Oak Park, IL 60301

Phone: 312-555-1212 E-mail: jfreeman123@gmail.com

www.jessicafreeman.com
www.linkedin.com/in/jessicafreeman

Objective	To obtain a position as a copywriter.
Education	**City State University,** Chicago, IL
	Bachelor of Science, Marketing 2010
Scholarships and Awards	Dean's List 2009, 2010
	2010 Loyola Scholarship Award

Marketing Experience

The Sage Group, Chicago, IL January–May 2010

Intern, Client Services

- Collaborated with the client services team that worked on the repositioning of Noah's Dairy Products.
- Created and sent weekly customer e-mails to 300,000 customers.
- Maintained customer e-mail segmentation lists using Blue Hornet e-mail tool.
- Monitored paid search budget and ROI by key word in Google Ad Words; identified 50 new key words that generated an additional 8% in revenue.
- Prepared weekly and monthly paid search reports that were used by the senior management team using Omniture web analytics tool.
- Assisted in analysis of consumer purchase patterns and report that was presented to the client.
- Participated in client and vendor meetings.
- Maintained client conference reports.

Work Experience

The Federal Reserve Bank, Chicago, IL Summer 2008–9

Currency Sorter

- Reviewed $150,000 of dollar bills daily with 100% accuracy; team leader of the student section.

Macy's, Chicago, IL Summer 2007

Sales Associate

- Served customers and resolved customer service issues in the Junior Department; completed Selling Stars sales training.

Community Service

Coats for Kids – Marketing Coordinator

- Raised contributions for $25,000 in new coats for 500 children.

Alpha Phil Sorority – Secretary

- Raised $3,000 for American Heart Association.

Skills

Microsoft Word, PowerPoint, Excel, Outlook, Adobe Acrobat, Google Ad Words, Blue Hornet E-mail Tool, Omniture Web Analytics Tool

Sample Cover Letter for Jonathan Vitale

Jonathan Vitale
541 North Elm Street
Dayton, OH 12345

April 18, 2011

Mr. Michael Woods
Account Director
Ludlow Interactive Advertising
4040 Century Boulevard; Suite 1501
Boston, MA 03456

Dear Mr. Woods:

Congratulations on landing the Domino's Pizza account. I'm sure it's an exciting time at the agency. If you are looking for a motivated individual with a passion for the Internet on your team, I am that person.

I am currently a junior at Brookstone College pursuing a major in Marketing with a focus in Interactive Marketing. I'd like to bring my energy and Internet savvy to Ludlow Interactive Advertising for a summer internship position on one of your client service teams. Some highlights of my background are as follows:

- **Marketing Trade Group Involvement** – I have gained exposure to the interactive advertising industry as a member of the local chapter of the American Marketing Association and a student member of the Boston Advertising Club.

- **Leadership Experience** – As the Student Chairperson of the Event Committee for the Saint Katherine's Youth Group, I have organized over 8 fund-raising events. As a result of the increased fund-raising, our group was able to provide financial assistance and personal support to over 300 local families in need.

- **Passion for the Internet** – I thrive on the fact that the Internet is continuously evolving and providing new and untapped opportunities for brands. I want to play a role in building brands online. As an experienced Internet and technology user, I have the experience and insight to understand how current interactive marketing works and ideas as to how it might work even better.

With Domino's as a new client, you need only the best people to support the brand. I am focused and willing to work hard in order to learn the business. I would like the opportunity to show you some examples of my work. I can be reached at 615-333-5555 or via e-mail at jvitale@brookstonecollege.edu. I will touch base the week of April 25 to see what day will be most convenient for you. I look forward to discussing your new challenges.

Sincerely,

Jonathan Vitale

Jonathan Vitale

Attachment

Sample Résumé for Jonathan Vitale

Jonathan Vitale
541 North Elm Street
Dayton, OH 12345
615-333-5555 jvitale@brookstonecollege.edu
www.jonathanvitale.com
www.linkedin.com/in/jonathanvitale

Objective

To obtain an internship position at a digital advertising agency.

Education

Brookstone College, Boston, MA
Bachelor of Science in Marketing, expected May 2012

Marketing Experience

American Marketing Association, Boston, MA   2010 to Present
Student Member
- Created a social networking strategy to increase student membership of the American Marketing Association on campus.
- Organized five student events sponsored by the American Marketing Association; increased student attendance by 22% compared to last year.
- Designed and implemented an ongoing student e-mail campaign; increased e-mail database by 12%.
- Developed and launched Facebook and Twitter pages for the student American Marketing Association.
- Increased student membership by 17%.

Boston Advertising Club, Boston, MA   2010 to Present
Student Member
- Wrote a weekly blog for the Boston Advertising Club Web site.
- Researched and contributed to regular articles in the Boston Advertising Club bi-monthly magazine.
- Updated the Boston Advertising Club Web site regularly with events, news, and job postings.
- Maintained member e-mail list.
- Sent out monthly member e-mail newsletters.
- Participated in the annual ADDY Awards event.

Work Experience

Janis Construction Company, Dayton, OH   Summer 2008–9
Construction Worker
- Worked on new home construction sites; learned electrical skills.

Activities

Saint Katherine of Siena, Dayton, OH
Youth Group, Student Chairperson—Event Committee
- Organized eight fundraising events in 2008–2010.
- Raised money to support over 300 local families in need.

Dayton Run for the Cure, Dayton, OH
- Ran in 5K race and raised $800 in sponsorships.

Skills

Microsoft Word, PowerPoint, Excel, Mac Pages, Numbers, and Keynote.

Portfolios and Professional Web Sites

Portfolios

No matter what position you are seeking, a portfolio can impress your interviewer. If you are interviewing for a creative position such as copywriter or designer, you'll need a portfolio. If you are interviewing for any other position in marketing, advertising, politics, education, accounting, IS, or even public service, samples of your work can go a long way on an interview.

Here are some tips for an effective portfolio:

- Use a professional binder or portfolio (most art supply stores have a good selection at reasonable prices)
- Include three to six samples of your best work from:
  - Class projects
  - Internship projects
  - Volunteer projects
  - Campus activities
  - Political campaigns
  - Blogs or other social networking for a cause or project
  - Any other work that demonstrates your skills
- Include only clean samples of your work (no grades or comments)
- Samples should not be shopworn (request a clean copy from your employer for any printed materials)

Bring your portfolio with you on every interview and let your interviewer know that you have some samples of your work to show him or her. Reviewing your work samples on an interview makes you stand out and makes you more memorable. It's a good idea to practice how you will show your work samples on an interview so that you can cover the highlights quickly and concisely.

Professional Web Sites

In addition to bringing samples of your work to an interview, you can make your personal brand story available to prospective employers 24/7 by creating a professional Web site to showcase samples of your work.

Your professional Web site should include some of the same elements that you would include in your portfolio. Here are some things to consider for your professional Web site:

- Résumé
- Work samples
- Links to online work samples
- Link to your blog (if appropriate for professional purposes)
- Link to video résumé (only if you are very comfortable in front of the camera)
- Link to your LinkedIn.com profile

A Web site doesn't need to be complex. You can build a Web site using iWeb on a Mac or visit www.GoDaddy.com for easy-to-use templates and hosting.

You can also include work samples as part of your LinkedIn.com profile. Choose "Profile" on the top navigation bar, then choose "Edit Profile," and then "Add Applications." You can choose from several different applications such as Twitter, WordPress, SlideShare, and several others.

Include your Web site URL and LinkedIn.com URL on your résumé and as part of your signature on your e-mails. That way, professionals will be able to view your work at any time of the day.

> Note: Hear Karen Carroll, Executive Recruiter at Blue Plate Minds, talk about the value of portfolios and professional Web sites at www.mypearsonmarketinglab.com.

Interview Checklist: Be Ready for Every Interview

Review this list before each interview. If you follow these steps, you'll increase your chances of getting the job offer you want!

Before the Interview

- Research the company so you can relate your skills and experience to its products or services. Review the company Web site, go to any stores or retail locations, and use their product or service, if possible. Read articles about the company by searching at **www.google.com**, **www.hoovers.com**, **www.bizjournals.com**, or the local newspaper Web site.

- Set up a Google News alert at **www.google.com/alert** so you can get any breaking news about the company. Also, news can be important when you are doing your follow-up. It's a great way to let the interviewer know you are current about what's going on with the company. And, if it's news about a new client, new office, or increased sales or earnings, you can use that as a reason to follow-up.

- Ask for a job description, if available.

- Analyze the job description and the information you gathered about the company. If you were doing the hiring, what skills, attitudes, and characteristics would you be looking for?

- Complete a NAB (Need, Action, Benefit) worksheet for the position. Develop memorable stories that describe your accomplishments and the benefits.

- Practice your answers to questions out loud. If you've ever given a speech, you know there can be a big difference between what your brain thinks and what your mouth says.

- Develop questions you will ask. Bring them with you in a professional folder or portfolio.

- Print at least three extra copies of your résumé on 24-lb. paper and put them in your folder or portfolio. Even though the interviewer has a copy, it might not be handy at the time of the interview. Also, you may be asked to meet someone who was not originally on the interview schedule. It's always best to be prepared.

- Look up directions to the location of the interview. If possible, do a dry run to be sure of the transportation time including parking, public transit, and so on. Be sure you know exactly which building and floor you will be visiting, as well as the name of the person with whom you are meeting.

- Dress professionally. You only have one chance to make a good first impression. If the workplace is casual, dress one step above. It's best to wear business attire. Don't display body piercings or tattoos.

- Plan to arrive early. This allows you time to relax (try deep breathing) and to review the information you want to emphasize. Stop in the restroom and do one last check to be sure you look your best. Have a mint and smile!

During the Interview

- Greet the interviewer with a smile and a firm handshake.

- Make eye contact and smile. This will actually help you relax and enjoy the interview.

- Express a positive attitude and show enthusiasm in your responses.

- Consider the interview a 50/50 exchange—evaluate how well the company fits you.

- Ask good questions.

- Ask about the next steps in the process.

- Ask for the job!

After the Interview

- Send a thank-you note to each person with whom you interviewed within 24 hours. Refer to something specific that you discussed in the interview so the person can connect your note with you. Reiterate your interest in the job. See sample thank-you notes later in the *Brand You* **Toolkit.**

- Call the interviewer one week after the interview to check on progress. It shows your interest, and it's better to know where you stand than to keep wondering.

Letters of Recommendation and References

Letters of Recommendation

There's nothing more powerful than to have someone recommend you because of your skills, character, and work ethic. **When you do an outstanding job at work, in class, or in a volunteer organization or other activity, it's a good idea to ask your professor, supervisor, or leader to write a letter of recommendation.** This is a letter that you can show during an interview (you can include letters of recommendation in your portfolio and have extra copies to leave behind). Letters of recommendation are the traditional version of LinkedIn.com recommendations. It's appropriate to ask for either one. The best time to ask for a letter of recommendation or LinkedIn.com recommendation is at the time of your accomplishment. For example, when you complete an internship it's a good idea to ask your supervisor for a letter of recommendation. That's when your performance is fresh in his or her mind and it's easy for you to ask. Having three to four letters of recommendation is a good way to impress a prospective employer on an interview.

References

References are different than letters of recommendation. It's good to have letters of recommendation to demonstrate your experience during an interview. **However, employers also want to talk to references personally.**

Most employers will request professional references. These are people who can attest to your professional skills—employers, co-workers, professors, and colleagues. Some employers also ask for personal references—people who have known you personally, preferably for five years or more, and can vouch for your character. It's best to select professionally employed people to use as personal references. Don't use your relatives; everyone expects your mother to give you a glowing report.

Lukewarm references can be as damaging as negative ones. Be sure that yours are excellent by asking people if they feel comfortable allowing you to use them as a reference.

Here are the best practices to secure references:

- Call each person you want to use as a reference shortly before you begin your job or internship search. You should have at least three professional references.

- Provide each person on your reference list with a copy of your résumé so he or she can be fluent with the details of your background.

- Explain to each person on your reference list the types of positions for which you are applying.

- Send a handwritten thank-you note to each person on your reference list thanking him or her for speaking on your behalf.

- Keep each person up to date on your job search. These people are interested in your career progress, and it's a good reason to touch base even if you have no news.

- Let each person on your reference list know when you have accepted a position.

Do not include references in your résumé or cover letter. Also, do not include "References available upon request" on your résumé; it's understood that employers will check references. Employers will ask for references at the point of the interviewing process when they plan to contact your references. If you provide references too early in the process, it is only distracting.

Following is a suggested format in which to provide references when requested by a prospective employer.

Katherine Sullivan
5524 Wanewright Way
Columbus, OH 43578

234-444-5555

Professional References

Mr. Jamal Robertson
Marketing Director
ABC Advertising, Inc.
5700 Corporate Drive
Willow Grove, PA 19086
610-888-9076
jrobertson@abcadv.com

Mr. Robertson was my supervisor at ABC Advertising, Inc.

Ms. Ying Lee
Marketing Manager
Jessup + Jessup
1500 Market Street
Philadelphia, PA 19131
215-939-4444
ylee@jessup.com

Ms. Lee was my supervisor at Jessup + Jessup

Dr. Sean Sursky
Professor of Marketing
PA State University
5050 N. First Avenue
Philadelphia, PA 19876
610-873-9028
s.sursky@pa.state.edu

Dr. Sursky is my academic advisor and professor of Marketing 101 (which I am taking during the Fall, 2010 semester)

Sample Thank-You Notes

It's always a good idea to send a thank-you note after an interview, when someone provides a reference for you, or any time someone has helped you. A thank-you note makes you stand out and says a lot about you as a person.

Following are some sample thank-you notes for different situations. Keep in mind that these are samples; you should adapt them and put them into your own words.

Sample Thank-You Note to Interviewer

Dear Janice,

I wanted to say thank you for taking the time to meet with me today. I thoroughly enjoyed our conversation. I was especially excited to hear about the new initiative to reposition Advance Insurance Group. It sounds as if there is a lot of work and reward ahead.

My experience at the Sage Group working on repositioning brands sounds like a perfect fit for the Marketing Specialist position. Based on our meeting, I already have some ideas about how I can add value to your team.

Thank you again for your time and insight. I look forward to the next steps in the interview process.

Sincerely,
Jessica Freeman

Sample Thank-You Note to HR/Recruiter

Dear Jason,

I wanted to send you a note to thank you for arranging all the logistics for my interviews today. I realize that it's not easy to coordinate everyone's schedule, but you did it with ease and good humor.

My meetings with Janice Phillips, John Kisko, Lou Hernandez, and Ty Rowen were interesting and informative. I learned so much about the company and the plans for the future. And even though I didn't get a chance to meet you in person, I feel as if I already know you. You are an excellent ambassador for Advance Insurance Group and a true professional.

Thanks again.

Sincerely,
Jessica Freeman

Sample Thank-You Note to Someone Who Provides a Professional Reference

Dear Lee,

Thank you so much for agreeing to provide a reference for me.

I'm very excited about the potential of being offered the position of Marketing Specialist at Advance Insurance Group. After doing my research and going through the interview process, I believe I could bring a lot to the company. And I think it would be a great environment for me to get my first full-time job in marketing. I'll keep you posted on the outcome of the interview.

A copy of my current résumé is attached for your reference.

Thanks again. I really appreciate and value your support.

Sincerely,
Jessica Freeman

FAQs—Frequently Asked Questions about Career Planning and Work Search

If you think you are the only one who has questions about planning your future, your career, and getting a job, think again! Many of the same questions you are asking are the same ones other students are also asking. You will find the most frequently asked questions below along with the page number and chapter reference in *Brand You* where you can find the answers. The questions are organized to follow the flow of **The 5 Steps to Real Success**.

Step 1—Choosing Your Path

Q. **I don't even know what my major will be; shouldn't I wait until I choose my major before I use *Brand You*?**

A. It's never too early to start planning your future. *Brand You* can help you identify areas in which you have interest and skills. It can help you decide on your major and a direction for your future. It's never too early to start understanding the process of career planning. Read Chapters 1–3 in *Brand You* to see how **The 5 Steps to Real Success** can help you make some important life choices.

Q. **I'm only a sophomore. Do I really need to make a choice now about what I'm going to do after I graduate?**

A. You don't have to make a commitment now about what you are going to do in the future. But you do need to learn more about what is available, what is most interesting to you, and how you can go about getting an internship and ultimately the full-time job you want. Start with Chapter 1 of *Brand You* and see how planning your future now can help you later.

Q. **I'm an accounting major. I'm not going to look for a job in marketing, so why would I use *Brand You*?**

A. Branding isn't just for marketing majors. Branding is the approach of identifying and communicating your unique talents and skills so that you can set yourself apart from the other candidates and land the internship or full-time job you want. And *Brand You* contains activities and resource information that will help you in your job search, no matter what career path you are pursuing. Start by reading Chapter 1 and don't stop there.

Q. Will I ever find a job I really like?

A. Yes! When you identify the type of environment, industry, and company that best fits you, you will be surprised at how much you will enjoy working. Check out Chapter 3 to see how *Brand You* can help you identify your direction.

Step 2—Researching the Market

Q. I think I'm interested in more than one industry. Do I have to choose just one?

A. You are not restricted to choosing only one industry. You may want to pursue a career in a few different industries. The research, interviewing, and internship process can help you get a better understanding of the direction you want to take. Don't limit yourself. Do your research and pursue the areas that interest you. Chapters 4, 5, and 7 in *Brand You* will help give you some ideas as to how you can approach multiple targets.

Q. Where do I find information about companies that are good to work for?

A. Chapter 4 provides invaluable information about how to research industries and identify companies that might be a good fit for you.

Q. What if I choose an industry now that I think I want to work in, and then change my mind next year?

A. You can't make a mistake. You may choose one or two industries now and change your mind before you graduate. Or you can change your mind after an internship or even after you start working. Read Chapter 5 to understand that your decisions will guide you and your experience will serve you well.

Step 3—Creating Your Value Proposition

Q. I don't have any experience. What can I put on my résumé?

A. Putting together your résumé takes thought and research. Take the time to read Chapter 8 in *Brand You* to see how you can identify your personal brand's features, benefits, and extras that can become the foundation for your résumé.

Q. Where do I start looking for an internship?

A. Chapter 9 and Internships 101 in the Toolkit in *Brand You* are good places to start. You can get some ideas about how to approach your search for an internship. Don't forget, you'll need a résumé and cover letter, so be sure to read all of *Brand You* to understand how you can get the internship you want.

Q. I'm not sure I want to work for a traditional company. What if I want to start my own company or work on my own?

A. There are many, many opportunities outside the corporate world. Read Chapter 10 in *Brand You* to explore some alternatives to a corporate job. You will also find some good Web sites that can provide information and resources to help you discover some appealing options.

Q. How much can I expect to get paid for an internship or full-time job?

A. The best way to determine how much you can expect to get paid is to read Chapter 11 in *Brand You*. This will help you determine how you establish how much you are worth. When you get an offer, be sure to read Chapter 16 so you can evaluate, negotiate, and accept the offer appropriately.

   If you are looking for an internship, keep in mind that not every internship is a paid internship. And some of the best internships are not paid. Read Internships 101 in the *Brand You* **Toolkit** to find out what factors to consider when you are pursuing an internship.

Step 4—Communicating Your Value Proposition

Q. What's the right format for a résumé?

A. There is no single format that is right or wrong when it comes to a résumé. However, there are some guidelines and tips in Chapter 13 of *Brand You* that can help make your résumé stand out. Don't forget, your résumé should never travel without your cover letter. Chapter 13 of *Brand You* also includes how to write a powerful cover letter.

Q. How should I get my résumé and cover letter to prospective employers?

A. You have the benefit of using a combination of online and traditional methods to let your target employers know that you are in the market for an internship or a full-time job. Read Chapter 12 in *Brand You* and put together an integrated marketing communications plan for your brand. And the Do's and Don'ts of Online Job Searching in the *Brand You* **Toolkit** is also helpful to avoid the pitfalls of using the Internet for your job search.

Q. Everyone says that most jobs are filled by networking, but I don't have a network. What else can I do?

A. You'll be surprised at how many people you know when you read Chapter 14 in *Brand You* and learn how to master your networking skills.

Step 5—Delivering Your Value Proposition

Q. How do I prepare for an interview?

A. An interview is an opportunity for the company to learn about you and for you to learn about the company, whether you are interviewing for an internship or a full-time job. But you only have one chance to make a good first impression, so read Chapter 15 in *Brand You* before every interview to be ready to impress.

Q. What if I'm interviewing at two companies and get an offer from one of them? How can I get an offer from the other company before I accept the first offer?

A. It's perfectly acceptable to ask for some time to consider an offer before you accept it. Find out how to handle this situation in Chapter 16 of *Brand You*.

Q. What's the best way to negotiate an offer?

A. Salary is not the only element of compensation. Read Chapter 16 to understand other benefits that can be a part of your negotiation.

Epilogue

You did it! You created your personal brand, charted your direction, and made your brand story come alive. Believe it or not, this is not the end, it's really the beginning of your career. Whether you are pursuing a profession in marketing, finance, economics, education, law, or any other field, you are now prepared to find the full-time job or internship you want.

Your brand will take shape and will continue to grow and be developed. The concepts in *Brand You* will serve you throughout your career and throughout your life. Whether you are looking for a new job or competing for a promotion, the concept of building and communicating a unique and relevant brand never changes.

This semester may be over, but the concepts covered in *Brand You* will continue to guide you. Don't get discouraged if you initially don't get the phone call you want. Go back through **The 5 Steps to Real Success** and redo the key activities. Make adjustments to your cover letter, résumé, professional Web site, networking list, target company list, and your communication plan. Use the campus career center, alumni association, and library as resources and keep going. Your job is out there.

Keep *Brand You* handy and revisit **The 5 Steps to Real Success** regularly. You'll be surprised at how helpful it will be as you go through the steps when you search for your internship, your first full-time job, and even when you are making a job change.

Enjoy creating and developing your brand. The world is waiting for brand YOU!